*Critical Essays on*

# HAWTHORNE'S

## *THE HOUSE OF*
## *THE SEVEN GABLES*

# CRITICAL ESSAYS
## ON
# AMERICAN LITERATURE

James Nagel, General Editor
*University of Georgia, Athens*

# Critical Essays on
# HAWTHORNE'S
# *THE HOUSE OF*
# *THE SEVEN GABLES*

*edited by*

BERNARD ROSENTHAL

*G. K. Hall & Co.*
*An Imprint of Simon and Schuster Macmillan*
*New York*

*Prentice Hall International*
*London Mexico City New Delhi Singapore Sidney Toronto*

G. K. Hall & Co.
An Imprint of Simon & Schuster Macmillan
866 Third Avenue
New York, N.Y. 10022

---

**Library of Congress Cataloging-in-Publication Data**

Critical essays on The house of the seven gables / edited by Bernard
Rosenthal.
    p.   cm.—(Critical essays on American literature)
   ISBN 0-7838-0014-2
   1. Hawthorne, Nathaniel, 1804–1864.  House of the seven gables.
I. Rosenthal, Bernard, 1934–  .  II. Series.
PS1861.C75   1995
813'.3—dc20                                94-41082
                                               CIP

---

10    9    8    7    6    5    4    3    2    1

Printed in the United States of America

# Contents

♦

MODERN CRITICISM, INCLUDING ORIGINAL ESSAYS

# General Editor's Note

◆

This series seeks to anthologize the most important criticism on a wide variety of topics and writers in American literature. Our readers will find in various volumes not only a generous selection of reprinted articles and reviews but original essays, bibliographies, manuscript sections, and other materials brought to public attention for the first time. This volume, *Critical Essays on Hawthorne's The House of the Seven Gables*, is the most comprehensive collection of essays ever published on this classic American novel. It contains both a sizable gathering of early reviews and comments and a broad selection of more modern scholarship as well. Among the authors of reprinted articles and reviews are Henry James, Evert Augustus Duyckinck, Nina Baym, and Bruce Michelson. In addition to a substantial introduction by Bernard Rosenthal, there are also three original essays commissioned specifically for publication in this volume: Joseph Flibbert on the novel as "Hawthorne's Portrait of Benevolence," Allan Emery on the historical background of Salem, and, in a related study, Thomas Woodson on the thematic role of the community. In addition, David Callaway has constructed a comprehensive annotated bibliography of secondary criticism. We are confident that this book will make a permanent and significant contribution to the study of American literature.

JAMES NAGEL
*University of Georgia, Athens*

# *Publisher's Note*

◆

Producing a volume that contains both newly commissioned and reprinted material presents the publisher with the challenge of balancing the desire to achieve stylistic consistency with the need to preserve the integrity of works first published elsewhere. In the Critical Essays series, essays commissioned especially for a particular volume are edited to be consistent with G. K. Hall's house style; reprinted essays appear in the style in which they were first published, with only typographical errors corrected. Consequently, shifts in style from one essay to another are the result of our efforts to be faithful to each text as it was originally published.

# *Introduction*

BERNARD ROSENTHAL

In 1850 Nathaniel Hawthorne published *The Scarlet Letter*, receiving both public success and critical approval. He had turned to authorship, having long ago rejected traditional professions such as the ministry or medicine.[1] In 1828, three years after his graduation from Bowdoin College, he had anonymously published his first novel, *Fanshawe*, at his own expense, a decision he regretted for the rest of his life. Nevertheless, his unhappiness with his first major literary attempt did not prevent him from actively pursuing a career as an author.

Between the appearances of *Fanshawe* and *The Scarlet Letter*, Hawthorne had published a variety of works, including children's tales, magazine pieces, and collections of his work in *Twice-Told Tales* (1837), a revised edition of this book in 1842, and *Mosses from an Old Manse* (1846). By the time *The Scarlet Letter* appeared, he was already an author with a solid literary reputation, and the acclaim that he received for this novel helped solidify his position in his own time as a major American author.

Fresh from this success, in the late spring of 1850 he began *The House of the Seven Gables*, which Ticknor, Reed, and Fields published on 9 April 1851.[2] Coming as it did so quickly after the triumphant achievement of *The Scarlet Letter*, *The House of the Seven Gables* was inevitably measured against *The Scarlet Letter* by critics. Although Hawthorne would publish two more novels (or "romances," as he defined them), *The Blithedale Romance* in 1852 and *The Marble Faun* in 1860, as well as other books, the comparison of *The House of the Seven Gables* to *The Scarlet Letter* continued through the years as a major motif in critical commentary.

In his new romance Hawthorne departed from the historical setting of *The Scarlet Letter* and placed his story in a contemporary milieu. Nevertheless, he rooted his story of the Pyncheon and Maule families in an event from the Puritan era. As with *The Scarlet Letter*, he had his story unfold from the consequences of an original sin. In April 1851, the prominent contemporary reviewer Evert Augustus Duyckinck observed, "The story of the House of the Seven Gables is a tale of retribution, of expiation extending over a period of two hundred years, it taking all that while to lay the ghost of the earliest victim, in the time of the Salem witchcraft; for, by the way, it is to Salem that this blackened old dwelling, mildewed with easterly scud, belongs. The yeoman who originally struck his spade into the spot, by the side of a crystal spring, was hanged for a wizard, under the afflictive dispensation of Cotton Mather."[3] In searching for the title of his book, Hawthorne had at one point considered "Maule's Well,"[4] referring to the theme of property dispute and the Salem witch trials.

Roughly 100 years later, Daniel G. Hoffman incisively articulated once again the inextricable link between a story of the present and a Puritan history: "*The House of the Seven Gables* is built on an implicit sub-structure of Puritan myth. On this is erected an historical reconstruction of folk belief in witchcraft as it varied over two centuries. This witchcraft—and the sins it represents—is superseded by the ebullient optimism of the contemporary Yankee character. Doubtless this is among the reasons for the book's great popularity among his contemporaries."[5] Whether or not Hoffman is accurate in so closely linking the popularity of *The House of the Seven Gables* with the motif of witchcraft cannot be definitively established. Nevertheless, the conclusion is certainly plausible, given the context in which Hawthorne's book appeared. Arlin Turner has pointed out that "during the years when Hawthorne was reading colonial New England history, others in Salem were learning that history with particular attention to the hanging of the witches."[6]

As Turner points out, Robert Calef's *More Wonders of the Invisible World* had been reprinted in 1823, and Charles W. Upham had published his *Lectures on Witchcraft* in 1831.[7] In 1867, Upham eventually published his two-volume study, *Salem Witchcraft; with An Account of Salem Village, and a History of Opinions on Witchcraft and Kindred Subjects*. During the years between the new edition of Calef's work and Upham's classic treatise, a broad interest in the trials had emerged, and Hawthorne certainly played on that in the premise of his book, which identified the original sin with the fictional execution of Matthew Maule.[8]

For his core myth, Hawthorne used the epithet that Sarah Good in 1692 uttered in response to the Reverend Nicholas Noyes. According to Robert Calef: "At Execution, Mr. Noyes urged Sarah Good to Confess, and told her she was a Witch, and she knew she was a Witch, to which she replied, you are a lyer; I am no more a Witch than you are a Wizard, and if you take away my Life, God will give you Blood to drink."[9] In the novel, of course, Hawthorne has a man utter the curse, a transposition that has recently aroused the ire of at least one feminist critic.[10] The condemned Matthew Maule confronts his persecutor, Colonel Pyncheon. " 'God,' said the dying man, pointing his finger with a ghastly look at the undismayed countenance of his enemy, 'God will give him blood to drink!' "[11] In substituting Matthew Maule for Sarah Good, Hawthorne conflated the witch trials with the persecution of the Quakers, for there was a Quaker named Thomas Maule who attacked the Puritan establishment for persecuting innocent people as witches.

Relying on what in *The House of the Seven Gables* he called "fireside tradition," Hawthorne also found another piece of lore to connect his tale to a Puritan past.[12] By placing Colonel Pyncheon on horseback at the execution and by having him urge it on, Hawthorne drew upon the account given by Robert Calef of Cotton Mather on horseback urging the execution of the minister George Burroughs, thus providing the Mather connection that Duyckinck noted in his review. Another theme linking the novel to the Salem witch trials is the matter of property disputes, to which Turner referred. One of the emerging assumptions in Hawthorne's day was that property disputes were at the core of the witch trials. If his allusions seem dim and out of reach to some modern readers, Hawthorne had every reason to expect that his audience knew his "fireside tradition." The same tradition told of how Nicholas Noyes, like Judge Pyncheon, died of apoplexy and spit up blood. The titillation of this Salem story, widely known to his audience, offered Hawthorne a context for playing out the eerie, supernatural spell that hovers over the inevitable death of Judge Pyncheon and the house that was built through what the Puritans called "the shedding of innocent blood."

That Hawthorne rooted his story in such grim origins seems ironic in view of his concern, which Arlin Turner noted, that he "had grown self-conscious about the gloom in his writing." Worried that *The House of the Seven Gables* would continue this pattern, Hawthorne wrote that "he would 'try hard to pour some setting sunshine over' " his new book.[13] He seems generally to have succeeded as far as his contemporary reviewers were concerned. In assessing *The House of the Seven Gables*, they often found it tempting to juxtapose the darkness of *The Scarlet Letter* against the later novel's light. A writer in the *Boston Daily Evening Transcript* observed that the book "will be welcomed all over the country as another evidence of Hawthorne's marked and brilliant genius."[14] The writer proceeded to compare *The House of the Seven Gables* favorably to *The Scarlet Letter*. The new book, wrote the reviewer, "will give greater satisfaction" than his earlier novel. This was because *The House of the Seven Gables* had more "glowing sunlight" and was marked by "a lively humor."

The perception of *The House of the Seven Gables* as offering a shift from darkness to sunshine appeared in other contemporary responses to the book. Thus one reviewer found it "much pleasanter" than *The Scarlet Letter*.[15] Yet the perception of Hawthorne as a writer of darkness persisted in the contemporary reviews. One reviewer, though finding the novel "exquisitely relieved by charming portraitures of character, and quaint and comic descriptions of social eccentricities," nevertheless found it "more terrific in its conception, and not less intense" than *The Scarlet Letter*.[16] Another reviewer observed that "[t]he fault of the book, indeed of all Hawthorne's books, in a moral aspect, is the sombre coloring which pervades them, and which leaves an effect more or less morbid on even healthy minds."[17]

Such concerns notwithstanding, the general critical response was overwhelmingly favorable. Melville praised it profusely, and Edwin Percy Whipple called it "Hawthorne's greatest work."[18] Initial sales of the book reflected such enthusiasm. Indeed, American sales of *The House of the Seven Gables* came to 6,710 in the first year of publication, as opposed to initial sales of 6,000 for *The Scarlet Letter*. Thus, Hawthorne did well with the book, receiving royalties of 15 percent, with the book selling for a dollar. Sales in England, where the book sold for a shilling and sixpence were also apparently good, although pirated editions cut into Hawthorne's royalties.[19] Yet in spite of this early success, in Hawthorne's lifetime sales of *The Scarlet Letter* exceeded those of *The House of the Seven Gables*.[20]

The early reviews of *The House of the Seven Gables* addressed issues that would concern critics in the years to follow. The comparison with *The Scarlet Letter* has persisted, with the latter generally judged superior, a judgement prompted in part by frequent dissatisfaction with the ending of *The House of the Seven Gables*. Although there has been some dissent from this view, it has been the prevalent one. In June 1851, in his generally highly enthusiastic review of the book, E. P. Whipple remarked "that the movement of the author's mind betrays a slight fitfulness toward the conclusion, and, splendid as is the supernaturally grotesque element which this ideal impatience introduces, it still somewhat departs from the integrity of the original conception, and interferes with the strict unity of the work."[21] In 1980, James R. Mellow observed that "Whipple . . . was to become Hawthorne's favorite critic," and Arlin Turner wrote that in Whipple's observation, "Hawthorne had confirmation of what he might have said he had known all along, that he must let a story follow its own logic to the end, as he had done in *The Scarlet Letter*—and as he would do in the two romances he published afterward."[22]

As the second half of the nineteenth century saw an emerging interest in literary "realism," discussions of *The House of the Seven Gables* turned in that direction. From the outset, though, realism had been a theme in the critical response. One reviewer, writing in July 1851, considered the work as "inferior to the 'Scarlet Letter' in artistic proportion, compactness and stained power"; nevertheless the reviewer deemed it "nearer actual life, and more comprehensively true to human nature, than any former work of its author."[23] As another writer observed in a complaint a few years later, "[e]verything is dwelt upon with a tedious minuteness."[24]

Among Hawthorne's nineteenth-century critics was Henry James, who saw in Hawthorne "the most valuable example of the American genius," even as he denigrated the value of American literature in general.[25] For

James, Hawthorne lacked a sense of realism, but wrote a literature suitable to his country.

I have alluded to the absence in Hawthorne of that quality of realism which is now so much in fashion, an absence in regard to which there will of course be more to say; and yet I think I am not fanciful in saying that he testifies to the sentiments of the society in which he flourished almost as pertinently (proportion observed) as Balzac and some of his descendants—MM. Flaubert and Zola—testify to the manners and morals of the French people. He was not a man with a literary theory; he was guiltless of a system, and I am not sure that he had ever heard of Realism, this remarkable compound having (although it was invented some time earlier) come into general use only since his death.[26]

In writing specifically about *The House of the Seven Gables*, James, like many other critics, juxtaposed it against *The Scarlet Letter*, and found it a lesser novel. Indeed, he thought *The House of the Seven Gables* "more like a prologue to a great novel than a great novel itself."[27] Nevertheless, James praised the book. While emphasizing again "that Hawthorne was not a realist," he observed that compared to Hawthorne's other writings the book has "more literal actuality," particularly in "that it renders, to an initiated reader, the impression of a summer afternoon in an elm-shadowed New England town."[28]

Ironically, future literary criticism would take for granted that Hawthorne was something of a literary "theoretician," that he explored and defined an area of fiction that he called "romance," one that openly rejects the very "realism" that James found missing in his work. Even in James's own day, the distinction between the romance and the novel had already achieved significance. Terence Martin pointed out that William Dean Howells, in reviewing James's book on Hawthorne, "objected to the manner in which James failed to distinguish between the romance and the novel in speaking of Hawthorne's fiction."[29] Martin also pointed out what has come to be a standard critical assumption about Hawthorne's romances: "The prefaces to his major romances contain what is, in effect, a theory of fiction based on the supposition that art requires a domain of its own if it is to flourish. Thus, he explains in the preface to *The House of the Seven Gables*, the latitude of fashion and material afforded by the romance is congenial to his imagination."[30] The preface to *The House of the Seven Gables* has more than any of Hawthorne's prefaces defined the nature of the "romance" for future critics. While James opposed romance to realism, Hawthorne shaped the matter somewhat differently, juxtaposing the novel against the romance, and defining himself as a writer of romances. The distinction that he drew in his preface to *The House of the Seven Gables*, would become standard in future critical assessments of the concept of romance. "The latter form of composition [the novel] is presumed to aim at a very minute fidelity, not merely to the possible, but to the probable and ordinary course of man's experience. The former [the romance]—while, as a work of art, it must rigidly subject itself to laws, and while it sins unpardonably, so far as it may swerve aside from the truth of the human heart—has fairly a right to present that truth under circumstances, to a great extent, of the writer's own choosing or creation."[31]

Much of later criticism has accepted this assessment, along with the rest of the preface, as a classic statement on romance. For the most part, whether praising or criticizing the novel, critics have accepted Hawthorne's own definition of his fiction as articulated in *The House of the Seven Gables*.

Criticism of *The House of the Seven Gables*, however, has not dwelt simply on matters of realism versus romance. Some of the main themes have included commentary on the characters, the weight of history upon the present, and the question of whether Hawthorne's ending violated the logic of his story. Of the characters, Phoebe has probably generated the most enthusiasm as well as the most negative criticism. Much of this discrepancy stems from a function of time, a difference between the values of Hawthorne's day and those of our own. Early reviewers were charmed by her, and later readers, including Henry James, fell under her spell. "Nothing," he writes, "can be more charming than the manner in which the soft, bright, active presence of Phoebe Pyncheon is indicated, or than the account of her relations with the poor, dimly sentient kinsman for whom her light-handed sisterly offices, in the evening of a melancholy life, are a revelation of lost possibilities of happiness."[32] More measured and less effusive than some of the many others who wrote of Phoebe, James shared none of our contemporary concerns with the problems and politics of sexual stereotyping and followed the more extravagant tradition that eulogized her charms. This tradition was perhaps exemplified by the reviewer in 1852 who wrote: "Phoebe is a bright and beautiful name; one full of the happiest significance. Phoebe, *light of life*! What more or better can a lover or husband desire? Those who have read Hawthorne's 'House of the Seven Gables' (and who has not?) will here recall to their minds the sweet-tempered, cheerful, and warm-hearted country maiden who brought the sunshine and the fragrance of the fields with her, to enliven and purify the dark, damp, and mouldy old mansion of the Pyncheons. She was rightly named, *Phoebe*."[33]

If many a nineteenth-century critic was able to expostulate on the glow of Phoebe, modern critics have seen other implications. Cathy N. Davidson, writing of Holgrave's objectivization of Phoebe, observed that "In effect, Holgrave renounces his earlier reluctance to objectify Phoebe in order to objectify her again, this time by casting her as the Eternal Feminine. . . . Phoebe becomes the substitute for Holgrave's itinerant observing, his patho-logical art making, his earlier Emersonian commitment to the inner life. She becomes a new kind of sundrawn picture, reflecting back Holgrave's new identity—ironically, an identity as a smiling, conservative, public man."[34] Louise DeSalvo saw Phoebe as shrewdly ingratiating herself into the Pyncheon household even as neither Hepzibah nor Hawthorne recognize her exploitation.[35] Nina Baym presented an incisive assessment of Hawthorne's female characters and patriarchy that offers a valuable connection between Phoebe and the others.[36] In a very useful summary of some of the critical trends concerning Phoebe, Judith A. Gustafson described the range of critical response, citing the approving "Richard H. Fogle's view of this forerunner of Doris Day" as " '[a] conservative in the best sense [who] represents the truth of the human heart,' " and the dubious Hyatt Waggoner, who "complains that her portrayal 'is both sentimental and frivolous, with a frivolity characteristic of the "playful" side of Hawthorne's fancy at its weakest.' "[37] Gustafson herself saw Hawthorne as mocking the idealized presentation of women so common in his day.[38]

In a much more traditional view of Hawthorne's feelings about Phoebe, James R. Mellow wrote "that Phoebe, with her chirrupy temperament, her sunny disposition, and incurable optimism, is drawn from Sophia [his wife], whom Hawthorne on several occasions addressed as Phoebe in his letters."[39] Given the fervor and ardency of Hawthorne's love letters to Sophia, it seems hard to believe that he would identify his wife with a character he did not admire. At the same time, Phoebe surely finds counterparts in numerous nineteenth-century representations of women.

Hawthorne, more than most male writers of his day, explored issues connected with the status of women, and made tentative probes toward addressing an active feminist movement of his day. In *The Scarlet Letter*, *The Blithedale Romance*, and *The Marble Faun*, he created respectively Hester, Zenobia, and Miriam, as strong-willed women searching for their own way in a world dominated by men. Hester achieves a kind of triumph; Zenobia is destroyed; Miriam endures. But in *The House of the Seven Gables*, Phoebe, provided with a few fainting spells, might be mistaken for a Cooper "female."[40] Unlike his other heroines, she faces no serious moral crisis and confronts no evil, except perhaps in having to deal with Pyncheon. This she does by simply behaving well.

While Phoebe may be seen in other guises in nineteenth-century fiction, Hepzibah represents a more unusual character. The early critics thought well of Hepzibah. Whipple saw Phoebe and Hepzibah as interconnected and as "masterpieces of characterization, in the felicity of their conception, their contrast, and their inter-action."[41] As one writer observed, Hepzibah concealed under her "scowl the unutterable tenderness of a sister."[42] Amory Dwight Mayo saw in Hepzibah's depiction issues that subsequently came to pervade criticism of *The House of the Seven Gables*. "Hepzibah," he wrote, "steps across the gulf that divides two social states, in her way from the parlor to the counter."[43] Mayo saw Hepzibah as "ancient gentility gone to seed, toiling in vain to obey the dictates of a good heart and human necessities."[44] Henry T. Tuckerman, on the other hand, found her to be of only passing interest as he described "the old maid, in her lonely chamber, gazing on the sweet lineaments of her unfortunate brother."[45] In general, Hepzibah, sometimes seen as an object of humor, drew less attention than did Phoebe.

On the whole, later critics followed this pattern, although British reviewers seemed to show more interest in Hepzibah. In a generally unflattering review of the book in *Blackwood's Edinburgh Magazine* (1855), the reviewer described Hepzibah as "perhaps, the most touching picture Mr. Hawthorne has made, and her first attempt at shopkeeping, with all its little humiliations and trials, is a pitiful picture, true enough to reach the heart."[46] The reviewer was sharply critical of Hawthorne's tolerance or approval of Clifford's rejecting Hepzibah's love because she lacks the beauty he seeks. Some years later, Hepzibah also won high praise from Anthony Trollope, who in 1879 found her the best character in the book. "Her timidity, her affection, her true appreciation of herself, her ugliness, her hopelessness, and general incapacity for everything,—cent-shop-keeping included,—are wonderfully drawn."[47]

In general, though, criticism of Hepzibah over the years has been connected to discussions of the Pyncheon family and its decline, of the weight of history bearing down on a collapsing present. Thoughtful exceptions to this view, of course, have been presented, as in Darrel Abel's view that "*The House of the Seven Gables* cannot be understood as a history of particular persons in a specific place at a definite time; it is, instead, a series of *tableaux vivants et parlants* showing phases and types of humanity embodied in different generations of two families which live in significantly revelatory relationship with each other within an ancient but changing tradition."[48] Thus, "the gentility of Hepzibah is a grotesque shadow of that of Alice Pyncheon. Hawthorne favored the vital over the moribund tradition."[49] Lawrence Sargent Hall, however, had earlier focused on a view of Hawthorne's purpose that would gain broader acceptance. For Hall, "the selfish individualism of a family so jealously guarding its interests through successive epochs, in defiance of newer trends and mores to which men at large are susceptible, is shown to be self-destructive. By preserving Colonel Pyncheon's proud egocentricity, the heirs cherished the very corrosive evil which eventually ate away their humanity."[50] Seen this way, Hepzibah's attempt to engage an emergent democratic culture fails as she retained "her aristocratic arrogance, and inwardly despised the people by whose pennies she hoped to be sustained."[51]

The aristocratic engagement with an emergent democratic culture, however, represented only one way in which the past impinged on the present. A Freudian model, articulated most forcefully by Frederick Crews, saw Hepzibah as submitting to "the imposing portrait of the first Colonel Pyncheon" with an "admittedly dim suggestion of incestuous feeling."[52] Henry Nash Smith found Crews's Freudian reading of *The House of the Seven Gables* "persuasive."[53] Whether seen in Freudian terms or not, however, critics have seen the centrality of guilt as a motif in *The House of the Seven Gables*. Roy Harvey Pearce observes that "*The House of the Seven Gables*, then, is to be a Romance in which history—the continuity of communal guilt in history—is manifested in such a way that the past is connected dynamically, in moral actuality, to the present."[54] Previously, Michael Davitt Bell had articulately pointed out that *The House of the Seven Gables* furthers the exploration of guilt and sin earlier put forth in *The Scarlet Letter*. In comparing the two works he argued that "what in *The Scarlet Letter* was applied to the life span of a single woman is extended, in *The House of the Seven Gables*, to the full span of American history. Under Maule's curse history would seem to entail the endless repetition of past acts."[55] In focusing on this repetition of history Bell pointed to the resemblance between Judge Pyncheon and his ancestor, Colonel Pyncheon. The significance of this resemblance, seen in "Holgrave's daguerreotype . . . is clear in Hepzibah's denunciation of the Judge as he attempts to force an interview with Clifford. 'You are but doing over again,' she declares to her cousin, 'in another shape, what your ancestor before you did, and sending down to your posterity the curse inherited from him!' "[56] Also using Hepzibah to articulate a central premise, Everett Carter, describing *The House of the Seven Gables* as Hawthorne's "most dramatic statement of the permanence of the past," calls attention to the moment of collapsed euphoria at the end of the journey of Clifford and Hepzibah:[57]

> Clifford subsided; his hectic fantasy over, he murmured to Hepzibah: "You must take the lead now." And Hepzibah, falling to her knees, ejaculated: "Oh, God—our Father—are we not thy children? Have mercy on us!"
> This was Hawthorne's most brilliant description of the pervasive powers of the past.[58]

The relation of past to present took another form in 1984 when John P. McWilliams saw in *The House of the Seven Gables* Hawthorne's attempt "to redeem the present from insignificance by uncovering within it a gradual reforming of Puritan character."[59]

Because of this attempt at redemption, "Hepzibah is never transformed into a plebian woman, the Pyncheon family never drowns, and a splendid establishment is restored to them."[60]

If some critics have expressed concern over Hawthorne's resolution of this engagement with history, Kriston Herzog saw a possible balance between present and past. "Hawthorne locates hope within human history without denying the power of the past."[61] While the "book leaves us only with a qualified and personal hope," Herzog forcefully argued that "the hope for redemption is found in primitive elements: in women who emerge from the realm of ghosts, fairy tales, and myth," one of them being Hepzibah.[62] Perhaps it is in this spirit of redemption that Susan L. Mizruchi has more recently asserted "that Hepzibah's deeper response to the Pyncheon view of history is subversive" and that in Hepzibah's "random images of family history" Hawthorne suggests "that the past can be conceived apart from the processes of historical change, as an eternal fulfillment of human desire."[63]

The continuing critical interest in Hawthorne's engagement with the past in *The House of the Seven Gables* has necessarily given rise to much commentary on the character who most embodies it, Judge Pyncheon. His delineation evoked contrasting responses among early reviewers, especially in connection with his death scene. Whipple found the scene "a masterpiece of fantastic description," while another reviewer complained that "there is scarcely such another piece of over-description in the language. The situation is fairly warn to pieces."[64] Whether critics liked the scene or not, it evoked frequent response. Although almost all critics have accepted Pyncheon's death, the fulfillment of Maule's curse, within the context of Hawthorne's idea of "romance," attempts have been made to define the episode in a more realistic mode. Most prominently, Alfred H. Marks has speculated that Pyncheon died as a result of his excessive imagination, from the sight of Clifford as a ghost.[65] Pursuing the avenue of inquiry opened by Marks, Clara B. Cox rejected his view and argued for Holgrave as a more probable precipitating agent of Judge Pyncheon's death.[66] Others, such as Gloria C. Erlich, engaged the death of Judge Pyncheon without joining in this particular kind of argument. Erlich saw the portrayal of Pyncheon as "a calculated mixture of ancestral Hathorne and contemporary Manning."[67] On the implications of Pyncheon's death, Eric J. Sundquist has argued that *"The House of the Seven Gables* revenges the death of Matthew Maule by gleefully presiding over the demise of Judge Pyncheon, only to turn around and implicate its narrator, through his association with Holgrave, in the necromantic act with which the cycle of guilt originated."[68]

Of the Pyncheons, Clifford has been the most complex character for critics to treat. He does not easily fit into the categories of the others: Judge Pyncheon, a representative of overreaching evil; Hepzibah, a decaying, pathetic, though deeply decent aristocracy; and Phoebe, the energizing force of an idealized nineteenth-century woman. For the modern critic, Clifford offers many possibilities for psychological insight, for probing into Hawthorne's sense of art and decay, as an odd variation of his "Artist of the Beautiful." Early critics, although quite interested in Clifford, could not agree on whether he represented a magnificent tribute to the love of art and beauty, or rather reflected a contemptible selfishness in shunning his benefactress, Hepzibah, because of some misplaced idea of beauty. The ambivalence is nicely reflected in Amory Dwight Mayo's review in 1851:

> Upon the character of Clifford, Mr. Hawthorne has evidently wreaked all his acuteness. The result is such a felicity of mental analysis as we never before witnessed. The manner in which this artist-soul, hovering alternately upon

the verge of insanity and idiocy, is pictured with all its relations to nature and healthy and diseased mind, is truly amazing. The theory that Clifford is made to suggest, would doubtless be true if a purely artistic spirit ever did or could exist; but since every human being has a heart as well as an imagination, we suspect the moral law must hold yet, in place of its artistic substitute.[69]

Future critics would expand upon the issues Mayo observed, although his basic view of Clifford has persisted. In modern times, J. F. Ragan has put a finer point on Mayo's assessment in observing that "Clifford is Hawthorne's criticism of what has been happening to man's love of Beauty at the hands of a utilitarian American aristocracy of wealth builders, [falling] into place as part of the beauty-versus-practicality theme."[70] For Richard H. Fogle, "Clifford is not ready to face the broad sunshine of reality, whether humor or divine," while Rita Gollin saw redemption for Clifford who ultimately "can leave the gloomy Pyncheon house and its counterpart, the dungeon of his heart."[71]

Into this decaying house of Pyncheon, some manifestation of the ghost of Maule appears in the form of Holgrave, the character who has probably caught the imagination of critics more than any other. Oddly, early reviewers tended either to ignore him or to find him unattractive. As Whipple observed in 1851, "It is impossible for the reader to like him, and one finds it difficult to conceive how Phoebe herself can like him. The love scenes accordingly lack love, and a kind of magnetic influence is substituted for affection."[72] More than one reviewer saw his presence as a flaw in the novel. If praised, the approval tended to be cursory. This early dismissal of Holgrave has not held up through the years. In the twentieth century, critics have become increasingly interested in Holgrave, both as a character and for the literary problem that he presents the critic. This has most frequently taken the form of questioning the plausibility of his transformation from a sardonic, alienated social commentator whose one redeeming virtue is kindness to Hepzibah, into a votary of Phoebe. Under her spell, he throws over all his revolutionary impulses and seems to march off to the countryside, content with marital bliss. Discussion has often centered on whether such a representation of him is accurate, with numerous inquiries into Holgrave's real function in relation to the novel's artistic integrity.

Criticism has focused on Holgrave from a variety of perspectives. He has frequently been discussed in the context of tensions between new and old social orders. In spite of early reservations about Holgrave, the social implications connected with him appeared in nineteenth-century criticism.[73] In more modern times, Arthur Sherbo has suggested that in depicting Holgrave Hawthorne drew on the social critic, Albert Brisbane, while Daniel R. Barnes suggested that Holgrave's depiction is a satire directed at Orestes

Brownson.[74] Luther S. Luedtke, on the other hand, has found the source for Holgrave in Hawthorne himself, as had Jeffrey Steinbrink and Amy Louise Reed.[75]

Holgrave has also attracted much attention in his role as artist, and in his connection to issues of great interest to Hawthorne's nineteenth-century audience, in his roles as mesmerist and daguerreotypist. These subjects often interconnect with Holgrave's relation to Phoebe and with the tale of Alice Pyncheon.

Linked to the past as a Maule, but breaching the family hostilities with the Pyncheons, Holgrave has provoked critics to radically different but nevertheless plausible interpretations. Brook Thomas, for example, argued for Holgrave's "affinity with the judge," while Jerome F. Klinkowitz argued for his essential decency.[76] Similarly, in a particularly valuable essay, Nina Baym saw him "presented as an admirable person, the most unequivocally heroic of Hawthorne's generally weak male characters."[77] As to Holgrave's definition as an artist, R. K. Gupta rejected such identity "because he presents reality in its crude, raw form, untransformed by the shaping process of imagination."[78] Conversely, Coleman W. Tharpe saw Holgrave's capacity to reveal the truth through art.[79] Taking another perspective, Maria M. Tatar saw him as surrendering his role as artist. "Rooted entirely in the present," she argued "he has lost those qualities that might have transformed him into the inspired reformer or the visionary artist."[80] Some of these conflicting perceptions simply represent critical differences, but Millicent Bell offered an interpretation that argued for a dual Holgrave: "His descent from the wizard of colonial times, Matthew Maule, is a deliberate metaphor. Holgrave, like his ancestor, possesses an acuity concerning the inner workings of the soul which seems somehow illicit and dangerous, and which is repre- sented in his skill as a mesmerist. But Holgrave also exists on the realist level suggested by his appearance not under the Maule name, but under a new, ancesterless one. Throughout the novel we are made aware of the double nature of this Maule-Holgrave."[81]

Other themes have attracted critics to Holgrave, including the motif traditionally associated with Hawthorne, the balance between the head and the heart. Arguing that Holgrave finds salvation through the right balance, Donald Ringe presented his case in "Hawthorne's Psychology of the Head and the Heart."[82] The criticism on Holgrave is rich and varied, and the interest in him in modern times largely represents an attraction to "realism" and social and psychological issues over the "moral" issues that nineteenth- century critics tended to find more interesting.

In its variety, however, critical response to Holgrave has moved in numerous other directions. Robert Emmet Whelan, Jr., for example, has argued for *The House of the Seven Gables* as an allegory in the tradition of Bunyan, with Holgrave representing "Intellect."[83] On the other hand, Evan

Carton asserted Holgrave's "blithe innocence," while Leland S. Person, Jr. argued that "Holgrave actually internalizes and acts out the conflict men experienced in nineteenth-century America between the aggressive, domineering ideology of Jacksonian heroism and the comparatively selfless ideal of Christian gentility."[84]

Since Alice Pyncheon is closely connected to Holgrave in both the novel and its criticism critics have tended to define her in relation to their assessment of Holgrave. Thus, those arguing for Holgrave's decency point to his refusal to possess Phoebe as Maule had possessed Alice Pyncheon. Commentary on Holgrave generally crosses over into discussions of Alice, although in the early responses she was rarely even mentioned. Later critics would find her story more interesting, as their interest in Holgrave increased. Nina Baym's assessment in *The Shape of Hawthorne's Career* is particularly useful in examining the connections between Holgrave and Phoebe, Maule, and Alice.[85]

On the whole, the minor characters in *The House of the Seven Gables* have attracted little attention. Uncle Venner was received with some enthusiasm by the early reviewers, but subsequent critics have not dwelt heavily upon him, although he has received some attention as, for example, from Everett Carter, who links Venner to Franklin and Emerson.[86] In general, the racial implications of the book have received little comment, although Richard Clark Sterne offered a notable exception.[87]

The structure of *The House of the Seven Gables* has been much more interesting to modern critics, an issue essentially inseparable from the recurring discussions about the ending of the story. As F. O. Matthiessen observed: "The conclusion of this book has satisfied very few."[88] Matthiessen, seeing unresolved issues in *The House of the Seven Gables*, felt "that Hawthorne could conceive evil in the world, but not an evil world. As a result his final pages drift away into unreal complacence."[89] Twenty years later, Daniel Hoffman, while conceding that the book's "unity is flawed" nevertheless argued for "an almost-successful ethical consistency."[90]

Subsequently, Francis Joseph Battaglia confronted the argument for the flawed ending by asserting "that the ending of Hawthorne's novel is neither artificial nor forced" and "that the plot of the novel has been in a very important particular generally misread. The whole structure of the novel is thus implicated in a discussion of its ending."[91] In part, Battaglia saw the problem as rooted in the flawed text of the standard edition prior to the appearance of the Centenary Edition.[92]

As Battaglia accurately observed, the structure of *The House of the Seven Gables* and its ending are inextricably linked. To see the end as a failure invites a similar judgment on the book as a whole, a judgment Kenneth Dauber seemed to make in writing that "Hawthorne, no longer invested in what he writes, will write anything to accomplish a goal that is beyond writing. The middle in which he has luxuriated, from which, for so long, he would not get out, the middle, indeed, that so successfully for a while resisted the pressures of development toward anything beyond itself, is reconceived as a stage in the progress of a form which develops toward an end."[93] Dauber adds: "The ending, of course, as most critics agree, is forced."[94]

For the most part, and on a variety of grounds, critics have continued to see the ending as a symptom of larger difficulties in *The House of the Seven Gables*. Thus, Claudia D. Johnson argued that "the ending of the novel is unsatisfactory," and presented a cogent case for the ending as working against "symbols . . . so convincingly set up" earlier in the novel.[95] Bruce Michelson also presented a cogent argument, although on somewhat other grounds. Michelson, examining issues of romance and gothic writing, stated that the "most striking, and perhaps most unsettling" aspect of "the ending . . . is how uneventful and undoctrinaire it really is. Lacking dramatic intensity, lacking even an air of finality, the novel trails off rather than closes, and as the end of a proper gothic tale, this may be the chief shortcoming of the last pages."[96]

Seeking to reconcile the text with its ending, Robert Clark addressed "thematic oppositions" in the text that in a sense become reconciled in the marriage of Holgrave and Phoebe. "There is an admission of a unity which the text has tried to keep at bay: the marriage occurred long ago between an ideology that has legitimised the expropriation of the Indians and a myth of nature that has stood as an alibi for building farms on another people's ground."[97] Yet the case against the novel continued. Gordon Hutner argued in 1988 "that the novel is divided in its purposes," leading to *The House of the Seven Gables* collapsing "under the weight of its unresolved contradictions."[98]

More recently, William J. Scheick has offered an interpretation of *The House of the Seven Gables* that involves a unifying approach to the novel consistent with its generally perceived "sunny" ending, except that in Scheick's interpretation there is no sunshine after all. Rooted in Humean philosophy, Scheick's reading argued that the underlying motif of the novel rests in an absence of identity shared by the author and his characters. At the core of this absence is death:

> The Pyncheon house, the human heart, and the house of fiction are each a corresponding "stately edifice," "beneath [which] . . . may lie a corpse, half-decayed, and still decaying, and diffusing its death-scent all through the palace" (pp. 229–30). This suggestion of a decaying corpse at the core of every stately edifice, including every "man himself" (p. 229), images essential non-being, its lack of "real" personal identity, in Humean terms. People, however stately in their own or others' opinion, are fundamentally nonentities because they always remain "slaves . . . to Death" (p. 183), their ultimate

past and future. In short, nonexistence (death) paradoxically defines the very core of our utterly mortal phenomenal being.[99]

Scheick builds his case around this centrality of death in the novel and in Hawthorne's definition of his place in the world. Seen this way, Holgrave's marriage at the end offers a way to "temporarily forget death" without redeeming his situation, or that of the author or other characters, from "the blight at the center of all life."[100] If Scheick is right, the ending of the novel is not false; only our understanding of it has been. It is a reading that evokes Melville's famous assessment of Hawthorne:

> You may be witched by his sunlight,—transported by the bright gildings in the skies he builds over you;—but there is the blackness of darkness beyond; and even his bright gildings but fringe, and play upon the edges of thunder-clouds.—In one word, the world is mistaken in this Nathaniel Hawthorne. He himself must often have smiled at its absurd misconception of him. He is immeasurably deeper than the plummet of the mere critic. . . .
>
> Now it is that blackness in Hawthorne, of which I have spoken, that so fixes and fascinates me. It may be, nevertheless, that it is too largely developed in him. Perhaps he does not give us a ray of his light for every shade of his dark. But however this may be, this blackness it is that furnishes the infinite obscure of his back-ground. . . .[101]

Melville wrote this before the existence of *The House of the Seven Gables*, before Hawthorne tried to write a book that would take him from the gloom of *The Scarlet Letter*. How well he succeeded, and on what terms, necessarily remains at the core of critical debates.

In addition to the rich array of criticism about *The House of the Seven Gables*, valuable biographies of Hawthorne have helped place this and other works by him in the context of his life. The best biographies are those by James R. Mellow, Edwin Haviland Miller, and Arlin Turner.[102] Turner's study is generally regarded as the standard scholarly biography, although Mellow's life of Hawthorne, like Turner's, is rich in its use of sources and its placement of Hawthorne in his time. It is also perhaps the most accessible to readers less familiar with Hawthorne. Miller also offered a comprehensive study of Hawthorne's life and times while presenting a more psychologically oriented approach than either Turner or Mellow. All three offered an excellent overview of Hawthorne's life. A valuable introductory study that includes biographical material is Terrence Martin's *Nathaniel Hawthorne*.[103] The standard text for *The House of the Seven Gables* is the Centenary Edition, which in addition to presenting the most accurate text offers valuable background information.[104]

The essays reprinted in *Critical Essays on Hawthorne's The House of the Seven Gables* have been selected both for variety and for quality, although, inevitably, other valuable essays could not be included. Nineteenth-century essays offer a counterpoint to more contemporary responses. In addition to the reprinted essays, an original bibliography appears by David Callaway, as do previously unpublished essays by Allan Emery and Thomas Woodson on the crucial relation of the town of Salem to *The House of the Seven Gables*, and by Joseph Flibbert on the major issue of Hawthorne's moral terms. William J. Scheick's reprinted essay had originally been solicited for this collection, but complicating circumstances led to its appearance in *Studies in the Novel*, which has generously given permission for his provocative study on Hawthorne and identity to be reprinted here. For assistance in the preparation of my collection of essays, I am grateful to David Callaway, Irene Burgess and Peter Sands. For reading an earlier version of this introduction, I express my appreciation to Joseph Flibbert. Any errors are, of course, my own responsibility.

## Notes

1. Arlin Turner, *Nathaniel Hawthorne: A Biography* (New York: Oxford University Press, 1980), 45–46.

2. *The Centenary Edition of the Works of Nathaniel Hawthorne: House of the Seven Gables*, ed. William Charvat, Roy Harvey Pearce, and Claude M. Simpson et al. (Columbus: Ohio State University Press, 1965), xxix.

3. Evert Augustus Duyckinck, review of *The House of the Seven Gables*, *Literary World* 8: 17 (26 April 1851): 334–35.

4. Turner, 222.

5. Daniel G. Hoffman, *Form and Fable in American Fiction* (New York: Oxford University Press, 1961), 188–89.

6. Turner, 65.

7. Turner, 65–66.

8. For the Salem witch trials and cultural responses to the overall episode see Bernard Rosenthal, *Salem Story: Reading the Witch Trials of 1692* (Cambridge: Cambridge University Press, 1993).

9. Robert Calef, *More Wonders of the Invisible World* (1700), reprinted in *Narratives of the Witchcraft Cases 1648–1706*, George Lincoln Burr, ed. (New York: Charles Scribner's Sons, 1914), 358.

10. Louise DeSalvo, *Nathaniel Hawthorne* (Atlantic Highlands, New Jersey: Humanities Press International, 1987), 80. DeSalvo incorrectly attributes the original curse as directed by Rebecca Nurse against Judge Hathorne. Actually, the curse came from Sarah Good and was directed at the Reverend Nicholas Noyes. DeSalvo's indication of the gender switch, however, remains valid.

11. *Gables*, 8.

12. *Gables*, 8.

13. Turner, 224.

14. "Hawthorne's New Romance," *Boston Daily Evening Transcript* 22 (8 April 1851): 1.

15. "Notices of Recent Publications," *Christian Examiner* (May 1851): 509.

16. "Literary Notices," *Harper's New Monthly Magazine* 2 (May 1851): 855.

17. "Review of New Books," *Peterson's Magazine* (June 1851): 283.

18. Herman Melville, letter to Hawthorne, 16? April 1851, in *The Letters of Herman Melville*, ed. Merrell R. Davis and William H. Gilman (New Haven: Yale University Press, 1960), 123–25; Edwin Percy Whipple, review of *The House of the Seven Gables*, *Graham's Magazine* (June 1851): 467.

19. *Gables*, xix, and "The Literary Guild," *North American Miscellany* (28 June 1851): 432.

20. For a discussion of sales and royalties, see *Gables*, xix–xx.

21. Whipple, 467.

22. James Mellow, *Nathaniel Hawthorne in His Times* (Boston: Houghton Mifflin Company), 315; Turner, 227.

23. Amory Dwight Mayo, "The Works of Hawthorne," *Universalist Quarterly* 8 (July 1851): 290–91.

24. "Modern Novelists—Great and Small," *Blackwood's Edinburgh Magazine* (May 1855): 564.

25. Henry James, *Hawthorne* (1879; reprint, Ithaca: Cornell University Press, 1967), 2.

26. James, 3.

27. James, 97.

28. James, 98.

29. Terence Martin, *Nathaniel Hawthorne* (Boston: Twayne Publishers, 1965), 44.

30. Martin, 38.

31. *Gables*, 1.

32. James, 100.

33. D. H. Jacques, "A Chapter on Names," *Knickerbocker* 40 (August 1852): 121.

34. Cathy N. Davidson, "Photographs of the Dead: Sherman, Daguerre, Hawthorne," *South Atlantic Quarterly* 89 (Fall 1990): 694.

35. DeSalvo, 89.

36. Nina Baym, "Hawthorne's Women: The Tyranny of Social Myths," *Centennial Review* 15 (Summer 1971): 250–72.

37. Judith A. Gustafson, "Parody in *The House of the Seven Gables*," *Nathaniel Hawthorne Journal* 6 (1976): 295.

38. Gustafson, 294–302.

39. Mellow, 359.

40. For a general discussion of women in *The House of the Seven Gables* and for a view on the connection with Cooper see Mary Suzanne Schriber, "Nathaniel Hawthorne: A Pilgrimage to a Dovecote," in *Gender and the Writer's Imagination: From Cooper to Wharton* (Lexington: Univ. Press of Kentucky, 1987), 45–85.

41. Whipple, 467.

42. "Literary Notices," 855.

43. Mayo, 291.

44. Mayo, 292.

45. Henry Theodore Tuckerman, "Nathaniel Hawthorne," *Southern Literary Messenger* 17 (June 1851): 348.

46. "Modern Novelists—Great and Small," 563.

47. Anthony Trollope, "The Genius of Nathaniel Hawthorne," *North American Review* 129 (September 1879): 215.

48. Darrel Abel, "Hawthorne's House of Tradition," *South Atlantic Quarterly* 52 (October 1953): 565.

49. Abel, 575.

50. Lawrence Sargeant Hall, *Hawthorne, Critic of Society* (1944; reprint, Gloucester, Mass.: P. Smith, 1966), 166.

51. Hall, 165.

52. Frederick Crews, *The Sins of the Fathers: Hawthorne's Psychological Themes* (New York: Oxford University Press, 1966), 183.

53. Henry Nash Smith, "The Morals of Power: Business Enterprise as a Theme in Mid-Nineteenth-Century American Fiction," in *Essays on American Literature in Honor of Jay B. Hubbell* (Durham, North Carolina, 1967), 94.

54. Roy Harvey Pearce, *Gesta Humanorum: Studies in the Historicist Mode* (Columbia: University of Missouri Press, 1987), 59.

55. Michael Davitt Bell, *Hawthorne and the Historical Romance of New England* (Princeton: Princeton University Press, 1971), 215–16.

56. Bell, 221.

57. Everett Carter, *The American Idea: The Literary Response to American Optimism* (Chapel Hill, North Carolina: University of North Carolina Press, 1977), 141.

58. Carter, 144.

59. John P. McWilliams, *Hawthorne, Melville, and the American Character: A Looking-Glass Business* (Cambridge: Cambridge University Press, 1984), 107.

60. McWilliams, 115.

61. Kriston Herzog, *Women, Ethnics, and Exotics: Images of Power in Mid-Nineteenth-Century American Fiction* (Knoxville: University of Tennessee Press, 1983), 28.

62. Herzog, 17.

63. Susan L. Mizruchi, *The Power of Historical Knowledge: Narrating the Past in Hawthorne, James, and Dreiser* (Princeton: Princeton University Press, 1988), 91.

64. Whipple, 468; "Modern Novelists—Great and Small," 565.

65. Alfred H. Marks, "Who Killed Judge Pyncheon? The Role of the Imagination in *The House of the Seven Gables*," *PMLA* 71 (June 1956): 355–69.

66. Clara B. Cox, " 'Who Killed Judge Pyncheon?' The Scene of the Crime Revisited," *Studies in American Fiction* 16 (Spring 1988): 99–103.

67. Gloria C. Erlich, *Family Themes and Hawthorne's Fiction* (New Brunswick, New Jersey: Rutgers University Press, 1984), 139.

68. Eric J. Sundquist, *Home as Found: Authority and Genealogy in Nineteenth-Century American Literature* (Baltimore: The Johns Hopkins University Press, 1979), 93.

69. Mayo, 292.

70. J. F. Ragan, "Social Criticism in *The House of the Seven Gables*," in *Literature and Society: Nineteen Essays by Germaine Bree and Others*, ed. Bernice Slote (Lincoln: University of Nebraska Press, 1964), 117.

71. Richard H. Fogle, *Hawthorne's Imagery: The "Proper Light and Shadow" in the Major Romances* (Norman: University of Oklahoma Press, 1969), 75–76; Rita Gollin, *Nathaniel Hawthorne and the Truth of Dreams* (Baton Rouge: Louisiana State University Press, 1979), 159.

72. Whipple, 468.

73. For example, "Reading Raids. I.—American Literature: Poe; Hawthorne," *Tait's Edinburgh Magazine* 22 (January 1855): 33–41, and Herbert Moore Hill, "Hawthorne's *House of the Seven Gables*," *Nassau Literary Magazine* 54 (December 1898): 253–57.

74. Arthur Sherbo, "Albert Brisbane and Hawthorne's Holgrave and Hollingsworth," *New England Quarterly* 27 (December 1954): 531–34; Daniel R. Barnes, "Orestes Brownson and Hawthorne's Holgrave," *American Literature* 45 (May 1973): 272.

75. Luther S. Luedtke, *Nathaniel Hawthorne and the Romance of the Orient* (Bloomington: Indiana University Press, 1989), 188; Jeffrey Steinbrink, "Hawthorne's Holgravian Temper: The Case Against the Past," *American Transcendental Quarterly* 31 (Summer 1976): 21–23; Amy Louise Reed, "Self-Portraiture in the Work of Nathaniel Hawthorne," *Studies in Philology* 23 (January 1926): 46–47.

76. Brook Thomas, *Cross-Examinations of Law and Literature: Cooper, Hawthorne, Stowe,*

*and Melville* (Cambridge: Cambridge University Press, 1987), 74; Jerome F. Klinkowitz, "In Defense of Holgrave," *Emerson Society Quarterly* 62 (Winter 1971): 6.

77.   Nina Baym, "Hawthorne's Holgrave: The Failure of the Artist-Hero," *JEGP* 69 (October 1970): 587.

78.   R. K. Gupta, "Hawthorne's Treatment of the Artist," *New England Quarterly* 45 (March 1972): 74.

79.   Coleman W. Thorpe, "The Oral Storyteller in Hawthorne's Novels," *Studies in Short Fiction* 16 (1979): 205–14.

80.   Maria M. Tatar, *Spellbound: Studies in Mesmerism and Literature* (Princeton: Princeton University Press, 1978), 215.

81.   Millicent Bell, *Hawthorne's View of the Artist* (New York: State University of New York Press, 1962), 159.

82.   Donald Ringe, "Hawthorne's Psychology of the Head and the Heart," *PMLA* 65 (March 1950): 120–32.

83.   Robert Emmet Whelan, Jr., "*The House of the Seven Gables*: Allegory of the Heart," *Renascence* 31 (Winter 1979): 71.

84.   Evan Carton, "The Prison Door," in *The Rhetoric of American Romance: Dialectic and Identity in Emerson, Dickinson, Poe, and Hawthorne* (Baltimore: The Johns Hopkins University Press, 1985), 224; Leland S. Person, Jr., *Aesthetic Headaches: Women and a Masculine Poetics in Poe, Melville, and Hawthorne* (Athens: University of Georgia Press, 1988), 141.

85.   Nina Baym, *The Shape of Hawthorne's Career* (Ithaca: Cornell University Press, 1976), 159–63.

86.   Carter, 141.

87.   Richard Clark Sterne, "Hawthorne's Politics in *The House of the Seven Gables*," *Canadian Review of American Studies* 6 (Spring 1975): 74–83.

88.   F. O. Matthiessen, *American Renaissance: Art and Expression in the Age of Emerson and Whitman* (New York: Oxford University Press, 1941), 331.

89.   Matthiessen, 334.

90.   Hoffman, 187.

91.   Francis Joseph Battaglia, "*The House of the Seven Gables*: New Light on Old Problems," *PMLA* 82 (December 1967): 579.

92.   Battaglia, 583. The Centenary Edition appeared in 1965.

93.   Kenneth Dauber, *Rediscovering Hawthorne* (Princeton: Princeton University Press, 1977), 147–48.

94.   Dauber, 148.

95.   Claudia D. Johnson, *The Productive Tension of Hawthorne's Art* (University: The University of Alabama Press, 1981), 76–77.

96.   Bruce Michelson, "Hawthorne's House of Three Stories," *New England Quarterly* (June 1984):181. For more on the gothic motif, see Jonathan Arac, "The House and the Railroad: *Dombey and Son* and *The House of the Seven Gables*," in *Commissioned Spirits: The Shaping of Social Motion in Dickens, Carlyle, Melville, and Hawthorne* (New Brunswick: Rutgers University Press, 1979), 94–113.

97.   Robert Clark, *History, Ideology and Myth in American Fiction, 1823–1852* (London: Macmillan, 1984), 130.

98.   Gordon Hutner, *Secrets and Sympathy: Forms of Disclosure in Hawthorne's Novels* (Athens: University of Georgia Press, 1988), 65.

99.   William J. Scheick, "The Author's Corpse and the Humean Problem of Personal Identity in Hawthorne's *The House of the Seven Gables*," *Studies in the Novel* 24 (Summer 1992): 144. Page references in the passage cited are to *The Centenary Edition of the Works of Nathaniel Hawthorne: The House of the Seven Gables*, ed. William Charvat, Roy Harvey Pearce, and Claude Simpson (Columbus: Ohio State University Press, 1965).

100. Scheick, 147.

101. From "Hawthorne and His Mosses" (1850), in *The Piazza Tales and Other Prose Pieces 1839–1860*, ed. Harrison Hayford, Hershel Parker, and G. Thomas Tanselle (Evanston and Chicago: Northwestern University Press and The Newberry Library, 1987), 243–44.

102. James R. Mellow, *Nathaniel Hawthorne in His Times* (Boston: Houghton Mifflin Company, 1980); Edward Haviland Miller, *Salem Is My Dwelling Place* (Iowa City: University of Iowa Press, 1991); and Arlin Turner, *Nathaniel Hawthorne: A Biography* (New York: Oxford University Press, 1980).

103. Terrence Martin, *Nathaniel Hawthorne* (Boston: Twayne Publishers, 1965).

104. See *The Centenary Edition*, cited above (note 99).

# REVIEWS AND EARLY CRITICISM

◆

# Letter of Herman Melville
# to Nathaniel Hawthorne
# 16? April 1851

Pittsfield, Wednesday morning.
My Dear Hawthorne,—Concerning the young gentleman's shoes, I desire
to say that a pair to fit him, of the desired pattern, cannot be had in all
Pittsfield—a fact which sadly impairs that metropolitan pride I formerly
took in the capital of Berkshire. Henceforth Pittsfield must hide its head.
However, if a pair of *bootees* will at all answer, Pittsfield will be very happy
to provide them. Pray mention all this to Mrs. Hawthorne, and command
me.

"The House of the Seven Gables: A Romance. By Nathaniel Hawthorne.
One vol. 16mo, pp. 344." The contents of this book do not belie its rich,
clustering, romantic title. With great enjoyment we spent almost an hour
in each separate gable. This book is like a fine old chamber, abundantly,
but still judiciously, furnished with precisely that sort of furniture best fitted
to furnish it. There are rich hangings, wherein are braided scenes from
tragedies! There is old china with rare devices, set out on the carved buffet;
there are long and indolent lounges to throw yourself upon; there is an
admirable sideboard, plentifully stored with good viands; there is a smell
as of old wine in the pantry; and finally, in one corner, there is a dark little
black-letter volume in golden clasps, entitled "Hawthorne: A Problem." It
has delighted us; it has piqued a re-perusal; it has robbed us of a day, and
made us a present of a whole year of thoughtfulness; it has bred great
exhilaration and exultation with the remembrance that the architect of the
Gables resides only six miles off, and not three thousand miles away, in
England, say. We think the book, for pleasantness of running interest,
surpasses the other works of the author. The curtains are more drawn; the
sun comes in more; genialities peep out more. Were we to particularize
what most struck us in the deeper passages, we would point out the scene

Letter of Herman Melville to Nathaniel Hawthorne, 16? April 1851, reprinted from Merrell R. Davis
and William H. Gilman, eds. *The Letters of Herman Melville* (New Haven: Yale University Press, 1960),
123–25, by permission of Yale University Press.

where Clifford, for a moment, would fain throw himself forth from the window to join the procession; or the scene where the judge is left seated in his ancestral chair. Clifford is full of an awful truth throughout. He is conceived in the finest, truest spirit. He is no caricature. He is Clifford. And here we would say that, did circumstances permit, we should like nothing better than to devote an elaborate and careful paper to the full consideration and analysis of the purport and significance of what so strongly characterizes all of this author's writings. There is a certain tragic phase of humanity which, in our opinion, was never more powerfully embodied than by Hawthorne. We mean the tragicalness of human thought in its own unbiassed, native, and profounder workings. We think that into no recorded mind has the intense feeling of the visable truth ever entered more deeply than into this man's. By visable truth, we mean the apprehension of the absolute condition of present things as they strike the eye of the man who fears them not, though they do their worst to him,—the man who, like Russia or the British Empire declares himself a sovereign nature (in himself) amid the powers of heaven, hell, and earth. He may perish; but so long as he exists he insists upon treating with all Powers upon an equal basis. If any of those other Powers choose to withhold certain secrets, let them; that does not impair my sovereignty in myself; that does not make me tributary. And perhaps, after all, there is *no* secret. We incline to think that the Problem of the Universe is like the Freemason's mighty secret, so terrible to all children. It turns out, at last, to consist in a triangle, a mallet, and an apron,—nothing more! We incline to think that God cannot explain His own secrets, and that He would like a little information upon certain points Himself. We mortals astonish Him as much as He us. But it is this *Being* of the matter, there lies the knot with which we choke ourselves. As soon as you say *Me*, a *God*, a *Nature*, so soon you jump off from your stool and hang from the beam. Yes, that word is the hangman. Take God out of the dictionary, and you would have Him in the street.

There is the grand truth about Nathaniel Hawthorne. He says NO! in thunder; but the Devil himself cannot make him say *yes*. For all men who say *yes*, lie; and all men who say *no*,—why, they are in the happy condition of judicious, unincumbered travellers in Europe; they cross the frontiers into Eternity with nothing but a carpet-bag,—that is to say, the Ego. Whereas those *yes*-gentry, they travel with heaps of baggage, and, damn them! they will never get through the Custom House. What's the reason, Mr. Hawthorne, that in the last stages of metaphysics a fellow always falls to *swearing* so? I could rip an hour. You see, I began with a little criticism extracted for your benefit from the "Pittsfield Secret Review," and here I have landed in Africa.

Walk down one of these mornings and see me. No nonsense; come. Remember me to Mrs. Hawthorne and the children.

H. Melville.

P. S. The marriage of Phoebe with the daguerreotypist is a fine stroke, because of his turning out to be a *Maule*. If you pass Hepzibah's cent-shop, buy me a Jim Crow (fresh) and send it to me by Ned Higgins.

# Review in *The Literary World*

## EVERT AUGUSTUS DUYCKINCK

In the preface to this work, the anxiously looked-for successor to the Scarlet Letter, Mr. Hawthorne establishes a separation between the demands of the novel and the romance, and under the privilege of the latter, sets up his claim to a certain degree of license in the treatment of the characters and incidents of his coming story. This license, those acquainted with the writer's previous works will readily understand to be in the direction of the spiritualities of the piece, in favor of a process semi-allegorical, by which an acute analysis may be wrought out and the truth of feeling be minutely elaborated; an apology, in fact, for the preference of character to action, and of character for that which is allied to the darker elements of life—the dread blossoming of evil in the soul, and its fearful retributions. The House of the Seven Gables, one for each deadly sin, may be no unmeet adumbration of the corrupted soul of man. It is a ghostly, mouldy abode, built in some eclipse of the sun, and raftered with curses dark; founded on a grave, and sending its turrets heavenward, as the lightning rod transcends its summit, to invite the wrath supernal. Every darker shadow of human life lingers in and about its melancholy shelter. There all the passions allied to crime,—pride in its intensity, avarice with its steely gripe, and unrelenting conscience, are to be expiated in the house built on injustice. Wealth there withers, and the human heart grows cold: and thither are brought as accessories the chill glance of speculative philosophy, the descending hopes of the aged laborer, whose vision closes on the workhouse, the poor necessities of the humblest means of livelihood, the bodily and mental dilapidation of a wasted life.

> A residence for woman, child, and man,
> A dwelling place,—and yet no habitation;
> A Home,—but under some prodigious ban
> Of excommunication.
>
> O'er all these hung a shadow and a fear;
> A sense of mystery and spirit daunted,

Reprinted from *The Literary World* 8:17 (26 April 1851): 334–36.

And said, as plain as whisper in the ear.
The place is haunted.

Yet the sunshine casts its rays into the old building, as it must, were it only to show us the darkness.

In truth there is sunshine brought in among the inmates, and these wrinkled, cobwebbed spiritualities with gentle Phoebe,—but it is a playful, typical light of youth and goodness,—hardly crystallizing the vapory atmosphere of the romance into the palpable concretions of actual life.

Yet, withal, these scenes and vivid descriptions are dramatic and truthful; dramatic in the picturesque and in situation rather than in continuous and well developed action; true to the sentiment and inner reality, if not to the outer fact. The two death scenes of the founder of the family and of his descendant, Judge Pyncheon, possess dramatic effect of a remarkable character; and various other groupings at the fountain and elsewhere, separate themselves in our recollection. The chief, perhaps, of the dramatis personae, is the house itself. From its turrets to its kitchen, in every nook and recess without and within, it is alive and vital, albeit of a dusty antiquity. We know it by sunlight and moonlight; by the elm which surmounts its roof, the mosses in its crevices, and its supernatural mist-swept blackness. Truly is it an actor in the scene. We move about tremblingly among its shadows,— the darkness of poverty and remorse dogging ruthlessly at our heels.

Verily this Hawthorne retains in him streaks of a Puritan ancestry. Some grave beater of pulpit cushions must lie among his ancestry; for of all laymen he will preach to you the closest sermons, probe deepest into the unescapable corruption, carry his lantern, like Belzoni among the mummies, into the most secret recesses of the heart; and he will do this with so vital a force in his propositions that they will transcend the individual example and find a precedent in every reader's heart. So true is it that when you once seize an actual thing you have in it a picture of universal life.

His Old Maid (Hepzibah) sacrificing pride to open her shop of small wares in one of the gables of the building, and her reluctant experiences of the first day, is not only a view of family pride in its shifts and reluctance, but covers all the doubts and irresolutions which beset a sensitive mind on the entrance upon any new sphere of duty in the great world.

These pictures are clear, distinct, full. The description is made out by repeated touches. There is no peculiar richness in the style: in some respects it is plain, but it flows on pellucid as a mountain rivulet, and you feel in its refreshing purity that it is fed by springs beneath.

You must be in the proper mood and time and place to read Hawthorne, if you would understand him. We think any one would be wrong to make the attempt on a rail-car, or on board a steamboat. It is not a shilling novel that you are purchasing when you buy the *House of the Seven Gables*, but a book—a book with lights and shades, parts and diversities, upon which you may feed and pasture, not exhausting the whole field at an effort, but returning now and then to uncropped fairy rings and bits of herbage. You may read the book into the small hours beyond midnight, when no sound breaks the silence but the parting of an expiring ember, or the groan of restless mahogany, and you find that the candle burns a longer flame, and that the ghostly visions of the author's page take shape about you. Conscience sits supreme in her seat, the fountains of pity and terror are opened; you look into the depths of the soul, provoked at so painful a sight—but you are strengthened as you gaze; for of that pain comes peace at last, and these shadows you must master by virtuous magic. Nathaniel Hawthorne may be the Cornelius Agrippa to invoke them, but you are the mirror in which they are reflected.

The story of the House of the Seven Gables is a tale of retribution, of expiation extending over a period of two hundred years, it taking all that while to lay the ghost of the earliest victim in the time of the witchcraft; for by the way it is to Salem that this blackened old dwelling, mildewed with easterly scud, belongs. The yeoman who originally struck his spade into the spot, by the side of a crystal spring, was hanged for a wizard, under the afflictive dispensation of Cotton Mather. His land passed by force of law under cover of an old sweeping grant from the State, though not without hard words and thoughts and litigations, to the possession of the Ahab of the Vineyard, Colonel Pyncheon, the founder of the house, whose statuesque death scene was the first incident of the strongly ribbed tenement built on the ground thus suspiciously acquired. It was a prophecy of the old wizard on his execution at Gallows Hill, looking steadfastly at his rival, the Colonel, who was there, watching the scene on horseback, that "God would give him blood to drink." The sudden death of apoplexy was thereafter ministered to the great magnates of the Pyncheon family. After an introductory chapter detailing this early history of the house, we are introduced to its broken fortunes of the present day, in its decline. An Old Maid is its one tenant, left there with a life interest in the premises by the late owner, whose vast wealth passed into the hands of a cousin, who, immediately, touched by this talisman of property, was transformed from a youth of dissipation into a high, cold, and worldly state of respectability. His portrait is drawn in this volume with the repeated limnings and labor of a Titian, who, it is known, would expend several years upon a human head. We see him in every light; walk leisurely round the vast circle of that magical outline, his respectability just mentioned, till we close in upon the man, narrowing slowly to his centre of falsity and selfishness. For a thorough witch laugh over fallen hollow-heartedness and pretence, there is a terrible sardonic greeting in the roll-call of that man's uncompleted day's performances as he sits in the fatal chamber, death-cold, having drunk the blood of the ancient curse. But this is to anticipate. Other inmates gather round Old Maid Hepzibah. A remote gable is rented to a young artist, a daguerreotypist, and then comes upon the scene the brother of the Old Maid, Clifford Pyncheon, one day let out from life incarceration for—what circumstantial evidence had brought home to him—the murder of the late family head. Thirty years had obliterated most of this man's moral and intellectual nature, save in a certain blending of the two with his physical instinct for the sensuous and beautiful. A rare character that for our spiritual limner to work upon! The agent he has provided, nature's ministrant to this feebleness and disease, to aid in the rebuilding of the man, is a sprig of unconscious, spontaneous girlhood—"a thing of beauty, and a joy for ever"—who enters the thick shades of the dwelling of disaster as a sunbeam, to purify and nourish its stagnant life. Very beautiful is this conception; and subtly wrought the chapters in which the relation is developed. Then we have the sacrifice of pride and solitary misanthropy in the petty retail shop Hepzibah opens for the increasing needs of the rusty mansion. This portion, as we have intimated, reaches the heart of the matter; and the moral here is as healthy as the emotion is keenly penetrated. What the tale-writer here says of his picture of the dilapidated figure of the Old Maid, applies to the poor and humble necessities of her position—"If we look through all the heroic fortunes of mankind, we find an entanglement of something mean and trivial with whatever is noblest in joy or sorrow. Life is made up of marble and mud. What is called poetic insight is the gift of discerning, in this sphere of strangely-mingled elements, the beauty and the majesty which are compelled to assume a garb so sordid." So, when gentility, and family decency, and the pride of life, seemed all to be sacrificed in the degradation and low vulgarities of the shop for boys and servant maids, a new ray of light breaks in upon the scene, quite unexpected and more noble than any form of magnificent selfishness. Note the crisis: "The new shop-keeper dropped the first solid result of her commercial enterprise into the till." . . . [Here Duyckinck quotes from the description of Hepzibah's new situation .]

The scene passes on, while Hepzibah, her life bound up in the resuscitation of Clifford, supported by the salient life of the youthful womanhood of Phoebe, fulfils her destiny, the "dukkeripens," as that lay-divine, the eminent Lavengro, has it in mystic, gipsy dialect, in the cent-shop—where, for a little sprinkling of pleasantry to this sombre tale, comes a voracious boy to devour the gingerbread Jim Crows, elephants, and other seductive fry of the quaintly-arranged window. His stuffed hide is a relief to the empty-waistcoated ghosts moving within. There is a humble fellow too, one Uncle Venner, a good-natured servitor at small chores—a poor devil in the eye of the world—of whom Hawthorne, with kindly eye, makes something by digging down under his tattered habiliments to his better-preserved human heart. He comes to the shop, and is a kind of out-of-door appendant to the fortunes of the house.

The Nemesis of the House is pressing for a new victim. Judge Pyncheon's thoughts are intent on an old hobby of the establishment, the procurement of a deed which was missing and which was the evidence wanting to complete the title to a certain vast New Hampshire grant—a portentous and arch-deceiving ignis fatuus of the family. Clifford is supposed to know something of this matter; but, knowledge or not, the Judge is the one man in the world whom he will not meet. Every instinct of his nature rises within him, in self-protection of his weak, sensitive life, against the stern magnetic power of the coarse, granite judge. More than that lies underneath. Clifford had been unjustly convicted—by those suspicious death-marks of his suddenly deceased relative—and the Judge had suffered it, holding all the time the key which would have unlocked the mystery, besides some other shades of criminality. To escape an interview with this man, Clifford and Hepzibah leave the house in flight, while Judge Pyncheon sits in the apartment of his old ancestor, waiting for him. And how sits he there? . . . [Here Duyckinck quotes from the death scene of Pyncheon.]

This, we conceive to be taking a pretty strong grip of Judge Pyncheon. It is a spiritual lashing of the old man, grievous as any material one Dickens ever inflicted in paying off an immitigable scoundrel at the close of a twenty months' cruise of sin and wickedness, in the last number of a long serial novel. The fortunes of the House, after this tremendous purgation, look more brightly for the future. The diverted patrimony of his ex-respectability—the Governor in posse of Massachusetts—returns to its true channel to irrigate the dry heart of the Old Maid, and furnish Clifford the luxuries of the Beautiful. The daguerreotypist, who turns out to be the descendant of the wizard,—the inventor of the curse—marries Phoebe, of course, and the parties have left the Old House, mouldering away in its by-street, for the summer realm of a country summer retreat.

Such is the material of Hawthorne's legend—with every "coigne of vantage" for his procreant, melancholy fancy to work in, hanging his airy cobwebs about, not without a glitter on them of dew and sunshine. In tenderness and delicacy of sentiment, no writer of the present day can go beyond this book. This is Hawthorne's province of the world. In it his life is original, fanciful, creative.

# [Review in *The International Magazine of Literature, Art, and Science*]

## Rufus Wilmot Griswold*

Mr. Hawthorne's last work is *The House of Seven Gables*, a romance of the present day. It is not less original, not less striking, not less powerful, than The Secret Letter. We doubt indeed whether he has elsewhere surpassed either of the three strongly contrasted characters of the book. An innocent and joyous child-woman, Phoebe Pyncheon, comes from a farm-house into the grand and gloomy old mansion where her distant relation, Hepzibah Pyncheon, an aristocratical and fearfully ugly but kind-hearted unmarried woman of sixty, is just coming down from her faded state to keep in one of her drawing-rooms a small shop, that she may be able to maintain an elder brother who is every moment expected home from a prison to which in his youth he had been condemned unjustly, and in the silent solitude of which he has kept some lineaments of gentleness while his hair has grown white, and a sense of beauty while his brain has become disordered and his heart has been crushed and all present influences of beauty have been quite shut out. The House of Seven Gables is the purest piece of imagination in our prose literature.

*Reprinted from *International Magazine of Literature, Art, and Science* 3 (May 1851):159.

# [Review in *Christian Examiner*]

The Twice-Told Tales were the first fruits of Mr. Hawthorne's genius; and their simple beauty and quiet pathos are doubtless familiar to many of our readers. They display the same mental characteristics that he has shown in his later works; and in the present elegant edition, which is enriched with an original Preface and a finely engraved head of the author, they can hardly fail of finding many new admirers.

In the Preface to The House of the Seven Gables, our author claims for the book "a certain latitude, both as to its fashion and material, which he would not have felt himself entitled to assume, had he professed to be writing a Novel"; and he further tells us, that "it had been no part of his object, however, to describe local manners, nor in any way to meddle with the characteristics of a community for whom he cherishes a proper respect and a natural regard." He has, however, a moral constantly in view, which is, to show that "the wrong-doing of one generation lives into the successive ones, and, divesting itself of every temporary advantage, becomes a pure and uncontrollable mischief"; and the same idea is presented once and again in the course of the romance itself. The work whose character and aim are thus described is a production of great power, though inferior in interest to The Scarlet Letter. The impression which it leaves on the reader's mind is, indeed, much pleasanter than that produced by its predecessor; but its plot is more complex, the characterization more exaggerated, and the artistic execution less perfect. Viewed as a whole, it will stand much higher than when considered in its separate parts; for the general outline is well conceived, but the filling up is not of equal excellence. There is too much of disquisition, and too little of narrative and dialogue. Consequently we have fewer descriptive passages of so great beauty and so tender pathos as we find in the Scarlet Letter and in some of the Twice-Told Tales, while there are scattered through the volume many sparkling gems of thought and incidental sketches of character which are alike striking and admirable. It will add to Mr. Hawthorne's reputation, and be greatly admired by a large class of readers.

Reprinted from *Christian Examiner* 50 (May 1851): 508–9.

We may say here, what we should have said at greater length had we noticed The Scarlet Letter, that it contains the grossest and foulest falsification of truth in history and personal character, that we have ever encountered, in romance or narrative.

# [Review in *Harper's New Monthly Magazine*]

Ticknor, Reed, and Fields have issued *The House of the Seven Gables*, a Romance, by Nathaniel Hawthorne, which is strongly marked with the bold and unique characteristics that have given its author such a brilliant position among American novelists. The scene, which is laid in the old Puritanic town of Salem, extends from the period of the witchcraft excitement to the present time, connecting the legends of the ancient superstition with the recent marvels of animal magnetism, and affording full scope for the indulgence of the most weird and somber fancies. Destitute of the high-wrought manifestations of passion which distinguished the "Scarlet Letter," it is more terrific in its conception, and not less intense in its execution, but exquisitely relieved by charming portraitures of character, and quaint and comic descriptions of social eccentricities. A deep vein of reflection underlies the whole narrative, often rising naturally to the surface, and revealing the strength of the foundation on which the subtle, aerial inventions of the author are erected. His frequent dashes of humor gracefully blend with the monotone of the story, and soften the harsher colors in which he delights to clothe his portentous conceptions. In no former production of his pen, are his unrivalled powers of description displayed to better advantage. The rusty wooden house in Pyncheon street, with its sharp-pointed gables, and its huge clustered chimney—the old elm tree before the door—the grassy yard seen through the lattice-fence, with its enormous fertility of burdocks—and the green moss on the slopes of the roof, with the flowers growing aloft in the air in the nook between two of the gables—present a picture to the eye as distinct as if our childhood had been passed in the shadow of the old weather-beaten edifice. Nor are the characters of the story drawn with less sharp and vigorous perspective. They stand out from the canvas as living realities. In spite of the supernatural drapery in which they are enveloped, they have such genuine expression of flesh and blood, that we cannot doubt we have known them all our days. They have the air of old acquaintance—only we wonder how the artist got them to sit for their likeness. The grouping of these persons is managed with admirable artistic skill. Old Maid Pyncheon, concealing under her verjuice scowl the unutter-

Reprinted from *Harper's New Monthly Magazine* 2:12 (May 1851): 855–56.

able tenderness of a sister—her woman-hearted brother, on whose sensitive nature had fallen such a strange blight—sweet and beautiful Phebe, the noble village-maiden, whose presence is always like that of some shining angel—the dreamy, romantic descendant of the legendary wizard—the bold, bad man of the world, reproduced at intervals in the bloody Colonel, and the unscrupulous Judge—wise old Uncle Venner—and inappeasable Ned Higgins—are all made to occupy the place on the canvas which shows the lights and shades of their character in the most impressive contrast, and contributes to the wonderful vividness and harmony of the grand historical picture. On the whole, we regard "The House of the Seven Gables," though it exhibits no single scenes that may not be matched in depth and pathos by some of Mr. Hawthorne's previous creations, as unsurpassed by any thing he has yet written, in exquisite beauty of finish, in the skillful blending of the tragic and comic, and in the singular life-like reality with which the wildest traditions of the Puritanic age are combined with the every-day incidents of modern society.

# [Review in *Peterson's Magazine*]

When we had read the first twenty pages of this romance, we felt inclined to dissent from the prevalent opinion of the press, that it was inferior to "The Scarlet Letter." As we proceeded, however, we were forced to acknowledge that our contemporaries were correct, and that "The House of Seven Gables" was, as one of the ablest of them characterized it, only another "Twice Told Tale." In short, though superior in the finish of some of its details, the romance, as a whole, is not equal to its predecessor. Nevertheless it is a work of genius. No living American author but Hawthorne could have drawn such a character as Clifford, described such a quaint old house as the Pyncheon Mansion, or imagined such a wild, half unearthly legend as that connected with the wizard's curse. The fault of the book, indeed of all Hawthorne's books, in a moral aspect, is the sombre coloring which pervades them, and which leaves an effect more or less morbid on even healthy minds. The only really loveable character in the book is Phebe, who comes, like a gleam of summer sunshine, to the old house and its legendary horrors. The volume is very elegantly printed.

Reprinted from *Peterson's Magazine* 19 (June 1851): 282–83.

# [Review in *Graham's Magazine*]

## EDWIN PERCY WHIPPLE*

"The wrong-doing of one generation lives into the successive ones, and, divesting itself of every temporary advantage, becomes a pure and uncontrollable mischief;" this is the leading idea of Hawthorne's new romance, and it is developed with even more than his usual power. The error in "The Scarlet Letter," proceeded from the divorce of its humor from its pathos— the introduction being as genial as Goldsmith or Lamb, and the story which followed being tragic even to ghastliness. In "The House of the Seven Gables," the humor and the pathos are combined, and the whole work is stamped with the individuality of the author's genius, in all its variety of power. The first hundred pages of the volume are masterly in conception and execution, and can challenge comparison, in the singular depth and sweetness of their imaginative humor, with the best writing of the kind in literature. The other portions of the book have not the same force, precision, and certainty of handling, and the insight into character especially, seems at times to follow the processes of clairvoyance more than those of the waking imagination. The consequence is that the movement of the author's mind betrays a slight fitfulness toward the conclusion, and, splendid as is the supernaturally grotesque element which this ideal impatience introduces, it still somewhat departs from the integrity of the original conception, and interferes with the strict unity of the work. The mental nerve which characterizes the first part, slips occasionally into mental nervousness as the author proceeds.

We have been particular in indicating this fault, because the work is of so high a character that it demands, as a right, to be judged by the most exacting requirements of art. Taken as a whole, it is Hawthorne's greatest work, and is equally sure of immediate popularity and permanent fame. Considered as a romance, it does not so much interest as fasten and fascinate attention; and this attractiveness in the story is the result of the rare mental powers and moods out of which the story creatively proceeds. Every chapter proves the author to be, not only a master of narrative, a creator of character, an observer of life, and richly gifted with the powers of vital conception and combination, but it also exhibits him as a profound thinker and skillful

*Reprinted from *Graham's Magazine* 38 (June 1851): 467–68.

metaphysician. We do not know but that his eye is more certain in detecting remote spiritual laws and their relations, than in the sure grasp of individual character; and if he ever loses his hold upon persons it is owing to that intensely meditative cast of his mind by which he views persons in their relations to the general laws whose action they illustrate. There is some discord in the present work in the development of character and sequence of events; the dramatic unity is therefore not perfectly preserved; but this cannot be affirmed of the unity of the law. That is always sustained, and if it had been thoroughly embodied, identified, and harmonized with the concrete events and characters, we have little hesitation in asserting that the present volume would be the deepest work of imagination ever produced on the American continent.

Before venturing upon any comments on the characters, we cannot resist the temptation to call the attention of our readers to the striking thoughts profusely scattered over the volume. These are generally quietly introduced, and spring so naturally out of the narrative of incidents, that their depth may not be at first appreciated. Expediency is the god whom most men really worship and obey, and few realize the pernicious consequences and poisonous vitality of bad deeds performed to meet an immediate difficulty. Hawthorne hits the law itself in this remark: "The act of the present generation is the germ which may and must produce good or evil fruit, in a far distant time; for, together with the seed of the merely temporary crop, which mortals term expediency, they inevitably sow the acorns of a more enduring growth, which may darkly overshadow their posterity." In speaking of the legal murder of old Matthew Maule for witchcraft, he says that Matthew "was one of the martyrs to that terrible delusion, which should teach us, among its other morals, that the influential classes, and those who take upon themselves to be leaders of the people, are fully liable to all the passionate error that has ever characterized the maddest mob." In reference to the hereditary transmission of individual qualities, it is said of Colonel Pyncheon's descendants, that "his character might be traced all the way down, as distinctly *as if the colonel himself, a little diluted, had been gifted with a sort of intermittent immortality on earth.*" In a deeper vein is the account of the working of the popular imagination on the occasion of Col. Pyncheon's death. This afflicting event was ascribed by physicians to apoplexy; by the people to strangulation. The colonel had caused the death of a reputed wizard; and the fable ran that the lieutenant-governor, as he advanced into the room where the colonel sat dead in his chair, *saw a skeleton hand* at the colonel's throat, which vanished away as he came near him. Such touches as these are visible all over the volume, and few romances have more quotable felicities of thought and description.

The characters of the romance are among the best of Hawthorne's individualizations, and Miss Hepzibah and Phoebe are perhaps his master-pieces of characterization, in the felicity of their conception, their contrast, and their inter-action. Miss Hepzibah Pyncheon, the inhabitant of the gabled house, is compelled at the age of sixty to stoop from her aristocratic isolation from the world, and open a little cent shop, in order that she may provide for the subsistence of an unfortunate brother. The chapters entitled "The Little Shop-Window," "The First Customer," and a "Day Behind the Counter," in which her ludicrous humiliations are described, may be placed beside the best works of the most genial humorists, for their rapid alternations of smiles and tears, and the perfect April weather they make in the heart. The description of the little articles at the shop-window, the bars of soap, the leaden dragoons, the split peas, and the fantastic Jim Crow, "executing his world-renowned dance in gingerbread;" the attempts of the elderly maiden to arrange her articles aright, and the sad destruction she makes among them, crowned by upsetting that tumbler of marbles, "all of which roll different ways, and each individual marble, devil-directed, into the most difficult obscurity it can find;" the nervous irritation of her deportment as she puts her shop in order, the twitches of pride which agonize her breast, as stealing on tiptoe to the window, "as cautiously as if she conceived some bloody-minded villain to be watching behind the elm-tree, with intent to take her life," she stretches out her long, lank arm to put a paper of pearl-buttons, a Jew's harp, or what not, in its destined place, and then straitway vanishing back into the dusk, "as if the world need never hope for another glimpse of her;" the "ugly and spiteful little din" of the door-bell, announcing her first penny customer; all these, and many more minute details, are instinct with the life of humor, and cheerily illustrate that "entanglement of something mean and trivial with whatever is noblest in joy and sorrow," which it is the office of the humorist to represent and idealize.

The character of Phoebe makes the sunshine of the book, and by connecting her so intimately with Miss Hepzibah, a quaint sweetness is added to the native graces of her mind and disposition. The "homely witchcraft" with which she brings out the hidden capabilities of every thing, is exquisitely exhibited, and poor Uncle Venner's praise of her touches the real secret of her fascination. "I've seen," says that cheery mendicant, "a great deal of the world, not only in people's kitchens and back-yards, but at the street corners, and on the wharves, and in other places where my business calls me; but I'm free to say that I never saw a human creature do her work so much like one of God's angels as this child Phoebe does!" Holgrave, the young gentleman who carries off this pearl of womanhood, appears to us a failure. It is impossible for the reader to like him, and one finds it difficult to conceive how Phoebe herself can like him. The love scenes accordingly lack love, and a kind of magnetic influence is substituted for affection. The character of Clifford is elaborately drawn, and sustained with much subtle skill, but he occupies perhaps too much space, and lures the author too much into metaphysical analysis and didactic disquisition. Judge Pyncheon is powerfully delineated, and the account of his death is a masterpiece of fantastic description. It is needless, perhaps, to say that the characters of the book have, like those in "The Scarlet Letter," a vital relation to each other, and are developed not successively and separately, but mutually, each implying the other by a kind of artistic necessity.

The imagination in the "House of Seven Gables," is perhaps most strikingly exhibited in the power with which the house itself is pervaded with thought, so that every room and gable has a sort of human interest communicated to it, and seems to symbolize the whole life of the Pyncheon family, from the grim colonel, who built it, to that delicate Alice, "the fragrance of whose rich and delightful character lingered about the place where she lived, as a dried rose-bud scents the drawer where it has withered and perished."

In conclusion, we hope to have the pleasure of reviewing a new romance by Hawthorne twice a year at least. We could also hope that if Holgrave continues his contributions to the magazines, that he would send Graham some such story as "Alice Pyncheon," which he tells so charmingly to Phoebe. "The Scarlet Letter," and "The House of Seven Gables," contain mental qualities which insensibly lead some readers to compare the author to other cherished literary names. Thus we have seen Hawthorne likened for this quality to Goldsmith, and for that to Irving, and for still another to Dickens; and some critics have given him the preference over all whom he seems to resemble. But the real cause for congratulation in the appearance of an original genius like Hawthorne, is not that he dethrones any established prince in literature, but that he founds a new principality of his own.

# [Review in *Southern Literary Messenger*]

## Henry T. Tuckerman*

The scenery, tone and personages of the story are imbued with a local authenticity which is not, for an instant, impaired by the imaginative charm of romance. We seem to breathe, as we read, the air and be surrounded by the familiar objects of a New England town. The interior of the House, each article described within it, from the quaint table to the miniature by Malbone;—every product of the old garden, the street-scenes that beguile the eyes of poor Clifford, as he looks out of the arched window, the noble elm and the gingerbread figures at the little shop window—all have the significance that belong to reality when seized upon by art. In these details we have the truth, simplicity and exact imitation of the Flemish painters. So life-like in the minutiae and so picturesque in general effect are these sketches of still-life, that they are daguerreotyped in the reader's mind, and form a distinct and changeless background, the light and shade of which give admirable effect to the action of the story: occasional touches of humor, introduced with exquisite tact, relieve the grave undertone of the narrative and form vivacious and quaint images which might readily be transferred to canvass—so effectively are they drawn in words; take, for instance, the street-musician and the Pyncheon fowls, the judge balked of his kiss over the counter, Phœbe reading to Clifford in the garden, or the old maid, in her lonely chamber, gazing on the sweet lineaments of her unfortunate brother. Nor is Hawthorne less successful in those pictures that are drawn exclusively for the mind's eye and are obvious to sensation rather than the actual vision. Were a New England Sunday, breakfast, old mansion, easterly storm, or the morning after it clears, ever so well described? The skill in atmosphere we have noted in his lighter sketches, is also as apparent: around and within the principal scene of this romance, there hovers an alternating melancholy and brightness which is born of genuine moral life; no contrasts can be imagined of this kind, more eloquent to a sympathetic mind, than that between the inward consciousness and external appearance of Hepzibah or Phœbe and Clifford, or the Judge. They respectively symbolize the poles of human existence; and are fine studies for the psychologist. Yet this attraction is subservient to fidelity to local characteristics. Clifford represents,

*Reprinted from *Southern Literary Messenger* 17 (June 1851): 344–49.

though in its most tragic imaginable phase, the man of fine organization and true sentiments environed by the material realities of New England life; his plausible uncle is the type of New England selfishness, glorified by respectable conformity and wealth; Phœbe is the ideal of genuine, efficient, yet loving female character in the same latitude; Uncle Venner, we regard as one of the most fresh, yet familiar portraits in the book; all denizens of our eastern provincial towns must have known such a philosopher; and Holgrave embodies Yankee acuteness and hardihood redeemed by integrity and enthusiasm. The contact of these most judiciously selected and highly characteristic elements, brings out not only many beautiful revelations of nature, but elucidates interesting truth; magnetism and socialism are admirably introduced; family tyranny in its most revolting form, is powerfully exemplified: the distinction between a mental and a heartfelt interest in another, clearly unfolded: and the tenacious and hereditary nature of moral evil impressively shadowed forth. The natural refinements of the human heart, the holiness of a ministry of disinterested affection, the gracefulness of the homeliest services when irradiated by cheerfulness and benevolence, are illustrated with singular beauty. "He," says our author, speaking of Clifford, "had no right to be a martyr, and beholding him so fit to be happy, and so feeble for all other purposes, a generous, strong and noble spirit would methinks, have been ready to sacrifice what little enjoyment it might have planned for itself,—*it would have flung down the hopes so paltry in its regard—if thereby the wintry blasts of our rude sphere might come tempered to such a man:*" and elsewhere: "Phoebe's presence made a home about her,—that very sphere which the outcast, the prisoner, the potentate, the wretch beneath mankind, the wretch aside from it, or the wretch above it, instinctively pines after—a home. She was real! Holding her hand, you felt something; a tender something; a substance and a warm one: *and so long as you could feel its grasp, soft as it was, you might be certain that your place was good in the whole sympathetic chain of human nature.* The world was no longer a delusion."

Thus narrowly, yet with reverence, does Hawthorne analyze the delicate traits of human sentiment and character; and open vistas into that beautiful and unexplored world of love and thought that exists in every human being, though overshadowed by material circumstance and technical duty. This, as we have before said, was his great service; digressing every now and then, from the main drift of his story, he takes evident delight in expatiating on phases of character and general traits of life, or in bringing into strong relief the more latent facts of consciousness. Perhaps the union of the philosophic tendency with the poetic instinct is the great charm of his genius. It is common for American critics to estimate the interest of all writings by their comparative glow, vivacity and rapidity of action: somewhat of the restless temperament and enterprising life of the nation infects its taste: such terms as "quiet," "gentle" and "tasteful," are equivocal when applied in this country, to a book; and yet they may envelope the rarest energy of thought and depth of insight as well as earnestness of feeling; these qualities, in reflective minds, are too real to find melodramatic development; they move as calmly as summer waves, or glow as noiselessly as the firmament; but not the less grand and mighty is their essence; to realize it, the spirit of contemplation, and the recipient mood of sympathy, must be evoked, for it is not external but moral excitement that is proposed; and we deem one of Hawthorne's most felicitous merits—that of so patiently educing artistic beauty and moral interest from life and nature, without the least sacrifice of intellectual dignity.

The healthy spring of life is typified in Phoebe so freshly as to magnetize the feelings as well as engage the perceptions of the reader; its intellectual phase finds expression in Holgrave, while the state of Clifford, when relieved of the nightmare that oppressed his sensitive temperament, the author justly compares to an Indian-summer of the soul. Across the path of these beings of genuine flesh and blood, who constantly appeal to our most humane sympathies, or rather around their consciousness and history, flits the pale, mystic figure of Alice—whose invisible music and legendary fate overflow with a graceful and attractive superstition—yielding an Ariel-like melody to the more solemn and cheery strains of the whole composition. Among the apt though incidental touches of the picture, the idea of making the music-grinder's monkey an epitome of avarice, the daguerreotype a test of latent character, and the love of the reformer Holgrave for the genially practical Phœbe, win him to conservatism, strike us as remarkably natural yet quite as ingenuous and charming as philosophical. We may add that the same pure, even, unexaggerated and perspicuous style of diction that we have recognized in his previous writing, is maintained in this.

# Review in [*Southern Literary Messenger*]*

Our valued contributor, Mr. Tuckerman, has so fully and satisfactorily discussed the merits of Hawthorne and of the present—his latest—work, in preceding pages of this number of our magazine, that we deem it quite out of place to unfold its plot, or remark upon its excellences here, as we might otherwise have done. The book is really charming, not, perhaps, as strongly marked as "The Scarlet Letter," but full to overflowing of rare and peculiar beauties. There is, we think, error in the author's predisposition to represent wealth as always vicious and poverty always virtuous, which is not the case, but his genial, receptive, loving spirit is attuned to all that is good and beautiful in man and nature.

*Reprinted from *Southern Literary Messenger* 17 (June 1851): 391.

# The Works of Hawthorne

The "House of the Seven Gables," is inferior to the "Scarlet Letter" in artistic proportion, compactness and sustained power. It is not a jet of molten ore from a glowing furnace, but a work elaborated in thoughtful leisure, characterized by a more sober coloring, and less intensity of life than its predecessor. Yet whatever value the book may have lost by the absence of one class of peculiarities, is almost restored by the presence of another; for it cannot be denied, that as a whole, it is nearer actual life, and more comprehensively true to human nature, than any former work of its author.

Mr. Hawthorne has here attempted to describe the operation of spiritual laws in the midst of the modern life in New England. The tale is the development of the providential retribution for gain unrighteously acquired, while the social problem of aristocracy and democracy naturally branches out from the main idea. The "House of the Seven Gables," with its central solitudes, its shop door upon the street, and the room of the daguerreotypist in one corner, with the Pyncheon family, well represents the old order in the process of vexatious adjustment to the new. Hepzibah steps across the gulf that divides two social states, in her way from the parlor to the counter. The judge, the sister, and Clifford, each in their own way, represent the phases of a decaying order, while little Phoebe is its point of contact with the new incarnated in Holgrave. To illustrate, in this manner, a strictly moral and social fact, requires a delicacy of handling which might appal one less conscious of power than Mr. Hawthorne, and we cannot say that he has done it perfectly. The separate portions are happily executed, but the welding of the parts is not always complete. The analysis of character and revelation of spiritual forces are unexceptionable, and certainly we have never known such admirable rendering of American life as in many pages of the book; but we are occasionally at a loss to reconcile the two things, and a vague suspicion often haunts us that Pyncheon street is after all in dream-land. Had the romance been kept longer in the author's mind, it would probably not have provoked these strictures, but might have been more evidently a step forward than now.

The characters display the writer's usual habits of delineation. Judge

*Reprinted from *The Universalist Quarterly and General Review* (8) (July 1851): 291–93.

Pyncheon, the type of respectability, with his wide extended influence, his popular philanthropy, his common-place philosophy and his rotten heart; Hepzibah,—ancient gentility gone to seed, toiling in vain to obey the dictates of a good heart and human necessities; and Holgrave, a rickety caricature of the "good time coming," are as valueless specimens of individual reality as any of their father's children, yet well enough adapted to be the spokesmen of laws and institutions. Upon the character of Clifford, Mr. Hawthorne has evidently wreaked all his acuteness. The result is such a felicity of mental analysis as we never before witnessed. The manner in which this artist-soul, hovering alternately upon the verge of insanity and idiocy, is pictured with all its relations to nature and healthy and diseased mind, is truly amazing. The theory that Clifford is made to suggest, would doubtless be true if a purely artistic spirit ever did or could exist; but since every human being has a heart as well as an imagination, we suspect the moral law must hold yet, in place of its artistic substitute. But we forgive all the offence received from the ghostly family of our author, now that he has given us Phoebe. If he had picked her in pieces, we would have cursed him with all the heartiness of which an angry reader is capable. Thank Heaven, the beautiful creature comes out of the fire unsinged, the loveliest creation of American poetry, the truest delineation of American female character.

The author's propensity to symbolism, is here as strongly marked as elsewhere. The house and the garden, the elm, the street, the shop, Maule's well and Alice's posies, Mammon and Grimalkin, all do good service in the typical "line." The conception of the house and garden, is in this respect, one of the happiest in literature. Yet we are compelled occasionally to endure the old offence of melodramatic perversity in the dog-day smile of the Judge, the gurgle in the throat of the Pyncheons, and the ancestral race of hens. Grimalkin and Mammon, however, are genuine creatures. Nothing can be happier than the greediness of the little devil, and nothing out of Shakespeare more terrible than the cat looking through the window at the dead Judge.

In passages, this work is not inferior to any of the author's books. The picture of Maule's execution; the description of the house and garden; Hepzibah opening the shop; the crowd seen from the arched window; the analysis of Clifford; Phoebe waking, walking to church, and becoming conscious of her love in the moonlight arbor, and the death of Judge Pyncheon, present an ever-fresh claim upon our admiration. The style is every way worthy of the theme; and although in some respects inferior to the "Scarlet Letter," the book has peculiar merits of its own, and is by far the most pleasing of its author's productions.

If in these pages we have done injustice to any of the qualities of Mr. Hawthorne's genius, in our desire to present what seems to us its noblest characteristic, we regret the failure the less that it may be the more easily detected than if it were radical. With all the elements of ordinary success in novel-writing, he is the possessor of a higher gift than is often granted to a poet. That he should not yet have subdued his versatile endowments to perfect harmony of action, is not strange;—that he has written the "Scarlet Letter," and the "House of the Seven Gables," is a new repetition of the perpetually recurring miracle of genius. And it is with a sense of gratitude for what we have received, too sincere for adulation, that we close by giving utterance to the hope of many readers, that yet other works are to come from the same source, in which justice shall be done to individual character, social life, and the eternal laws of Providence. All this in one book he can yet achieve, and on the day when that volume comes from the genial press of Messrs. Ticknor, Reed & Fields, Nathaniel Hawthorne will be the first writer, in the English tongue, of the highest order of romance.

# Modern Novelists Great and Small*

*The House of the Seven Gables* is not less remarkable nor less unwholesome than its predecessor. The affectation of extreme homeliness and commonplace in the external circumstances, and the mystery and secret of the family with which these circumstances are interwoven, is very effective in its way; and if it were not that its horrors and its wonders are protracted into tedious long-windedness, we would be disposed to admire the power with which these figures were posed and these situations made. But we are never contented with manufactured stories. If they do not grow with a sweet progression of nature, they may please our eye, or flatter, with a sense of superiority to the multitude, our critical faculties; but we cannot take such productions into our heart. Hephzibah Pyncheon is, perhaps, the most touching picture Mr. Hawthorne has made, and her first attempt at shopkeeping, with all its little humiliations and trials, is a pitiful picture, true enough to reach the heart. We can understand how the poor old gentlewoman cries over the scattered sweetmeats which roll over the floor when she lets them fall. We can comprehend her nervousness, her pride, her self-humiliation. There is a spark of human kindness in her, as there is a touch of delicate art in the canker-eaten roses in the old desolate garden; and her devotion to her brother, uncouth and awkward as its demonstrations are, has something pathetic in it. The brother himself is one of those peculiar individuals who owe their existence to the spiritual anatomist whose business it is to "study" his neighbours. Clifford's perfect selfishness is only an intense development of love for the beautiful, says his biographer. Hephzibah's shy and awkward tenderness disgusts and irritates rather than delights him, because it is his natural instinct to seek beauty, and there is nothing lovely in the withered ancient lady, in spite of the deep love at her heart. If we are not mistaken, Mr. Hawthorne calls this "poetic," this heartlessness of his hero, and certainly endeavors to elevate it into something higher than the common hard selfishness which we are accustomed to, both in the world and in novels. Whatever it may be in America, we should be greatly disappointed to find the poetic temperament resolved into this vulgar sensualism in our own more sober world. A nice eye for external beauty, and a heart closed to all perception

*Reprinted from *Blackwood's Edinburgh Magazine* 77: 475 (May 1855): 563–64.

of the beauty of other hearts, may make a voluptuary, but will never, with any amount of talent added thereto, make a poet. The character is fit enough for Harold Skimpole, and comes in admirably to make up that capital sham; but we entirely reject and disbelieve it in any personage of more serious pretensions. It has just originality enough to strike a casual observer, or a rapid reader, as "something new;" but we know of nothing more repellant or obnoxious to common humanity, than a man who rejects, and is disgusted by, honest affections and tenderness of which he is entirely unworthy, because, forsooth, they are not lovely in their outward manifestations, and he has an "eye for beauty," and a fastidious taste, which cannot endure anything that is not attractive to the eye.

In the death-scene of Judge Pyncheon, we are wearied and worried out of all the horror and impressiveness which might have been in it, had its author only known when to stop. Perhaps there is scarcely such another piece of over-description in the language. The situation is fairly worn to pieces. Throughout the book this is the leading error. Everything is dwelt upon with a tedious minuteness. The motion is slow and heavy. The storyteller holds our buttons and pours out his sentences all in the same cadence. We feel ourselves compelled to submit and listen to the long story. But even the power and fascination it undoubtedly possesses, does not impel us to forgive the author for this interminable strain upon our patience. Like the wedding guest in the *Ancient Mariner*, we sit reluctantly to hear it out; and when it is done, and no adequate reward is forthcoming of either wisdom or pleasure, we are injured and indignant, and do not understand why we have been detained so long to so little purpose. For it is no particular gratification to us to know how Mr. Hawthorne studies his subjects—how he sets them in different lights, like a child with a new toy, and gets new glimpses of their character and capabilities—we want the result, and not the process—the story completed, but not the photographs from which it is to be made.

# The Genius of Nathaniel Hawthorne

### Anthony Trollope*

As a novel "The House of the Seven Gables" is very inferior to "The Scarlet Letter." The cause of this inferiority would, I think, be plain to any one who had himself been concerned in the writing of novels. When Hawthorne proposed to himself to write "The Scarlet Letter," the plot of his story was clear to his mind. He wrote the book because he had the story strongly, lucidly manifest to his own imagination. In composing the other he was driven to search for a plot, and to make a story. "The Scarlet Letter" was written because he had it to write, and the other because he had to write it. The novelist will often find himself in the latter position. He has characters to draw, lessons to teach, philosophy perhaps which he wishes to expose, satire to express, humor to scatter abroad. These he can employ gracefully and easily if he have a story to tell. If he have none, he must concoct something of a story laboriously, when his lesson, his characters, his philosophy, his satire, and his humor will be less graceful and less easy. All the good things I have named are there in "The House of the Seven Gables"; but they are brought in with less artistic skill, because the author has labored over his plot, and never had it clear to his own mind.

There is a mystery attached to the house. That is a matter of course. A rich man obtained the ground on which it was built by fraud from a poor man, and the poor man's curse falls on the rich man's descendants, and the rich man with his rich descendants are abnormally bad, though very respectable. They not only cheat but murder. The original poor man was hung for witchcraft,—only because he had endeavored to hold his own against the original rich man. The rich men in consequence die when they come to advanced age, without any apparent cause of death, sitting probably upright in their chairs, to the great astonishment of the world at large, and with awful signs of blood about their mouths and shirtfronts. And each man as he dies is in the act of perpetrating some terrible enormity against some poor member of his own family. The respectable rich man with whom we become personally acquainted in the story,—for as to some of the important characters we hear of them only by the records which are given of past times,—begins by getting a cousin convicted of a murder of which he knew

*Reprinted from *North American Review* 129:274 (September 1879): 212–15.

that his kinsman was not guilty, and is preparing to have the same kinsman fraudulently and unnecessarily put into a lunatic asylum, when he succumbs to the fate of his family and dies in his chair, all covered with blood. The unraveling of these mysteries is vague, and, as I think, inartistic. The reader is not carried on by any intense interest in the story itself, and comes at last not much to care whether he does or does not understand the unraveling. He finds that his interest in the book lies elsewhere,—that he must seek it in the characters, lessons, philosophy, satire, and humor, and not in the plot. With "The Scarlet Letter" the plot comes first, and the others follow as accessories.

Two or three of the characters here drawn are very good. The wicked and respectable gentleman who *drees* the doom of his family, and dies in his chair all covered with blood, is one Judge Pyncheon. The persistent, unbending, cruel villainy of this man,—whose heart is as hard as a millstone, who knows not the meaning of conscience, to whom money and respectability are everything,—was dear to Hawthorne's heart. He likes to revel in an excess of impossible wickedness, and has done so with the Judge. Though we do not care much for the mysteries of the Judge's family, we like the Judge himself, and we like to feel that the author is pouring out his scorn on the padded respectables of his New England world. No man had a stronger belief than Hawthorne in the superiority of his own country; no man could be more sarcastic as to the deficiencies of another,—as I had reason to discover in that affair of the peas; but, nevertheless, he is always throwing out some satire as to the assumed virtues of his own immediate countrymen. It comes from him in little touches as to every incident he handles. In truth, he can not write without satire; and, as in these novels he writes of his own country, his shafts fall necessarily on that.

But the personage we like best in the book is certainly Miss Hepzibah Pyncheon. She is a cousin of the Judge, and has become, by some family arrangement, the life-possessor of the house with seven gables. She is sister also of the man who had been wrongly convicted of murder, and who, when released after a thirty-years' term of imprisonment, comes also to live at the house. Miss Hepzibah, under a peculiarly ill-grained exterior, possesses an affectionate heart and high principles. Driven by poverty, she keeps a shop,— a cent-shop, a term which is no doubt familiar enough in New England, and by which it would be presumed that all her articles were to be bought for a cent each, did it not appear by the story that she dealt also in goods of greater value. She is a lady by birth, and can not keep her cent-shop without some feeling of degradation; but that is preferable to the receiving of charity from that odious cousin the Judge. Her timidity, her affection, her true appreciation of herself, her ugliness, her hopelessness, and general incapacity for everything,—cent-shop-keeping included,—are wonderfully drawn. There are characters in novels who walk about on their feet, who stand upright and move, so that readers can look behind them, as one seems to be able to do in looking at a well-painted figure on the canvas. There are others, again, so wooden that no reader expects to find in them any appearance of movement. They are blocks roughly hewed into some more or less imperfect forms of humanity, which are put into their places and which there lie. Miss Hepzibah is one of the former. The reader sees all round her, and is sure that she is alive,—though she is so incapable.

Then there is her brother Clifford, who was supposed to have committed the murder, and who, in the course of the chronicle, comes home to live with his sister. There are morsels in his story, bits of telling in the description of him, which are charming, but he is not so good as his sister, being less intelligible. Hawthorne himself had not realized the half-fatuous, dreamy, ill-used brother, as he had the sister. In painting a figure it is essential that the artist should himself know the figure he means to paint.

There is yet another Pyncheon,—Phoebe Pyncheon, who comes from a distance, Heaven knows why, to live with her far-away cousin. She is intended as a ray of sunlight,—as was Pearl in "The Scarlet Letter,"—and is more successful. As the old maid Pyncheon is capable of nothing, so is the young maid Pyncheon capable of everything. She is, however, hardly wanted in the story, unless it be that the ray of sunlight was necessary. And there is a young "daguerreotypist,"—as the photographer of the day used to be called,—who falls in love with the ray of sunlight, and marries her at the end; and who is indeed the lineal descendant of the original ill-used poor man who was hung as a witch. There is just one love-scene in the novel, most ghastly in its details; for the young man offers his love, and the girl accepts it, while they are aware that the wicked, respectable old Judge is sitting, all smeared with blood, and dead, in the next room to them. The love-scene, and the hurrying up of the marriage, and all the dollars which they inherit from the wicked Judge, and the "handsome dark-green barouche" prepared for their departure, which is altogether unfitted to the ideas which the reader has formed respecting them, are quite unlike Hawthorne, and would seem almost to have been added by some every-day, beef-and-ale, realistic novelist, into whose hands the unfinished story had unfortunately fallen.

But no one should read "The House of the Seven Gables" for the sake of the story, or neglect to read it because of such faults as I have described. It is for the humor, the satire, and what I may perhaps call the philosophy which permeates it, that its pages should be turned. Its pages may be turned on any day, and under any circumstances. To "The Scarlet Letter" you have got to adhere till you have done with it; but you may take this volume by bits, here and there, now and again, just as you like it. There is a description of a few poultry, melancholy, unproductive birds, running over four or five pages, and written as no one but Hawthorne could have written it. There are a dozen pages or more in which the author pretends to ask why the busy Judge does not move from his chair,—the Judge the while having dree'd his doom and died as he sat. There is a ghastly spirit of drollery about this which would put the reader into full communion with Hawthorne if he had not read a page before, and did not intend to read a page after. To those who can make literary food of such passages as these, "The House of the Seven Gables" may be recommended. To others it will be caviare.

# [Selection From *Hawthorne*]

## Henry James*

*The House of the Seven Gables* was written at Lenox, among the mountains of Massachusetts, a village nestling, rather loosely, in one of the loveliest corners of New England, to which Hawthorne had betaken himself after the success of *The Scarlet Letter* became conspicuous, in the summer of 1850, and where he occupied for two years an uncomfortable little red house which is now pointed out to the inquiring stranger. The inquiring stranger is now a frequent figure at Lenox, for the place has suffered the process of lionisation. It has become a prosperous watering-place, or at least (as there are no waters), as they say in America, a summer-resort. It is a brilliant and generous landscape, and thirty years ago a man of fancy, desiring to apply himself, might have found both inspiration and tranquillity there. Hawthorne found so much of both that he wrote more during his two years of residence at Lenox than at any period of his career. He began with *The House of the Seven Gables*, which was finished in the early part of 1851. This is the longest of his three American novels, it is the most elaborate, and in the judgment of some persons it is the finest. It is a rich, delightful, imaginative work, larger and more various than its companions, and full of all sorts of deep intentions, of interwoven threads of suggestion. But it is not so rounded and complete as *The Scarlet Letter*; it has always seemed to me more like a prologue to a great novel than a great novel itself. I think this is partly owing to the fact that the subject, the *donnée*, as the French say, of the story, does not quite fill it out, and that we get at the same time an impression of certain complicated purposes on the author's part, which seem to reach beyond it. I call it larger and more various than its companions, and it has indeed a greater richness of tone and density of detail. The colour, so to speak, of *The House of the Seven Gables* is admirable. But the story has a sort of expansive quality which never wholly fructifies, and as I lately laid it down, after reading it for the third time, I had a sense of having interested myself in a magnificent fragment. Yet the book has a great fascination, and of all of those of its author's productions which I have read over while writing this sketch, it is perhaps the one that has gained most by re-perusal. If it be true of the others that the pure, natural quality of the imaginative strain is

*Reprinted from *Hawthorne* (1879; reprinted, London: Macmillan & Co., Limited, 1902), 122–30.

their great merit, this is at least as true of *The House of the Seven Gables*, the charm of which is in a peculiar degree of the kind that we fail to reduce to its grounds—like that of the sweetness of a piece of music, or the softness of fine September weather. It is vague, indefinable, ineffable; but it is the sort of thing we must always point to in justification of the high claim that we make for Hawthorne. In this case of course its vagueness is a drawback, for it is difficult to point to ethereal beauties; and if the reader whom we have wished to inoculate with our admiration inform us after looking a while that he perceives nothing in particular, we can only reply that, in effect, the object is a delicate one.

*The House of the Seven Gables* comes nearer being a picture of contemporary American life than either of its companions; but on this ground it would be a mistake to make a large claim for it. It cannot be too often repeated that Hawthorne was not a realist. He had a high sense of reality—his Note-Books superabundantly testify to it; and fond as he was of jotting down the items that make it up, he never attempted to render exactly or closely the actual facts of the society that surrounded him. I have said—I began by saying—that his pages were full of its spirit, and of a certain reflected light that springs from it; but I was careful to add that the reader must look for his local and national quality between the lines of his writing and in the *indirect* testimony of his tone, his accent, his temper, of his very omissions and suppressions. *The House of the Seven Gables* has, however, more literal actuality than the others, and if it were not too fanciful an account of it, I should say that it renders, to an initiated reader, the impression of a summer afternoon in an elm-shadowed New England town. It leaves upon the mind a vague correspondence to some such reminiscence, and in stirring up the association it renders it delightful. The comparison is to the honour of the New England town, which gains in it more than it bestows. The shadows of the elms, in *The House of the Seven Gables*, are exceptionally dense and cool; the summer afternoon is peculiarly still and beautiful; the atmosphere has a delicious warmth, and the long daylight seems to pause and rest. But the mild provincial quality is there, the mixture of shabbiness and freshness, the paucity of ingredients. The end of an old race—this is the situation that Hawthorne has depicted, and he has been admirably inspired in the choice of the figures in whom he seeks to interest us. They are all figures rather than characters—they are all pictures rather than persons. But if their reality is light and vague, it is sufficient, and it is in harmony with the low relief and dimness of outline of the objects that surround them. They are all types, to the author's mind, of something general, of something that is bound up with the history, at large, of families and individuals, and each of them is the centre of a cluster of those ingenious and meditative musings, rather melancholy, as a general thing, than joyous, which melt into the current and texture of the story and give it a kind of moral richness. A grotesque old spinster, simple, childish, penniless, very humble at heart, but rigidly conscious of her pedigree; an amiable bachelor, of an epicurean temperament and an enfeebled intellect, who has passed twenty years of his life in penal confinement for a crime of which he was unjustly pronounced guilty; a sweet-natured and bright-faced young girl from the country, a poor relation of these two ancient decrepitudes, with whose moral mustiness her modern freshness and soundness are contrasted; a young man still more modern, holding the latest opinions, who has sought his fortune up and down the world, and, though he has not found it, takes a genial and enthusiastic view of the future: these, with two or three remarkable accessory figures, are the persons concerned in the little drama. The drama is a small one, but as Hawthorne does not put it before us for its own superficial sake, for the dry facts of the case, but for something in it which he holds to be symbolic and of large application, something that points a moral and that it behoves us to remember, the scenes in the rusty wooden house whose gables give its name to the story, have something of the dignity both of history and of tragedy. Miss Hephzibah Pyncheon, dragging out a disappointed life in her paternal dwelling, finds herself obliged in her old age to open a little shop for the sale of penny toys and gingerbread. This is the central incident of the tale, and, as Hawthorne relates it, it is an incident of the most impressive magnitude and most touching interest. Her dishonoured and vague-minded brother is released from prison at the same moment, and returns to the ancestral roof to deepen her perplexities. But, on the other hand, to alleviate them, and to introduce a breath of the air of the outer world into this long unventilated interior, the little country cousin also arrives, and proves the good angel of the feebly distracted household. All this episode is exquisite— admirably conceived, and executed with a kind of humorous tenderness, an equal sense of everything in it that is picturesque, touching, ridiculous, worthy of the highest praise. Hephzibah Pyncheon, with her near-sighted scowl, her rusty joints, her antique turban, her map of a great territory to the eastward which ought to have belonged to her family, her vain terrors and scruples and resentments, the inaptitude and repugnance of an ancient gentlewoman to the vulgar little commerce which a cruel fate has compelled her to engage in—Hephzibah Pyncheon is a masterly picture. I repeat that she is a picture, as her companions are pictures; she is a charming piece of descriptive writing, rather than a dramatic exhibition. But she is described, like her companions too, so subtly and lovingly that we enter into her virginal old heart and stand with her behind her abominable little counter. Clifford Pyncheon is a still more remarkable conception, though he is perhaps not so vividly depicted. It was a figure needing a much more subtle touch, however, and it was of the essence of his character to be vague and unemphasised. Nothing can be more charming than the manner in which the soft, bright, active presence of Phoebe Pyncheon is indicated, or than the account of her relations with the poor dimly sentient kinsman for whom her light-handed sisterly offices, in the evening of a melancholy life, are a revelation of lost possibilities of happiness. "In her aspect," Hawthorne says of the young girl,

> there was a familiar gladness, and a holiness that you could play with, and yet reverence it as much as ever. She was like a prayer offered up in the homeliest beauty of one's mother-tongue. Fresh was Phoebe, moreover, and airy, and sweet in her apparel; as if nothing that she wore—neither her gown, nor her small straw bonnet, nor her little kerchief, any more than her snowy stockings—had ever been put on before; or if worn, were all the fresher for it, and with a fragrance as if they had lain among the rose-buds.

Of the influence of her maidenly salubrity upon poor Clifford, Hawthorne gives the prettiest description, and then, breaking off suddenly, renounces the attempt in language which, while pleading its inadequacy, conveys an exquisite satisfaction to the reader. I quote the passage for the sake of its extreme felicity, and of the charming image with which it concludes.

> But we strive in vain to put the idea into words. No adequate expression of the beauty and profound pathos with which it impresses us is attainable. This being, made only for happiness, and heretofore so miserably failing to be happy—his tendencies so hideously thwarted that some unknown time ago, the delicate springs of his character, never morally or intellectually strong, had given way, and he was now imbecile—this poor forlorn voyager from the Islands of the Blest, in a frail bark, on a tempestuous sea, had been flung by the last mountain-wave of his shipwreck, into a quiet harbour. There, as he lay more than half lifeless on the strand, the fragrance of an earthly rose-bud had come to his nostrils, and, as odours will, had summoned up reminiscences or visions of all the living and breathing beauty amid which he should have had his home. With his native susceptibility of happy influences, he inhales the slight ethereal rapture into his soul, and expires!

I have not mentioned the personage in *The House of the Seven Gables* upon whom Hawthorne evidently bestowed most pains, and whose portrait is the most elaborate in the book; partly because he is, in spite of the space he occupies, an accessory figure, and partly because, even more than the others, he is what I have called a picture rather than a character. Judge Pyncheon is an ironical portrait, very richly and broadly executed, very sagaciously composed and rendered—the portrait of a superb, full-blown hypocrite, a large-based, full-natured Pharisee, bland, urbane, impressive, diffusing about him a "sultry" warmth of benevolence, as the author calls it again and again, and basking in the noontide of prosperity and the consideration of society; but in reality hard, gross, and ignoble. Judge Pyncheon is an elaborate piece of description, made up of a hundred admirable touches, in which satire is always winged with fancy, and fancy is linked with a deep sense of reality. It is difficult to say whether Hawthorne followed a model in describing Judge Pyncheon; but it is tolerably obvious that the picture is an impression—a copious impression—of an individual. It has evidently a definite starting-point in fact, and the author is able to draw, freely and confidently, after the image established in his mind. Holgrave, the modern young man, who has been a Jack-of-all-trades and is at the period of the story a daguerreotypist, is an attempt to render a kind of national type— that of the young citizen of the United States whose fortune is simply in his lively intelligence, and who stands naked, as it were, unbiased and unencumbered alike, in the centre of the far-stretching level of American life. Holgrave is intended as a contrast; his lack of traditions, his democratic stamp, his condensed experience, are opposed to the desiccated prejudices and exhausted vitality of the race of which poor feebly-scowling, rusty-jointed Hephzibah is the most heroic representative. It is perhaps a pity that Hawthorne should not have proposed to himself to give the old Pyncheon-qualities some embodiment which would help them to balance more fairly with the elastic properties of the young daguerreotypist—should not have painted a lusty conservative to match his strenuous radical. As it is, the mustiness and mouldiness of the tenants of the House of the Seven Gables crumble away rather too easily. Evidently, however, what Hawthorne designed to represent was not the struggle between an old society and a new, for in this case he would have given the old one a better chance; but simply, as I have said, the shrinkage and extinction of a family. This appealed to his imagination; and the idea of long perpetuation and survival always appears to have filled him with a kind of horror and disapproval. Conservative, in a certain degree, as he was himself, and fond of retrospect and quietude and the mellowing influences of time, it is singular how often one encounters in his writings some expression of mistrust of old houses, old institutions, long lines of descent. He was disposed apparently to allow a very moderate measure in these respects, and he condemns the dwelling of the Pyncheons to disappear from the face of the earth because it has been standing a couple of hundred years. In this he was an American of Americans; or rather he was more American than many of his countrymen, who, though they are accustomed to work for the short run rather than the long, have often a lurking esteem for things that show the marks of having lasted. I will add that Holgrave is one of the few figures, among those which Hawthorne created, with regard to which the absence of the realistic mode of treatment is felt as a loss. Holgrave is not sharply enough characterized; he lacks features; he is not an individual, but a type. But my last word about this admirable novel must not be a restrictive one. It is a large and generous production, pervaded with that vague hum, that indefinable echo, of the whole multitudinous life of man, which is the real sign of a great work of fiction.

# The Romances of Nathaniel Hawthorne

THOMAS BRADFIELD*

Although *The House of the Seven Gables* may not possess the intensity and interest of *The Scarlet Letter*, it is to us a lovelier and more fascinating story, and belongs to a higher region of imaginative art. From the first we seem spirited into another world—the characters and their surroundings possessing that indefinable charm which belongs to ideal scenes and personages. These are of the simplest and most attractive description. A sister, the elaborately delineated, delightfully aristocratic old maiden, Hepzibah Pyncheon, who is tenderly attached to her brother Clifford—the most exquisitely inspired and finely delineated of all Hawthorne's characters—but from whom she has long been separated by the falsity of a relative, the Judge Pyncheon of the story; a bright, nimble-minded, joyous-hearted maiden, Phœbe, brought by stress of circumstances into the circle; and an intelligent, interesting, if somewhat moody artist, Holgrave. These are the suggestive characters to which the ancient and picturesque domicile of the Pyncheon family, the House of the Seven Gables, forms an artistic and appropriate background. Slowly, leisurely, but always beautifully, the story unfolds itself, like one of the legendary flowers in the quaint old garden behind the memorable house—with, too, a fragrance all its own. Everything in connection with the little group of characters is old-world, lovely, attractive, with an awe and interest owing to a mysterious shadow hovering round the inmates of the grotesque mansion. After the most startling event in the story—the sudden death of Judge Pyncheon—the shadow vanishes, and the romance closes in light and joyance. The feature of Hawthorne's genius which here stands out with more than usual refinement and charm is the art by which the exquisite group of characters, brought together by the simplest device of interest, are portrayed as forming parts of a harmonious whole. Among the pictures left upon the memory when we have closed the story, that of the dreamy, idealistic Clifford, with his refined, fanciful sensibilities, and tender, lovable admiration of what is beautiful and pleasing, so that his very existence seems to depend upon sunshine, is the most original and striking. One leading trait of this æsthetic dreamer is nowhere more finely illustrated than in his intercourse with Phœbe, who to his sensitive epicurean nature

*Reprinted From *Westminster Review* (August 1894): 209–10.

is as the light and fragrance of a spiritual bloom. Further, in no other of his stories does Hawthorne's humour play with such genuine and spontaneous effect. Its bright and glancing flashes usually linger on the surface, as if they had no power to penetrate deeply or warm through and through. His humour, as a rule, does not spring from the heart, or call forth irresistible mirth. Like his pathos, it is generally reserved, almost steeled, as if shy of showing itself. But through this story ever and again there are indications of a freer and heartier impulse, as in the inimitable description of Hepzibah's experience on the first morning of her opening her little shop, with the references to the boy who devoured a whole caravan of gingerbread animals; and in such touches as those describing Holgrave's friends, who "ate no solid food, but lived on the scents of other people's cookery, and turned up their noses at that." But it is as a whole that the work impresses one with its irresistible beauty. It is not often that the flower of romance blossoms so luxuriantly, or, when it does, bears such refreshing as well as ennobling fruit.

# MODERN CRITICISM,
# INCLUDING ORIGINAL ESSAYS

◆

# Hawthorne's Holgrave: The Failure of the Artist-Hero

## NINA BAYM*

Nathaniel Hawthorne's four novels—*The Scarlet Letter, The House of the Seven Gables, The Blithedale Romance, The Marble Faun*—develop versions of the romantic conflict, at once social and private, between forces of passion, spontaneity, and creativity, and counterforces of regulation and control. In *The House of the Seven Gables* these forces are embodied respectively in Maule and Pyncheon and represented emblematically in Maule's fountain and Pyncheon's house. The fundamental action of the novel revolves around their struggle for possession of land first occupied by Maule but later appropriated by Pyncheon, and possession, in many senses, is the book's major metaphor. The antagonism of Pyncheon and Maule lends itself to a number of social and ideological readings—aristocrat vs. democrat, conservative vs. radical, institutionalist vs. transcendentalist, to name but a few[1]—but all these readings depend on and derive from the book's psychological core, where the struggle occurs within the world of the single self, with authority trying to suppress passion, and passion to depose authority. The apparent stability of the situation as it exists in the novel's present time is clearly unhealthy, for Maule's fountain has turned brackish, and Pyncheon's house has become a prison, a dead shell which expresses no one's nature and deforms the lives contained within it.[2]

Moreover, this stability is illusory. The Maules still retain and continue to exercise strange forms of control over the Pyncheons, who, "haughtily as they bore themselves in the noonday streets of their native town, were no better than bond-servants to these plebeian Maules, on entering the topsy-turvy commonwealth of sleep" (p. 26).[3] Though they may be repressed and distorted, the energies represented by Maule cannot die unless the self dies, for (as Hawthorne's historical account of the origins of the conflict demonstrates) they are the self's true and original core. Maule was not only the *first* owner of the land, but also the one who turned it from wild nature to

*Reprinted from Nina Baym, "Hawthorne's Holgrave: The Failure of the Artist-Hero," *JEGP* (October 1970), 584–98. Copyright 1970 by the Board of Trustees of the University of Illinois. Used with the permission of the University of Illinois Press.

garden ground and homestead with the labor of his own hands. Though he takes the land away from nature, Maule demonstrates his kinship with her by his creative powers; this is why the fountain which makes this plot of ground so valuable is rightly given his name. As a conduit for natural, creative vitality, Maule is vehicle for the life force itself.

In contrast to this, Pyncheon is a man of writs, deeds, and documents, one who arrives on the scene only with the expansion of the village boundaries, and who depends on institutions to achieve his goals and protect his achievements. He claims the land not from nature but the legislature, and his invariable recourse in all moments of crisis is the law. To Maule's surly independence he responds with suave respectability; but if we are tempted to assume that Hawthorne gives equal moral weight to the natural and the legal, the organic and the formal (even if he shows one as historically anterior to the other), we need only note that Pyncheon's acquisition of the land, though legal, is criminal. Thus Pyncheon wants to consolidate and extend an immoral reign, while Maule is only trying to regain what is rightfully his. In psychological terms, Maule has been denied his own identity; in some schizoid sense, an alien self has been imposed on him. Hawthorne's real concern and sympathy are not with Pyncheon, the most thoroughgoing villain he ever created, but with this dispossessed hero who is forced to hover, ghostlike, sinister, and misunderstood, on the periphery of his own character, a disembodied spirit literally beside or outside himself. In the book's present time, this dispossessed hero is Holgrave; it is he who must attempt to eliminate Pyncheon and thereby reassert his identity as Maule. In the truest sense *The House of the Seven Gables* is his story. His spectatorship, which Phoebe quite mistakenly takes for intellectual coldness, is in fact the traditional pose of the returned exile who bides his time waiting for the appropriate moment to strike or reveal himself—for example (to compare lesser with greater), Orestes and Odysseus. And Holgrave's true identity is concealed until Jaffrey Pyncheon is dead—not only as deliberate strategy on his part, but also because he is not truly Maule, not truly himself, until the judge is dead. Hawthorne's special and characteristic twist to this story of romantic triumph is that, at the moment he takes the name of Maule, Holgrave becomes in fact a Pyncheon—the author's sense of reality is such that he cannot, however he would like to, believe in such a victory.[4]

Maule, as has been said, is the agent of the life force; moreover, as the medium through which this general energy is turned to human expression, he is the artist. He thus gives Hawthorne the opportunity to develop his invariable secondary theme: the nature of art and the problems of the artist in a world where artistic expression is always inhibited and distrusted. Holgrave is regularly referred to as "the Artist" and is shown as master of a number of media—music, authorship, daguerreotyping. As artist, Holgrave is developed in contrast on the one hand to previous Maules, who represent a perversion of artistic energy, and on the other to Clifford, a pseudo-artist who is really a Pyncheon. Though a Maule, Holgrave is also quite clearly the "best" Maule, in whom the fountain seems to flow again with something of its original purity. In Holgrave the fundamental energies of the self are at their healthiest, strong in the sense of their own power and ability, fixed to no form and no medium but informing all, always progressive, impulsive, dynamic. These energies are unmaterial since they care nothing for fixity; they are nonacquisitive, and their inevitable social effect is radical and disruptive.

It is a commonplace of Hawthorne interpretation that he disapproves of radical reformers, and for this reason the portrait of Holgrave is usually assumed to be unfavorable. But Hawthorne defines Holgrave's radicalism as a sense of human possibility "which a young man had better never been born, than not to have, and a mature man had better die at once, than utterly to relinquish" (p. 179). If his radicalism is based on his innocence, and is therefore in error, the error is noble. Radicalism like Holgrave's is inseparable from the kind of spontaneous and impulsive energy he embodies. He is in fact presented as an admirable person, the most unequivocally heroic of Hawthorne's generally weak male characters. He is a courageous, high-principled, idealistic, kind-hearted, self-reliant, and sensitive youth, who has "never violated the innermost man," has "carried his conscience along with him," who combines "inward strength" with "enthusiasm" and "warmth" and gives a total "appearance of admirable powers" (pp. 177, 180).

The one quality he does not have is the one most frequently attributed to him in critical discussions—intellectuality; for though "he considered himself a thinker, and was certainly of a thoughtful turn," he "had perhaps hardly yet reached the point where an educated man begins to think" (p. 180). Since, in Hawthorne's ethic, intellectuality is by no means a desirable trait, being associated with emotional coldness, moral deformity, and temperamental morbidity, it is not surprising that Holgrave is lacking in this respect. From his first appearance in the novel, when, "coming freshly, as he did, out of the morning light, he appeared to have brought some of its cheery influence into the shop along with him" (p. 43), he functions as a source of vigor and joy in the pervasive atmosphere of gloom and fatigue. Tending and planting the Pyncheon garden, he is associated with metaphors of fertility and virility, especially in the remarkable image of the bean-poles vivid with scarlet blossoms and attracting to them multitudes of vibrating hummingbirds (p. 148). In other, less sensuously charged scenes he is found applying himself in the evening to "the task of enlivening the party" with such success that even Clifford's dull soul becomes animated and gives off winged thoughts (p. 157). Where everything turns to dead weight under the Pyncheon touch, everything comes to life under Holgrave's. He is as closely associated with the sun as Phoebe, harnessing its power for his daguerreotypes. Hawthorne's enthusiasm for him is qualified by only one doubt, which does indeed foreshadow the novel's conclusion—there is some question as to whether Holgrave will fulfil his splendid promise or, "like certain chintzes, calicoes, and ginghams," will "assume a very sober aspect after washing-day." Until the future reveals itself, Holgrave is a young man "for whom we anticipate wonderful things" (p. 181). Thus Holgrave represents a rejuvenescence of the Maule powers. In him the decline of the Maules into sadistic wizards has been arrested, the perversion of their energies into drives for spite and revenge has been halted.

Hawthorne illustrates Holgrave's superiority to previous Maules, his freedom from their corruptions, in the scene where Holgrave reads the narrative of Alice Pyncheon to Phoebe. As the story is read, the present-day characters assume the identities of characters from the past. Holgrave becomes the wizard Maule, and through Phoebe's susceptibility to his reading he is presented with the same opportunity for misuse of his gifts that Maule could not resist. Phoebe, too, by her response to Maule's reading, shows her kinship to Alice, whose room she occupies and whose flowers she tends. Moreover, since the story is supposed to have been written by Holgrave, we can take it as evidence of his comprehension of his own situation. In this sense the story constitutes a kind of self-analysis, which liberates through its insights.

In the fantasy, an observant and embittered Maule recognizes in the "pure" Alice Pyncheon an unacknowledged sexual attraction which he en-flames into a violent physical passion. Alice, as in all cases of demonic "possession," is less victimized by an external agency than she is controlled by internal, but invisible forces—invisible because denied. In this case it is her own sexual nature, whose responsiveness is evident to Maule, that she refuses to recognize. "This fair girl deemed herself conscious of a power—combined of beauty, high, unsullied purity, and the preservative force of womanhood—that could make her sphere impenetrable, unless betrayed by treachery within" (p. 203). Her inability to conceive of such internal treachery—her distorted self-understanding—delivers her to Maule. Like all Pyncheons, she rejects, suppresses, or denies the forces of passion and impulse that underly human nature. Her later torments, too, result from the continued frustration of this inadmissible and yet obvious passion, for "so lost from self-control, she would have deemed it sin to marry" (p. 209), and she is killed, aptly enough, by the irrevocable loss of her passion's object when Maule marries.

Alice, then, displays typical Pyncheon characteristics in a female mold. How do we interpret Maule, who chooses neither to possess Alice nor let her go, but settles rather on the meanest behavior, at once arousing and rejecting her? This nastiness figures his own degradation into an Eros that has become destructive instead of creative, and whose destructiveness mani-fests itself in acts of malice, subversive thrusts that produce no release. Northrop Frye outlines a similar mythology in Blake's works: "the innocent vision is then driven underground into the subconscious, as we now call it, where it becomes a subversive revolutionary force with strong sexual elements in it. . . . If this force is released, it permeates the world of experience with its energy; if it is suppressed, it turns demonic."[5] Denied free and open expression, the polluted fountain becomes a source of disease.

Holgrave's reading recreates Alice's erotic response in Phoebe; so Hawthorne demonstrates the sexual power of art and its near relation to witchcraft. Art and sex are both expressions of the creative energy which, ideally, they celebrate. The common origin of art and sex (neither of which, in this pre-Freudian mythology, is prior to the other) in the life force, or Eros, of the personality, makes sexual metaphors appropriate to art. Great works of art in Hawthorne's fictions are frequently unabashedly sensuous representations of beautiful women. The fate of art in a repressive society is exactly parallel to the fate of sex—it goes underground. Witchcraft is simply debased, perverse creativity. It destroys rather than creates, controls rather than liberates, degrades rather than celebrates the life force. The self-mocking and yet deadly serious wizard, seeking to "possess" through misuse of the powers of art, is an obscene parodist of the tyrant. He betrays his own nature by aping repressive forms, and he destroys art by making it an instrument of oppression.

The optimist Holgrave, while recognizing that he operates in a repressive society, refuses to turn his art to twisted purposes. He believes that the world is making strides toward a Utopia where Eros will have a place above ground, and he means to participate in the movement. Art in the interim, as he conceives of it, can have a liberating and constructive effect through its power to expose the truth. His daguerreotypes, taken with the help of the sunlight that is his friend and ally, show Pyncheon's true nature, illuminating his villainy and identifying him with his persecuting ancestor. His tale of Alice Pyncheon, developed with the help of the moonshine that for Hawthorne always accompanies romance, exposes the depravity of the Maules. Art, thus practiced, can be an agent of progress and reform. The story of Alice Pyncheon demonstrates Holgrave's understanding of his own situation; his refusal to succumb to the opportunity which Phoebe's response gives him demonstrates his moral worthiness. He withstands temptation, and not only Phoebe but art itself is saved by his forbearance. "Let us, therefore—whatever his defects of nature and education, and in spite of his scorn for creeds and institutions—concede to the Daguerreotypist the rare and high quality of reverence for another's individuality. Let us allow him integrity, also, forever after to be confided in; since he forbade himself to twine that one link more which might have rendered his spell over Phoebe indissoluble" (p. 212).

The cleansed vitality which Holgrave brings to the centuries-old conflict seems specifically attributable to his mobility. He has severed ties with the house, abandoned the place, and refused to commit himself to any fixed form of life. He has made the particularly American response to history—

he has moved away from his past, even to the extent of leaving behind an old self by creating a new identity with a new name. He has escaped the past by avoiding the forms in which it is preserved and transmitted. Distance has given him a stranger's objectivity toward his own origins. Holgrave must now discover whether freedom is possible on any terms other than perpetual motion and flight. He hopes to reattach himself to his sources without forfeiting any of his spiritual independence and flexibility, and like the fountain to be at once fixed and fluid.

This reattachment obviously requires that he return to Salem and confront the figure who has so long forced the Maules into exile and outlawry. Yet Holgrave's optimism and self-confidence give him a certain serenity in the face of this ordeal. He does not doubt that he will emerge triumphant from his confrontation, and he has absolutely no inkling of possible internal weakness, of "treachery within." Establishing himself in an attic gable, tending the garden—taking possession, so to speak, of the house's peripheries—he calmly bides his time, waiting, we must assume, for Maule's curse to claim its last victim. Pyncheon is naturally completely unaware of the other's presence and has no sense of impending doom. Hawthorne is more than usually coy, even for him, about the Pyncheon deaths. For the more sober-minded of his readers he supplies, as always, a "natural" explanation of his mysteries—in this case a hereditary disposition to apoplexy. At the same time, pointed remarks establish the *true* fact in this fantasy world— that the killer of the Pyncheons is Maule's curse. Adopting, as is his habit, Gothic and historical elements to his psychological purposes, Hawthorne makes the curse the channel (magical only because not understood) by which the power of a suppressed Eros is communicated to its oppressor. In any of the three readings of the drama—that every generation of Pyncheons and Maules repeats it, that there is really only one Pyncheon and Maule, or that both Pyncheon and Maule are parts of a single personality—Holgrave, as Maule, must assume some responsibility for Jaffrey's death. And Holgrave's serenity implies that he is ready to face that death and accept that responsibility.

In the meantime his attention focuses on Clifford, an even more unfortunate victim of Jaffrey's ruthless greed. He loses no opportunity to ask about him, spend time with him, observe him, until the uncomprehending Phoebe decides that he is heartlessly curious. But Clifford is an object of intense *personal* interest to Holgrave, who sees in his victimization a situation analogous to his own. As Holgrave cannot get into the house, Clifford cannot get out of it, and from this contrast Hawthorne develops another aspect of his consideration of art and the artist. Clifford is certainly no artist (he is a Pyncheon and not a Maule), but there is about him a sense of arrested potential. The idea of a castrated Eros is, in a sense, inconceivable because self-contradictory; yet some such idea as this is the source of the fearful interest that both Holgrave and Hawthorne find in Clifford. Although physically an old man, Clifford's psychic organization is infantile. The effect of the tyranny of his cousin has been to keep him forever passive and immature, dependent, absorbed in immediate sensual (but nonsexual) gratification, uncontrollably moody, irrevocably impotent, barely mentally awake. The Maules, at great price, have held to some sort of manhood however warped, but Clifford has never attained his. The prime of life has been denied him.

The simplest of all tests shows that Clifford is no artist. He is totally uncreative. He is characterized above all perhaps by his entire dependency, just as Holgrave is shown in contrast as completely independent. Clifford's satisfactions are achieved through a kind of omnivorous absorption of the world into the self—eating is the best image for this, and much is made of Clifford's voracious and indelicate appetite—Holgrave's by a kind of multiplication of the self into the world through created forms. The appetites that Clifford satisfies are the primary animal appetites for food, comfort, and the like, and his love of beauty is presented as a refinement of his animal nature. In Holgrave's case one must use the word "appetite" as a metaphor, for what he expresses is man's hunger not to absorb, but to produce. In the sense in which Clifford is hungry, indeed, Holgrave is not hungry at all; like the Puritan's Deity, he creates out of an overflowing sense of joy and fulness. This is to say that Clifford's appetites stem from his incompleteness, and Holgrave's from his "perfection." True transcendentalist that he is, Holgrave has no attachment to the works he has made, and no particular fondness for any one medium. Clifford is associated with beauty, to be sure—that is certainly what has led to the frequent misinterpretation of him as an artist—but the *artist* is associated with energy. Clifford indeed exhibits a set of characteristics that resemble materialism, the opposite of artistry. This presumably is why Hawthorne made him a Pyncheon. He loves things; he wants to possess them; he is satisfied by forms not of his own making.

Such distinctions show that Hawthorne is thinking about the connections between art and the infantile and is rejecting the idea that art is a preserve of infantilism in the adult personality. There is no art until the infant is left behind. At some point in its development, the child moves from a fascination with and dependence on forms to the desire to create them; after this, forms become dependent on him. If development is arrested before this point, the artist remains unborn. Art is the product of an informing spirit (theoretically all men are potentially artists) associated with the maturing of the personality, a progressive force which confronts reality rather than a regressive activity which tries to evade it.[6] The artist is a continual danger to the social structure, but *not* because of his desire to recreate infantile patterns of pleasure in the workaday world. It is rather that the continual flux of his energies operates against the stability and permanence required by institutions. Even if he were not consciously striving to destroy restrictive forms, the artist would be, albeit inadvertently, destructive, because form to him has no meaning in and for itself. Conversely,

Hawthorne finds no subversive threat to society in infantilism; the self-absorbed and passive Clifford can easily be pacified and more easily controlled.

Insofar as the conflict of Pyncheon and Maule can be understood as the conflict between form and energy (the idea of artist as formalist, brought into American literary theory by Henry James and popularized by the New Critics, is completely absent in Hawthorne's thought), Clifford shows himself quite clearly to be a Pyncheon. But this is not the whole story. Though he lacks the force that makes art, though he is indeed frightened of raw energy, he is at the same time greatly attracted to it. This attraction may be the seed from which, normally, the artist matures. As soon as he gets out of the house, for example, Clifford runs to the railroad that has always terrified him, recognizing on this occasion and sporadically at other times that his salvation can only come by embracing what he fears.[7] This sympathy to the force behind the form had led him, in the far past, to the secret by which the Maules kept the Maine lands away from the Pyncheons. Of course he has also forgotten the secret, for his insights are weak and intermittent—it is not for *him* to tumble the Colonel's picture from the wall. Yet the sympathy is real enough for him to constitute a danger to Jaffrey. Putting it differently, we may say that Clifford's discovery of the Maules' secret heralds his approaching maturity and is the signal for Jaffrey to take strong countermeasures. Jaffrey's death means liberation for Clifford, and his essentially light-weight nature, relieved of the pressures which have constricted it for so long, achieves some fraction of the pleasing development possible to it.

The same cannot be said for Holgrave. The long-awaited death of Jaffrey Pyncheon does not mean liberation for him. Something goes wrong. Between the time that he enters the parlor, prepared to face the judge and master him through the last symbolic gesture of taking his daguerreotype, and the time of Phoebe's return, Holgrave undergoes a striking change of character. His social radicalism has gone; he is prepared to abandon his art and take over the routines of a country squire. Instead of finding himself in the darkened parlor, he loses himself, for when he leaves he is prepared to follow in Pyncheon's path. He takes the name of Maule, but the form of Pyncheon. The change is first evident in his new attitude toward Phoebe. He at last declares his love for her, but he frames his declaration as a plea for solace and protection. "Could you but know, Phoebe, how it was with me, the hour before you came! A dark, cold, miserable hour. . . . I never hoped to feel young again! . . . But, Phoebe, you crossed the threshold; and hope, warmth, and joy, came in with you! The black moment became at once a blissful one. It must not pass without the spoken word. I love you!" (p. 306). It is entirely appropriate that his betrothal to Phoebe, undertaken in this frame of mind, becomes the means by which he repossesses the Pyncheon property, for despite her appealing freshness and softness Phoebe is a Pyncheon, law-abiding and limit-loving.[8] The best she *can* do for Hepzibah and

Clifford is to make life in the house tolerable; horrified of the untidy, the unorthodox, and the unknown, she cannot begin to act as an agent of release. Indeed, confined to the house she begins to droop and fade, and she must take a place along with her cousins as one liberated from its baleful influence by Holgrave.

At the same time, like Clifford, Phoebe feels an attraction for what she fears, and this is expressed in her love for Holgrave. Even as she tells him that she is afraid to marry him, she is seen "shrinking towards" him (p. 306), asking him without words to help her move beyond her own limits into the terrifying but exhilarating world of adult freedom. However, Holgrave can no longer help her; on the contrary, he is now asking for such help as she can give *him*—for talents that prettify and brighten the gloom, and arts that help one bear the unbearable. Whatever possibilities there might have been for a new era in relations between man and woman are over, for this couple, before they declare themselves to each other. They drive off to Pyncheon's country estate loaded with goods and dependents. Clifford, Hepzibah, Uncle Venner, and all the neighbors rejoice, but Holgrave has become a brooding and melancholy man. Would it have been a better symbol of his victory if he had built his own house, or, remaining in the house of the seven gables, had truly made it his own? This nice question need not be answered, for he does neither. On the one hand, he abandons the ground for which he has struggled; on the other, he moves into the judge's country mansion, astounding everyone by his lament that the wooden structure is not built of more durable material. What Holgrave has left behind in this ending is simply himself. Moving into Jaffrey Pyncheon's house, he identifies himself with all those parts of the personality he had previously been trying to overcome.

It is generally argued that Holgrave's conversion from radicalism to conservatism has been brought about by love; that his relationship with Phoebe, tying him for the first time to the human world, gives him a new appreciation of things in that world worth preserving. This interpretation, however, takes for granted that Holgrave's conversion is morally desirable, an assumption that Hawthorne's depiction of Pyncheon makes completely untenable. This reading also asserts that Holgrave finds a new happiness through love and stability, and Holgrave himself appears to concur when he says that "the world owes all its onward impulse to men ill at ease. The happy man inevitably confines himself within limits" (pp. 306–307). But whatever Holgrave's frame of mind before his conversion, he is certainly not happy afterward. In the beginning he brought the sunlight with him; now he has been darkened by the shadows of the house. He has turned to Phoebe for relief from his new misery and despair. And later, with a "half-melancholy laugh," he will himself call his conversion unpardonable: "It is especially unpardonable in this dwelling of so much hereditary misfortune, and under the eye of yonder portrait of a model-conservative, who, in that very character, rendered himself so long the Evil Destiny of his race" (p. 315). Holgrave's love for Phoebe is real enough but irrelevant to his alteration. He changes because of his encounter with the judge, who, even though dead, continues to exert his crushing influence. Indeed, in death he has a power over Holgrave that he never had in life.

Readers familiar with Hawthorne's preoccupations will recognize that Holgrave, believing himself responsible for Pyncheon's death, feels guilt over it. Assuming for the moment that because he is a Maule he truly is accountable for that death, we may still wonder why he should feel guilty about eliminating in self-defense someone who is thoroughly evil. The first Maule, who antedated society, was free to be himself; all the others would have had to strike through the iron framework of institutions and laws to find and express themselves. The first man, in this myth, had no father, but all subsequent men have found their paths to adulthood blocked by the father's presence.[9] To reach freedom they must commit an act which, ironically, implicates them in the guilt-ridden structure of society and forces them to perpetuate it. Those energies which were to be expended in self-expression are now diverted to the endless task of atonement. Feelings of guilt are assuaged by capitulating to the system one has just overthrown. Holgrave's rootless freedom, it appears, is all the freedom man can know; he comes into his own by a father-murder for which he must punish himself. So society and Pyncheon, phoenix-like, spring up from their own ashes.

Holgrave's sense of guilt has a metaphysical as well as a private dimension, for his new vision sees the whole world lying under its shadow. "The presence of yonder dead man threw a great black shadow over everything; he made the universe, so far as my perception could reach, a scene of guilt, and of retribution more dreadful than the guilt" (p. 306). Holgrave has become aware, for the first time, of the reality of death. Knowing the present only, and impelled by a transcendental idealism which holds the universe to be eternally animate, Holgrave has imagined himself as operating through an infinity of present moments—has believed himself immortal. In his impassioned radical speeches, he used death as a figure with the insouciance of ignorance: "The case is just as if a young giant were compelled to waste all his strength in carrying about the corpse of the old giant, his grandfather, who died a while ago, and only needs to be decently buried. Just think, a moment; and it will startle you to see what slaves we are to by-gone times— to Death, if we give the matter the right word!" (pp. 182–83). The rigid immobility of the corpse turns Holgrave's words back against him, demonstrating that we are indeed slaves to Death. The real existence of death is precisely what foredooms all radical attempts to transfigure reality, and it gives the conservative position whatever validity it may have. The judge has escaped his revenger by becoming, finally, Death itself. No longer a symbol of powerful but possibly vulnerable human authority, he has regressed into a symbol of the ultimate, unconquerable, tyrannizing form.

Accepting his destiny now to perpetuate forms, Holgrave can hardly be said to embrace that destiny; rather he sees it as inevitable in a universe structured around guilt and retribution. At the book's end he has not arrived at the orthodox belief that man is sinful and that death came into the world as a just punishment, but he realizes now that man is punished *as though* he were sinful. He does not become religious; he despairs. Phoebe supplies neither faith nor hope; she offers comfort, but that is all Holgrave looks for.

The life of the individual is thus chronicled as a journey away from the illusion of freedom. The life of society demonstrates the same futility. The conflict remains unresolved; Judge Pyncheon and Holgrave are their ancestors, ceaselessly cycling through history with exactly the same lack of progress as the barrel-organ: "Possibly, some cynic, at once merry and bitter, had desired to signify, in this pantomimic scene, that we mortals, whatever our business or amusement—however serious, however trifling—all dance to one identical tune, and, in spite of our ridiculous activity, bring nothing finally to pass" (p. 163).[10] Such cycling obliterates history. If he is successful, the revolutionary becomes a tyrant, the son a father, the romantic wanderer a man of property and propriety. The great American dream of making one's own history instead of inheriting it is delusory. There is no escape from history precisely because there is no progress in it.

The finale of *The House of the Seven Gables*, then, reflects both romanticism and pessimism. Such catastrophic endings—the debacle at Blithedale, Dimmesdale's death, Donatello's incarceration—are hallmarks of Hawthorne's fiction. *The House of the Seven Gables* resembles *The Marble Faun* and differs from the other two novels, however, in that Hawthorne is trying so hard to present the ending as a happy one. The ending attempts to reverse the book's values and to reinterpret events so that we understand Holgrave's absorption into the system as the end for which *he* was striving, as though the Maules had coveted the Pyncheon possessions instead of their own freedom. This is absurd, as is the idea that a finale in which the hero abandons all the best of himself can be called triumphant. Most recent Hawthorne critics are not convinced by the presentation, and the question of the purpose behind the author's strategy has become a crux in Hawthorne interpretation. One cannot explain the treatment of the ending by Hawthorne's so-called "ambiguity," for it does not result from a broad vision which grasps and represents both sides of an issue at once. On the contrary, Hawthorne insists on a single reading which is inadequate to the rendered facts, which flies in the face of the book's symbolism, and which contradicts the organization of its plot. It is less ambiguity than disguise, an effort on the author's part to conceal or even deny what the book has done. Hawthorne's less sympathetic critics have called this duplicity.[11]

By asserting that the ending, in which a romantic self dies and is reborn as a solid social citizen, is happy, Hawthorne undermines his own romanticism and identifies the narrative voice with the conservative side of the Pyncheon-Maule conflict. Hawthorne's concern at the end is less with the coherence of his story than with the sense the reader will get of its informing values, and by extension the author whose values these are. He does not want the reader to notice how romantic he is, and so he poses as a genteel writer. *The House of the Seven Gables* becomes a romantic story told by a genteel narrator. Many of Hawthorne's works exhibit this peculiar dissociation of plot and narrator; it was for him that D. H. Lawrence devised his famous dictum, "Never trust the teller, trust the tale." We may understand what Hawthorne is doing here in two ways, not necessarily mutually exclusive. On the one hand it may reflect his determination to avoid artistic suicide, not to dash himself to pieces on the rocks of public orthodoxy (as his friend Melville was so spectacularly doing with *Pierre* at about this time). On the other, it may well reflect a real conflict within the author, who wrote of his Puritan ancestors in "The Custom-House" that "strong traits of theirs have intertwined themselves with mine." The ending, then, would be both an attempt to deceive the public *and* to placate the inner judge. The strategy may seem clumsy or neurotic, and it certainly muddies the book's moral waters. But it permits Hawthorne to continue to function as an artist, and the alternative from his point of view might have appeared a good deal worse—Holgrave's death-in-life as a gentleman farmer.

*Notes*

1. Polarities such as these have been identified by most critics of the novel. Many Hawthorne critics prefer this novel to his others because of its lighter tone and generally more novelistic qualities; recently it has been interpreted mainly as a comic romance of redemption and regeneration with a poorly conceived and clumsily executed plot. The favorite technique of critical analysis has been explication of imagery and symbolism. The reader will find the following selection representative: F. O. Matthiessen, *American Renaissance* (New York, 1940); Austin Warren, *A Rage for Order* (New York, 1949); Clark Griffith, "Substance and Shadow: Language and Meaning in *The House of the Seven Gables*," *MP*, II (1954), 187–95; Maurice Beebe, "The Fall of the House of Pyncheon," *NCF*, XI (1956), 1–17; Alfred H. Marks, "Who Killed Judge Pyncheon? The Role of Imagination in *The House of the Seven Gables*," *PMLA*, LXXI (1956), 355–69; Roy R. Male, *Hawthorne's Tragic Vision* (Austin, 1957); Marius Bewley, *The Eccentric Design* (New York, 1959); William B. Dillingham, "Structure and Theme in *The House of the Seven Gables*," *NCF*, XIV (1959), 59–70; D. G. Hoffman, *Form and Fable in American Fiction* (New York, 1961); H. H. Waggoner, *Hawthorne* (Cambridge, Mass., 1963); R. H. Fogle, *Hawthorne's Fiction: The Light and the Dark* (Norman, 1964); Marcus Cunliffe, "*The House of the Seven Gables*," *Hawthorne Centennial Essays* (Columbus, 1964), pp. 79–100; Martin Green, *Reappraisals* (New York, 1967); Francis Joseph Battaglia, "*The House of the Seven Gables*: New Light on Old Problems," *PMLA*, LXXII (1967), 579–90; Joel Porte, *The Romance in America* (Middletown, Conn., 1969).

2. Several critics have constructed interpretations around the many passages wherein the house is compared to a human heart. In this metaphor the house represents not Pyncheon, but the enclosure within which both Pyncheon and Maule exist—in this paper's terminology, the self. Whether one centers the struggle on the house or the ground, the same relations

and priorities obtain. Maule owns the land which Pyncheon appropriates; Maule builds the house which Pyncheon calls his own.

3. Page references are to the Centennial Edition of *The House of the Seven Gables* (Columbus, 1965), with an introduction by William Charvat.

4. Rudolph Von Abele, in *The Death of the Artist* (The Hague, 1957), and Frederick C. Crews, in *The Sins of the Fathers: Hawthorne's Psychological Themes* (New York, 1965), both propose interpretations of *The House of the Seven Gables* in which Holgrave's alteration at the end is extremely important.

5. Northrop Frye, *A Study of English Romanticism* (New York, 1968), p. 33.

6. This observation may shed light on that problem story, "The Artist of the Beautiful." The satire with which Hawthorne develops Owen Warland's character, the stress he puts on his childishness, impotence, and effeminacy, does not extend to artists in general because Owen is not truly an artist. He is a fearful and timid creature terrified of Peter Hovenden, the intellectual father-figure, and the blacksmith who provides an alternate image of robust erotic energy. For him art *is* a way of evading reality and adult life, but the "masterwork" he produces is not art at all; it is no more than a miniature mechanical toy. Artists like Owen who pursue the otherworldly are in fact simply rationalizing their fear of the world; but a character like Holgrave proves that Owen does not represent all artists.

7. The railroad in *The House of the Seven Gables* does not stand for technology, nor is it employed with the same moral implications found in the story of eight years earlier, "The Celestial Railroad," where it satirizes spiritual optimism. In *The House of the Seven Gables* it is a symbol of "terrible energy" (p. 161). Like the fountain, it is a symbol contrasting with the house. The discussion between Clifford and the passenger about the uses of the telegraph oppose two views of the possibilities of these new forms of energy: as an expression of Eros— "I love you forever! My heart runs over with love!"—or as an instrument of social control, "a great thing . . . as regards the detection of bank-robbers and murderers!" (p. 264). As fast as energy finds forms to express itself, a restrictive society appropriates them.

8. Each of the Pyncheons demonstrates a different version of the family traits— materialism, acquisitiveness, conservatism. Only in Jaffrey are they developed to the point where they harm others, and only he therefore is truly evil. The fourth member of the family, Hepzibah (whose characterization suffers from Hawthorne's apparent indecision about whether or not to develop her as comic), shows herself a Pyncheon in her foolish pride in and reliance on her aristocratic lineage. In vain Holgrave tries to persuade her that to rely on her "title" is self-defeating; she persists in looking for life where none is and pays for it in her physical form, so frequently likened to rusty machinery, in an image combining both lack of life and lack of use. Nor does it imply a great revolution in her character when she takes to shopkeeping; Jaffrey is a prosperous businessman.

9. Though one is tempted to read this father-son conflict in an Oedipal fashion, it should be noted that Maule and Pyncheon are not embroiled over a woman. The son does not kill the father in order to possess the mother or a surrogate sister, but in order to possess himself.

10. It is true that at the end of this much-cited passage, Hawthorne's editorial voice repudiates the moral. However, it is impossible convincingly to reject in a single sentence the careful build-up of a couple of pages.

11. E.g., D. H. Lawrence, *Studies in Classic American Literature* (New York, 1923), and Leslie Fiedler, *Love and Death in the American Novel* (New York, 1960).

# Hawthorne's House of Three Stories

## BRUCE MICHELSON*

In its best moments, Nathaniel Hawthorne's fiction reveals an astonishing duality of mind, a broad awareness that is generally discussed only by halves. In recent years strong evidence has been gathered to show that Hawthorne was a deep questioner of the nature of fiction itself, that he was given to self-conscious puzzling over the problems of being understood, over the impreciseness of language and the pitfalls of communicating by means of stories, over the whole anomalous art of seeking and imparting truth by telling tales.[1] On the other side of a standing disagreement is the Hawthorne of old, the author who writes not to himself about fiction but directly to an American audience and who engages those social and moral issues that for a century have been taken as Hawthorne's essence: stasis and change, the past and the present, sin and retribution—problems that show up everywhere in the fiction and that no new wave of reinterpretation can or should displace. My position, and what I hope to demonstrate here, is that these two apparently opposite Hawthornes can in fact be one. As his readers, we are not faced with an either-or choice of accepting one idea of his achievement and rejecting the other; rather, in at least some of the major works, the older Hawthorne, the familiar moralist and social observer, reconciles himself elegantly with that self-reflexive writer who supposedly questions the validity of his own art.

*The House of the Seven Gables* is my case in point. In a real sense, the novel does show itself to be about fiction, about the very paradox of telling stories for high-serious reasons, but it is also about those classic Hawthornian matters we have supposed it to be involved with all along; moreover, the tale explores the relationship of each realm to the other. In a single novel, in other words, Hawthorne finds a way to challenge the creed on which the novel itself relies as it strives both to address and to take part in American life; and several different meditations—on the nature of art, on art's place in life, on life with and without the resonance of the imagination—are gracefully fused in the essential form of the tale.

At the center of *The House of the Seven Gables* is a strong governing idea

*Bruce Michelson, "Hawthorne's House of Three Stories," *New England Quarterly* (June 1984), 163–83. Reprinted with the permission of *The New England Quarterly* and Bruce Michelson.

that does much more than determine the plot and provide the suspense for that popular romance which, of course, the novel had to be on its most basic level. That idea also focuses the moral observations so evident in the book and, further, provides the matrix for a concern with romance itself, with the nature and the effect of shadowy fictions launched into an American world of broad daylight, blunt fact, practicality, materialism, and general distrust of dreams and the imaginative mind. As a ghost story—for after all Hawthorne does build his fiction on a tale of a haunted house—as a moral document, as (if the expression can be forgiven) a kind of metafiction, *The House of the Seven Gables* is about the loss of the self. It is about, in other words, the perils inherent in too much tradition, in too much change, in artistic detachment, in social immersion, and in the making and reading of romances. This overriding theme brings us to the book's most important paradox: the end result of too much reality, like the end result of imaginative excess, is a destructive, debilitating vertigo; to be fully alive, for Hawthorne, requires a careful balance between the power to see and suspect illusion *as* illusion and the wisdom to require the presence of illusion, of fantasy, of imagination and wonder, in a complete view of real life. One must keep one's allegiance both to romance and to that "Main Street" world with which Hawthorne's fictional storytellers must always reckon; one must possess a consciousness open to reverie, to imaginative literature, and to a contemporary, skeptical, practical America.

In order to see how Hawthorne balances the popular tale, the moral observation, and the inquiry into romance itself, one must begin with the face of the novel first, the story about the old mansion, the buried crime, the concealed will, the ghosts in the attic, the kitchen, the well, the mirror, the familiar New England story of a haunting. One must pause, as the narrator does on the first page of the novel, to look deliberately at an exterior; to take it for granted is not only to miss some crucial evidence but to make the mistake that the novel ultimately warns against, the mistake of failing to remain open to fantasies, as much for their own sake as for their value in making sense of intractable daily life. Readers of *The House of the Seven Gables* often recall Hawthorne's jibe at Whittier for his collection *The Supernaturalism of New England* (1847), that "If he cannot believe his ghost-story while he is telling it, he had better leave the task to somebody else."[2] Largely unanswered, though, is the question of how, or even whether, Hawthorne makes *The House of the Seven Gables* a ghost story he himself could believe while telling it, how the haunted house conventions, the variations, and the very intensity with which both are carried through connect to the novel's own larger ambitions. There is no question that this is one of the most thoughtfully haunted houses in American literature—but a purely abstract, intellectualized haunting was not at all what Hawthorne was after. The problem was to be not merely symbolic but genuinely eerie at the same time.

One can readily observe that a tale of a haunting will commonly raise two questions: how the ghosts came to be there, and what must be done by the living either to get rid of the ghosts, to escape, or to return the premises to some measure of normalcy and commerce with the outside world.[3] Hawthorne rarely showed any interest in ghost breaking either in real life or in his fiction. "Houses of any antiquity," he observes in his preface to *Mosses from an Old Manse*, "are so invariably possessed with spirits, that the matter seems hardly worth alluding to";[4] indeed, on the evidence of his notebooks, travel writings, and the tales themselves, Hawthorne often seems grateful for strange company. The Old Manse brought him into friendly acquaintance with two resident ghosts, the spectre of the old minister, agitating for the publication of his sermons, and the long-dead kitchen maid, who cleaned house and ground coffee all night without the slightest effect beyond the noise. In the Boston Athenæum, Hawthorne regularly encountered (so he reports) the ghost of one Dr. Harris, who seemed content to spend the first weeks of eternity reading quietly in the same room where he had contentedly passed the last weeks of life. The same general characteristics turn up in Hawthorne's most ghost-ridden short story—which also happens to be one of his stories about a storyteller and his efforts to impose his wild dreams on the real world. The crowd of graveyard spirits in "Alice Doane's Appeal" is caught in a kind of loop, living its worldly destiny over and over, with no result other than sheer spectacle.

The tales and the personal accounts suggest, in other words, that a ghost for Hawthorne is a "lost soul" in two very specific ways. It is first a soul that has lost its identity, its completeness; as a revenant, it has deteriorated from a personality into a repeated gesture, a daily habit, an obsession that meagerly replaces the individual. Second, the ghost is a soul "lost" because it has escaped from temporality into a vertiginous world beyond time, beyond change, beyond consequence, where repetitiveness resembles action, suggests movement of some sort, but is really nothing of the kind. It should not surprise, therefore, that Hawthorne was given to seeing ghosts where others saw living people. Not merely in his tales ("The Wedding Knell," "The Minister's Black Veil," "Old Esther Dudley," "The White Old Maid," "Wakefield") but in his sketches from life, he dwells upon those who become haunters and phantoms long before going to their tombs. He is eloquent on the subject in *Our Old Home*, in which entire English villages strike him as havens of the living dead.

Life is there fossilized in its greenest leaf. The man who died yesterday, or ever so long ago, walks the village-street to-day, and chooses the same wife that he married a hundred years since, and must be buried again, tomorrow, under the same kindred dust that has already covered him half a score of times. The stone threshold of his cottage is worn away with his hob-nailed footsteps, shuffling over it from the reign of the first Plantagenet to that of

Victoria. Better than this is the lot of our restless countrymen, whose modern instinct bids them tend always towards "fresh woods and pastures new."[5]

Such living phantoms are Hawthorne's truest, most disquieting ghosts; Dr. Harris, the dead minister, the kitchen maid of the Old Manse seem, in comparison, not only less consequential but less uncanny. They seem the more innocuous, even quaint, because they keep to their proper dimension and never try to pass themselves off as living men and women. This paradox intensifies in *The House of the Seven Gables*, in which the proper full-fledged ghosts of the Pyncheon mansion wander about the house harmlessly, quaintly, doing nothing more than what they must to be noticeable at all. Alice strikes a few notes from time to time on her harpsichord, tends the wildflowers on the roof; a few faces look out of a mirror that no one gazes into; other ghosts apparently amuse themselves by fouling the well water— these naturally supernatural folk provide a stable, almost comfortable background to the main story. The astonishment, the vertigo, the menace that go with a good haunted house story are in the foreground, with creatures who will not keep their place among either the living or the dead, who can inhabit both worlds at the same instant. In one cleverly balanced passage, the villain of the piece is at once the living man, the corpse, his own ghost, and the ghost of his colonial forefather. From the chapter titled "Governor Pyncheon":

Can we believe our eyes? A stout, elderly gentleman has made his appearance; he has an aspect of eminent respectability, wears a black coat and pantaloons, of roomy width, and might be pronounced scrupulously neat in his attire, but for a broad crimson-stain, across his snowy neckcloth and down his shirt-bosom. Is it the Judge, or no? How can it be Judge Pyncheon? We discern his figure, as plainly as the flickering moonbeams can show us anything, still seated in the oaken chair! Be the apparition whose it may, it advances to the picture, seems to seize the frame, tries to peep behind it, and turns away, with a frown as black as the ancestral one.[6]

When Clifford exclaims, "We are ghosts! We have no right among living beings—no right anywhere but in this old house, which has a curse on it, and which, therefore, we are doomed to haunt!" (p. 169), his remark suggests something more than that he and Hepzibah are too old to change or that they too much resemble the full-time revenants in the mansion.[7] In their ancient silks, turbans, and pallid, dreary gowns, in Hepzibah's scowl and Clifford's ravaged innocent visage, the two strongly recall the period's commonplace engravings of graveyard spirits,[8] but for Hawthorne the resemblance runs much deeper, down to what for Hawthorne was that true ghostliness in which he and we can believe. The vertiginous death-in-life condition of Clifford and Hepzibah—a limbo of ceaselessly repeated actions, of confining temperament, of the same old yearnings frustrated by the same old possibilities—is much more disturbing. The turn-about from the popular haunted house story, that these particular ghosts are more afraid of the outside world than the other way around, only intensifies the menace—which is throughout Hawthorne's work the only otherworldly menace worth worrying about—not that one may be harmed by a ghost but that one may become, by easy, almost imperceptible stages, a ghost oneself.

Through Hepzibah and Clifford, therefore, the popular tradition of the haunted house is linked to Hawthorne's special conception of the revenant and to the moral issue of self-loss through stasis and perseveration. Hepzibah and Clifford are the two real haunters of the house; the other two important ghosts in the novel are a good deal more complex, both in their presentation and their importance, and it is chiefly through them that the book takes on its manifold identity. Jaffrey Pyncheon is that special sort of ghost known as the shapeshifter,[9] a far more dangerous sort of spectre to deal with than consistent, timid, and retiring revenants and one that presents an altogether opposite peril to the soul. The danger here is not loss in singlemindedness, reminiscence, reverie but in the disintegration that comes with too much of the public life, of the business of the street, too much attention, in other words, not to the past but to the ideas and poses of the hour. We need not go all the way back to Spenser for shapeshifters; they are common enough in colonial mythology and are part and parcel of the New England ghost tradition. Cotton Mather, for example, frequently mentions their tempta-tions and vexings of the colonists,[10] and of course shapeshifters figure promi-nently in the "spectral evidence" of the Salem witch trials. The presence of one ghost behind all of Jaffrey's shifting, the ghost of the old Colonel, is established in Phoebe's very first encounter with him, when she recognizes not just family resemblance but premeditated disguise.

> The fantasy would not quit her, that the original Puritan, of whom she had heard so many sombre traditions—the progenitor of the whole race of New England Pyncheons, the founder of the House of the Seven Gables, and who had died so strangely in it—had now stept into the shop. In these days of off-hand equipment, the matter was easily enough arranged. On his arrival from the other world, he had merely found it necessary to spend a quarter-of-an-hour at a barber's, who had trimmed down the Puritan's full beard into a pair of grizzled whiskers; then, patronizing a ready-made clothing establishment, he had exchanged his velvet doublet and sable cloak, with the richly worked band under his chin, for a white collar and cravat, coat, vest, and pantaloons; and, lastly, putting aside his steel-hilted broadsword to take up a gold-headed cane, the Colonel Pyncheon, of two centuries ago, steps forward as the Judge, of the passing moment! [P. 120]

Among the offhand equipment available to the old Colonel are not only new suits and canes but a ready-made modern demeanor; what gives Jaffrey his special measure of uncanniness and evil is the array of public faces he takes up with his walking stick, his succession of disguises that hide his secret and allow him to pass unsuspected among most of his fellow townspeople. Like the traditional shapeshifter in the American folk tradition, the repulsive true form can be only glimpsed by mortals, and only when the dissembling spirit is caught off its guard. Even before Phoebe finds her way to the old Colonel lurking behind Jaffrey's masks, she takes fright at the quick changes those masks can undergo. "It was quite as striking, allowing for the difference of scale, as that betwixt a landscape under a broad sunshine, and just before a thunder-storm; not that it had the passionate intensity of the latter aspect, but was cold, hard, immitigable, like a day-long brooding cloud" [Pp. 118–19].

At this moment Phoebe recalls the miniature of Holgrave's that she had mistaken for the old Colonel; but she has barely made this connection, when Jaffrey shifts once again. Indeed, as she witnesses these transformations, Phoebe seems to be put in mind of Coleridge's Geraldine and Keats's Lamia, the two best-known shapeshifters in romantic literature. "But, as it happened, scarcely had Phoebe's eyes rested again on the Judge's countenance, than all its ugly sternness vanished; and she found herself quite overpowered by the sultry, dog-day heat, as it were, of benevolence, which this excellent man diffused out of his great heart into the surrounding atmosphere;—very much like a serpent, which, as a preliminary to fascination, is said to fill the air with his peculiar odor" [P. 119].

Henceforward, every time Jaffrey appears in the novel, even for an instant, we have a privileged view of one of his shape changes: from stern ancestor to affable cousin, from comforter to enemy and back again. Jaffrey practices his black magic not just on his relations but on everyone in town, for spectral power is a special advantage to a ghost running for public office. "As is customary with the rich, when they aim at the honors of a republic, he apologized, as it were, to the people, for his wealth, prosperity, and elevated station, by a free and hearty manner towards those who knew him; putting off the more of his dignity, in due proportion with the humbleness of the man whom he saluted; and thereby proving a haughty consciousness of his advantages, as irrefragably as if he had marched forth, preceded by a troop of lackeys to clear the way" [P. 130]. Such a moment brings us close to the thematic importance of shapeshifting in the novel, but Jaffrey's final transformations, as he sits down in the Colonel's death chair to await Clifford, illustrate this theme more strongly still. The first of these changes Hawthorne presents only as a possibility.

> From that hour of evil omen, until the present, it may be—though we know not the secret of his heart—but it may be, that no wearier and sadder man had ever sunk into the chair, than this same Judge Pyncheon, whom we have just beheld so immitigably hard and resolute. Surely, it must have been at

no slight cost, that he had thus fortified his soul with iron! Such calmness is a mightier effort than the violence of weaker men. And there was yet a heavy task for him to do! Was it a little matter—a trifle, to be prepared for in a single moment, and to be rested from, in another moment—that he must now, after thirty years, encounter a kinsman risen from a living tomb, and wrench a secret from him, or else consign him to a living tomb again? [P. 238]

Hawthorne may be making a sardonic gesture here in giving the Judge the benefit of the doubt and crediting him with more conscience and inner life than he actually has. But sardonic or not, speculation or not, this passage offers our one moment of insight into the dessicated soul and the essential misery of the shapeshifting ghost. If there is indeed any shred of integrity— in either sense of the word—left in Jaffrey, the time to redeem it and nurture it is past, for Jaffrey's very next change is his last one, his sudden, permanent cessation from changes of any kind. As Hawthorne has his prolonged sport, in the "Governor Pyncheon" chapter, with Jaffrey's seated corpse, the emphasis falls not simply on this peculiar new serenity, this end to the Judge's perpetual bustling, but also upon the end of all the role playing. The essential hollowness and invisibility of the dead man are harped upon over and over not as new qualities in Jaffrey but as old ones made clear by death. Jaffrey has always been an emptiness inside; the whole, long mock-elegy has as its theme that this void has now lost all disguise. So Hawthorne forestalls explicit revelation that Jaffrey has died, for the game he plays first reveals the dead moral sense of the living man and underscores the fact that as far as Jaffrey's true nature is concerned, the dead Judge is not much different from the live one, that the void at the center of Jaffrey, in the spot where the man's soul should be, is not caused but rather discovered by his end. Hawthorne's holiday in the company of Jaffrey's corpse painstakingly chronicles Jaffrey's utter disappearance from the world, the apotheosis of the perfectly invisible man.

The gloom has not entered from without; it has brooded here all day, and now, taking its own inevitable time, will possess itself of everything. The Judge's face, indeed, rigid, and singularly white, refuses to melt into this universal solvent. Fainter and fainter grows the light. It is as if another double-handful of darkness had been scattered through the air. Now it is no longer gray, but sable. There is still a faint appearance at the window; neither a glow, nor a gleam, nor a glimmer—any phrase of light would express something far brighter than this doubtful perception, or sense, rather, that there is a window there. Has it yet vanished? No!—yes!—not quite! And there is still the swarthy whiteness—we shall venture to marry these ill-agreeing words—the swarthy whiteness of Judge Pyncheon's face. The features are all gone; there is only the paleness of them left. And how looks it now? There is no window! There is no face! An infinite, inscrutable blackness has annihilated sight! Where is our universe? All crumbled away from us; and we, adrift in chaos, may hearken to the gusts of homeless wind, that go sighing and murmuring about, in quest of what was once a world! [Pp. 276–77]

In context these words are something other than an "all is vanity" pronouncement about worldly business. A shapeshifter is a swarthy whiteness, a hollowness made flesh, and to unmask such a ghost is ultimately to reveal the nothing inside, the inward emptiness that comes of too much concern with surfaces, too many rapid changes for the sake of profit, fashion, social advancement.

We have, so far, two revenants and one shapeshifter: too much reverie and romance on one hand, and much too little of them on the other, either kind of excess leading to a loss of the self. In a real sense, then, the suspense of the novel, as it gradually builds, centers on whether every one of the major characters, everyone in the world of the novel, must be either one sort of ghost or another, whether anyone can find a way to some condition afflicted by neither too much nor too little romance. It is not strange, then, that Hawthorne should require one more ghost—Maule's ghost—both to complete the haunting and to end it, that the last ghost should be, in a sense, both a revenant and a shapeshifter; in other words, that he should perform Hepzibah, Clifford, and Jaffrey's essential ghostlike duties—repeating ancient gestures, haunting the house in the custom of the Maules, and at the same time changing shape at will—but also that he should be able, at some point, to unghost himself, to escape that self-loss that would make him one of the novel's true spectres. The mystery of Holgrave, from his very first appearance in the novel as a customer in Hepzibah's cent shop, is established in an oblique and humorous way. Hepzibah's greeting to him shows us her best moment of second sight. " 'If old Maule's ghost, or a descendant of his, could see me behind the counter to-day, he would call it the fulfilment of his worst wishes. But I thank you for your kindness, Mr. Holgrave, and will do my utmost to be a good shopkeeper' " [P. 46].

Hepzibah's salutation puts the Holgrave question very neatly: Is he Maule's ghost or just distant posterity? Is he here to fulfill old Maule's worst wishes or to offer kindness? Is he the same old ill nature come round again, like Jaffrey—and changed, like Jaffrey, only upon the surface—or have the Maules finally made some escape from their own black arts and resentments, some reconciliation between the inherited temperament and the need to live in a new world? Will Holgrave, in short, prove yet another Maule ghost or a genuine living man? Coming near the close of the novel, Hawthorne's salute to Holgrave aims to settle these lingering questions.

> But what was most remarkable, and perhaps showed a more than common poise in the young man, was the fact, that, amid all these personal vicissitudes, he had never lost his identity. Homeless as he had been—continually changing his whereabout, and therefore responsible neither to public opinion nor to

individuals—putting off one exterior, and snatching up another, to be soon shifted for a third—he had never violated the innermost man, but had carried his conscience along with him. It was impossible to know Holgrave, without recognizing this to be the fact. Hepzibah had seen it. Phoebe soon saw it, likewise, and gave him the sort of confidence which such a certainty inspires. [P. 177]

Noteworthy is the emphasis that Hawthorne places on this integrity, a virtue that does not reveal itself in Holgrave's words or actions until much later in the narrative but that nonetheless establishes him, in Hawthorne's array of ghosts and near-ghosts, as the one best hope in the novel and the most precise and perfect contrast to Jaffrey. Holgrave is simply a much better sort of shapeshifter, perhaps the best we can hope for in the ever-changing creatures walking in the new world.

It has been said often that Holgrave is in the novel to represent the artist, the scientist, the new breed of man, the spiritual pilgrim, even the Red Cross Knight; and there is truth in all of these estimations. But it is also true that through this last embodiment of the Maules the novel most directly addresses the problem of romantic fiction and its place in life. Certainly Holgrave plays and sees himself both as scientist and as artist. He explains to Phoebe that, as he understands his own work, the sun tells the story on the daguerreotype plate, not the man who takes the picture; having studied both Mesmerism and the art of writing tales for women's magazines, however, he deals in enchantments as much as in the objective recording of the real. But the most interesting paradox about Holgrave, at the center of his work in both science and art, is that what he achieves always has a multiple identity, proving always both a misleading illusion *and* a representation of the truth. Furthermore, his creations invariably have escaped the controlling hand of their maker and have unforeseen and even undesired effects on his audiences. Holgrave makes a good many mistakes. His photograph of Jaffrey may reveal "the secret character" of the public man, but to Phoebe, the only person to whom he shows it, the picture does not suggest Jaffrey at all but rather a doctored version of the old portrait of the Colonel—and all the while, Holgrave has been trying to take a picture of Jaffrey that is recognizably the smiling Judge. Indeed, Holgrave has taken the picture "over and over again, and still with no better result" (p. 91). His mesmerizing of Phoebe is likewise a blunder, coming not of his intention but from gestures unconsciously produced by "plunging into his tale with the energy and absorption natural to a young author" (p. 211). His story of Alice may be good romance, or perhaps good history, but he has caused Phoebe to miss it. She recalls nothing except "an impression of a vast deal of trouble and calamity" (p. 212), the sort of impression that might be left by a poor piece of storytelling. Holgrave may be an enchanter in the Maule tradition, but his magic, scientific or otherwise, seems always to be getting away from him. Perfect scientific products, pictures made from sunshine, bewilder his audience just as thoroughly as his ventures into romance. In this new world that Holgrave inhabits, the young scientist, like the young romancer, had better get used to a career of unforeseen results, and of being misunderstood.

Holgrave's ultimate solution, of course, is to marry his audience, to join for life with the woman who understands almost nothing of what he does, either as a storyteller or as a realist. While the marriage to Phoebe may be a wry comment of sorts on the best fate that either a romancer or a believer in fact can hope for—love without understanding—the abiding, major question at the end of the novel is why Hawthorne ultimately allows Holgrave to escape, not from Phoebe but from the Maule past, the Pyncheon past, and (most disturbing, to some readers) from his own fiercely espoused ideologies.

To make better sense of the novel's conclusion, we must first notice that the residents of this haunted house, when they are all in their places, make up a striking picture of Hawthorne's own strange predicament as a modern writer of fiction, as Hawthorne himself conceived of that ambiguous, ambivalent condition and which the notebooks, the letters, and the major biographies of Hawthorne reveal again and again: his wish to be both reclusive and renowned, fantastic and factual, arcane and understood. Holgrave is only one of the tenants in *The House of the Seven Gables*, and to see him as the only one worth commenting on at the end is to finish the novel in an unbalanced way. High up under the roof, he represents an unbridled, improvising intellect, dabbling with art, with magic, with science; he is sometimes a renegade; he preaches, philosophizes, takes pictures, casts spells, professes no lasting allegiance to any political or aesthetic doctrine. Down in the gloomy heart of the house there is a world of enduring reverie, a dreamy yearning for the past, a childish perfectionism. Clifford and Hepzibah, the pale revenants, wish to escape time, to blow empty, beautiful bubbles, to evade the present, ultimately to escape the confinement of their own natures. The last tenant, the newcomer, makes the house complete as a portrait of the modern romancer, for in the cent shop, Phoebe addresses the daylight street of that very world that reverie denies and the improvising mind confounds. She is in fact the gingerbread figure placed carefully in the window, inviting commerce with everyday life.

No one has ever argued that any one of the tale's characters is, taken alone, a special achievement in realization. The point is that they are an ensemble, each a part of a whole, and that they must be looked at together if the book is to make much sense. When Holgrave stops being the ghost of the old Maules, when he proposes marriage to Phoebe, moves himself, Phoebe, Clifford, Hepzibah, and even Uncle Venner out of the house, and compromises his professed faith in newness and impermanence, he precipitates the long-running dispute about the ending of the book. The most common objections seem at times surprisingly severe and Pyncheonesque in temper, with their insistence, apparently, that Hawthorne, like one of his ghosts, should remain finally wedded to one professed ideology. While no single foray into such a dispute will resolve anything, three simple recognitions, growing out of the above discussion, ought to figure into our thinking.

First, it matters that the Maule and the Pyncheons quit the house *together*, as they have lived together. The improviser, the adaptable young woman, the reclusive aesthete, the scowling elegist are apparently off to seek some kind of mutual sensibility. Their different temperaments have, at the very last, become almost one, as the old residents take leave of the house with the same insouciance as the young ones. "The party came forth, and (with the exception of good Uncle Venner, who was to follow in a few days) proceeded to take their places. They were chatting and laughing very pleasantly together; and—as proves to be often the case, at moments when we ought to palpitate with sensibility—Clifford and Hepzibah bade a final farewell to the abode of their forefathers, with hardly more emotion than if they had made it their arrangement to return thither at tea-time" [P. 318].

Second, Holgrave's decision to start changing and improvising in his ideas, much as he has always done in his occupations, not only makes common sense (Holgrave is after all just twenty-two years old) but also recalls many attempts by Hawthorne to suggest the one best chance he sees for mankind in a world of entrapments, time-worn curses, inherited misfortunes, a life full of ghosts. Nowhere in Hawthorne's writings does he suggest that anyone, old or young, naive or worldly, can escape error or the miseries that error brings on; indeed, the recurring idea is that those who live in old stone houses, real or ideological, are no more nor less liable to such woe than those who live in huts. In one of Hawthorne's major short stories from the period, for example, Holgrave's old gospel of permanent impermanence comes off as another proof of human foolishness. "Earth's Holocaust" (1846) is the tale of a mob of Holgraves burning everything for the sake of renewal and gaining nothing by doing so.

> "There is one thing that these wiseacres have forgotten to throw into the fire, and without which all the rest of the conflagration is just nothing at all— yes; though they had burnt the earth itself to a cinder!"
>
> "And what may that be?" eagerly demanded the Last Murderer.
>
> "What, but the human heart itself!" said the dark-visaged stranger, with a portentous grin. "And, unless they hit upon some method of purifying that foul cavern, forth from it will re-issue all the shapes of wrong and misery— the same old shapes, or worse ones—which they have taken such a vast deal of trouble to consume to ashes. I have stood by, this live-long night, and laughed in my sleeve at the whole business. Oh, take my word for it, it will be the old world yet!"[11]

Hawthorne's best wish for this world, where the human heart is ever fallible and impure, is only a modest chance to start over—not to escape evil or burn it away but simply to live one's own life and make one's own blunders. His benedictions upon the young commonly have this idea at heart; they inveigh against moral fixity of any sort. Here is what he offers as a prayer for a "New Adam."

> But, blessed in his ignorance, he may still enjoy a new world in our worn-out one. Should he fall short of good, even as far as we did, he has at least the freedom—no worthless one—to make errors for himself. And his literature, when the progress of centuries shall create it, will be no interminably repeated echo of our own poetry, and reproduction of the images that were moulded by our great fathers of song and fiction, but a melody never yet heard on earth, and intellectual forms unbreathed upon by our conceptions. Therefore let the dust of ages gather upon the volumes of the library, and, in due season, the roof of the edifice crumble down upon the whole.[12]

To dust, says Hawthorne, with libraries and all their instructive cautionary fictions, for moral literature too can be a haunted house.

Young Holgrave's gospel of the new, congealed into an ideology and sustained against common sense and compromise, must prove no more than another interminably repeated echo, for a major idea both in this novel and throughout Hawthorne's tales and sketches, is that lessons taken too much to heart are dangerous lessons. Holgrave's little closing speech favoring stone houses and long traditions is not a sign of Hawthorne's "selling out to the marketplace," pandering to a middle-class American audience.[13] In the context of the novel, and in light of the fate that Hawthorne consistently doles out to his other young adventurers, it should be clear that where Holgrave lives now is of no consequence, whether or not he contradicts himself is of no consequence. Warned by the defeated refugees from the outside world, the young people of "The Canterbury Pilgrims" (1833) are nonetheless better off setting out to "mingle in an untried life," forsaking the safe consistencies of the Shaker village; the Old Year may have the last word, in "The Sister Years" (1839), about the miseries and vain hopes of mankind, but the New Year still begins not merely as she must but as she ought, in naive joy and perfect hope; in "The Maypole of Merrymount" (1837), Edgar and Edith learn that "systematic gayety" serves no better as a way of living than the "moral gloom" to which they finally return—just as the storytellers themselves, in "The Devil in Manuscript," "Main Street," and "Alice Doane's Appeal" all learn that moral and artistic fixity are the best guarantees of failure. If the problem of escaping from a haunted condition, from the loss of the self, serves both as an essential organizing principle and a key moral issue in *The House of the Seven Gables*, then the ending, in which Holgrave decides no more than to marry Phoebe, to quit the house with the others, and to forget ideologies for a while, fits the novel handsomely on its most important thematic level and restates that cautious, plausible human hope that turns up so often in Hawthorne's other work. At twenty-two, the last of the Maules weds, rather than bewitches, the last of the Pyncheons; in the process, he becomes a human being rather than an instrument of malice or a mouthpiece for popular transcendental ideas. He has cleansed the ancient house, and if at the end he is setting out on the road toward error, he affirms in doing so the essential human right in Hawthorne's universe—the right of every human being, and every artist, to make his or her own blunders rather than inherit them from someone else.

Still, the young experimenter from the upper rooms has more to offer than such a measured answer to the central moral problem in the novel. As he joins with the others, Holgrave comes to represent an equally sensible response to the literary problem that is part and parcel of the larger issue. The quitting of the house, with the living girl and the flesh-and-blood ghosts all now in Holgrave's company, is in fact a venturing back into the real world, into the life after romance, after *this* romance in particular. For both the romancer and his audience, this is the crucial moment: the closed-in reverie of the haunted house, the romantic fiction cut off from life beyond literature, is left behind cheerfully, if only incompletely. For to leave this house, this romance, is not to escape untouched; it is to take something along, the recognition that life after romance is at its best a life of improvisation, a life at peace with many sensibilities, with the romantic impulse, the detachment of the scientist, the urge to exist as both the private and the public creature.

What is most striking, and perhaps most unsettling, about the ending of *The House of the Seven Gables* is how uneventful and undoctrinaire it really is. Lacking dramatic intensity, lacking even an air of finality, the novel trails off rather than closes, and as the end of a proper gothic tale, this may be the chief shortcoming of the last pages. But as a book about romances and the place of romances, and as a meditation on the nature of ghosts, hauntings, and ghost stories, *The House of the Seven Gables* does close with a handsome expression of its abiding theme, that what makes people and stories into ghosts is their single-minded response to life. The tale has "a great deal more to do with the clouds overhead, than with any portion of the actual soil of the County of Essex," Hawthorne observes at the end of his famous preface to the second edition. In the last sentence of the novel the last important ghost in residence, Alice Pyncheon, strikes her harpsichord and ascends from the house into these clouds overhead, the clouds being, at the first and at the last, the realm of the imagination. The difference is that we do know, at the end, what those clouds have to do with the County of Essex, the true world. One more look, then, at the very first sentences of this famous, puzzling preface.

When a writer calls his work a Romance, it need hardly be observed that he wishes to claim a certain latitude, both as to its fashion and material, which he would not have felt himself entitled to assume, had he professed to be writing a Novel. The latter form of composition is presumed to aim at a very minute fidelity, not merely to the possible, but to the probable and ordinary course of man's experience. The former—while, as a work of art, it must rigidly subject itself to laws, and while it sins unpardonably, so far as it may swerve aside from the truth of the human heart—has fairly a right to present that truth under circumstances, to a great extent, of the writer's own choosing or creation. [P. 1]

A right, certainly—but what to do with it? The novel itself provides the answer, and the answer turns out to be, in a word, improvisation. Improvisation with popular romance, with scientific fact and method, social commentary, satire. The very blurriness of the preface, the imprecision that provokes such debate over where in its short span the stress ought to be laid and just where and how the clouds and the county are reconciled in the novel, this evasiveness serves the same purpose as the tale itself. To call that purpose artistic license is, in Hawthorne's case, to miss the real point, for freedom in *The House of the Seven Gables* is a necessity, the one real hope for answering the moral and aesthetic questions that come with trying to write a romance that is something more than a romance. Because the loss of the self in *The House of the Seven Gables* is as much a literary as a moral challenge, touching the writer and reader just as it does those who walk old halls and dream of lost fortunes, the novel from the first page to the last explores not merely romance as a moral act but the nature of the real itself, of life with and without reverie, ideas with too little and too much of the disordering touch of the imagination.

As the blunderer and the craftsman, the wizard and the sunshine man, Holgrave has made his peace with romance and with realism; with two ghosts and one genuine woman he will feel his way into the future. At the end of the novel the Maule and the Pyncheons, joining their meager forces, have begun collectively to balance the dream world and the real one, the individual consciousness and all codifications and reductions of it, the romance, the fiction, and the life beyond the spell of either. To see this complex idea in *The House of the Seven Gables* is really only to give Hawthorne credit for the insight that so many of his other stories confirm, his full recognition of the problems of being a storyteller. There is no need to disconnect him intellectually from his own time in the development of the American novel or to treat him as if he belonged in a more modern, more conspicuously self-conscious company of writers. The largest inference may simply be this: that if there has long been a conversation out at the limits of fiction, a conversation in which sensitive artists face the question of what place they and their stories ought to have in a larger world, what they can and cannot teach, what, as writers and audience alike, we can and cannot understand of either fiction or life, then in *The House of the Seven Gables* this questioning has found its way into the very form of the fiction itself and reconciled itself not only with the plot and features of a familiar kind of romance but with the undiminished moral force of the tale.

## Notes

1. Hyatt Waggoner reviews much of this recent scholarship in "Hawthorne Explained," *Sewanee Review* 86 (Winter 1978): 130–38.

2. Hawthorne's comment appears in a review in *Literary World*, 17 April 1847, p. 248.

3. One of the best discussions to date of the structure and obligations of a ghost story is Peter Penzoldt's *The Supernatural in Fiction* (London: P. Nevill, 1952), esp. pp. 18–25.

4. *Mosses from an Old Manse, The Centenary Edition of the Works of Nathaniel Hawthorne*, ed. William Charvat et al., 12 vols. (Columbus: Ohio State University Press, 1962–74), 10:17.

5. Hawthorne, *Our Old Home, Centenary Edition*, 5:59–60.

6. Hawthorne, *The House of the Seven Gables Centenary Edition*, 2:280–81. All subsequent references to *The House of the Seven Gables* are to this standard edition.

7. The ghosts in *The House of the Seven Gables* have been discussed before, most notably by Edgar Dryden and Ronald T. Curran. Curran's argument is that Hawthorne intends to democratize the traditional gothic romance and to treat gothic conventions, ghosts included, in an ironic manner. Dryden's interest in ghosts is likewise aimed at demonstrating Hawthorne's "nostalgic parody of a lost autonomous form, but also its will to regain them." Neither of these scholars treats the ghost motif as extensively or draws the inferences that I do here. Curran, " 'Yankee Gothic': Hawthorne's 'Castle of Pyncheon,' " *Studies in the Novel* 7 (Spring 1976): 69–80; Dryden, "Hawthorne's Castle in the Air: Form the Theme in *The House of the Seven Gables*," *ELH* 38 (June 1971): 294–317.

8. See, e. g., the illustrations in Raphael (pseud. for Robert C. Smith), *The Familiar Astrologer* (London: n.p., 1831), a popular book of the time on ghosts and hauntings.

9. For a general discussion of shapeshifting and its widespread presence in the folk tradition, see Maria Leach, ed., *Dictionary of Folklore, Mythology, and Legend*, 2 vols. (New York: Funk and Wagnalls, 1950), 2:1004–5. Also see the chapter "Cases of Conscience Concerning Witchcraft," in Increase Mather's *A Further Account of the Tryals of the New England Witches* (1693; reprinted, London: J. R. Smith, 1862), a chapter predominantly about the shapeshifting of Satan and his legions in colonial New England.

10. See, e. g., Cotton Mather's chapter, entitled "Enchantments Encountered," in *The Wonders of the Invisible World* (1693; reprinted London: J. R. Smith, 1862) in which he comments at length on the power of spectres and devils to take any shape they choose: "The Witches have not only intimated, but some of them acknowledge, That they have plotted the Representations of *Innocent Persons*, to cover and shelter themselves and their Witchcrafts; now, altho' our good God has hitherto generally preserved us from the Abuse therein design'd by the Devils for us, yet who of us can exactly state, *How far our God may for our Chastisement permit the Devil to proceed in such an Abuse?*" (pp. 17–18).

11. Hawthorne, "Earth's Holocaust," *Centenary Edition*, 10:403.

12. Hawthorne, "The New Adam and Eve," *Centenary Edition*, 10:265–66.

13. For the contrary viewpoint, see Michael T. Gilmore, "The Artist and the Marketplace in *The House of the Seven Gables*," *ELH* 48 (1981): 172–89.

# The Author's Corpse and the Humean Problem of Personal Identity in Hawthorne's *The House of the Seven Gables*

## WILLIAM J. SCHEICK*

Over the decades, readers of Hawthorne's fiction have detected a large number of influences on his thought and writings. One interesting example of these readings suggests that Hawthorne was an artist divided between a conscious philosophical agreement with eighteenth-century empirical thought (in which meanings are fixed) and an unconscious instinctual agreement with nineteenth-century Romantic thought (in which meanings are open-ended).[1] Although this formulation of a major tension in Hawthorne's writings has endured, critics have especially studied Hawthorne's sensitivity to philosophical and artistic developments during the nineteenth century, while they have paid relatively less attention to evidence of his eighteenth-century cultural inheritance.[2]

One particularly cogent assessment of Hawthorne's awareness of eighteenth-century thought detects his artistic use of certain arguments of David Hume, whose philosophical work Hawthorne might have read directly but whose thought he certainly knew at least second hand from his studies at Bowdoin College.[3] It is certain that in 1822, while a college student, he had tried to read Hume's famous *History of England*, but found it terribly dull and doubted that he would finish it.[4] In one way or another, Hawthorne was exposed to the concepts of Humean skeptical empiricism, which not only formed an important component of his intellectual heritage but also apparently, in his later years, suited his sense of life.

To propose that Humean concepts contributed to Hawthorne's understanding of the world is not to argue that he necessarily thought specifically of Hume as he wrote. Humean skeptical empiricism is part of a philosophical tradition he had inherited, as had his generation, and we can profitably annotate features of his work by means of Hume's philosophy without in the least intimating that the philosopher was consciously on Hawthorne's

*Reprinted from William J. Scheick, "The Author's Corpse and the Humean Problem of Personal Identity in Hawthorne's *The House of the Seven Gables*," *Studies in the Novel* 24 (Summer, 1992), 131–53. Copyright 1992 by University of North Texas. Reprinted by permission of the publisher.

mind much of the time. In other words, it is less useful to argue for Hawthorne's conscious or unconscious specific reliance on Hume, than to use his inheritance of Humean thought as one appropriate context for exploring and decoding features of Hawthorne's artistry. Such an application of Humean thought to Hawthorne's writings, for instance, closes the gap some have perceived in the seeming division between his conscious philosophical agreement with eighteenth-century empirical thought and his unconscious instinctual agreement with nineteenth-century Romantic thought; for Humean skeptical empiricism radically destabilizes meanings of the sort established by such empiricists as John Locke.[5]

Actually, in spite of efforts on the part of some critics to argue that Hawthorne was basically affirmative in his view of life, many scholars have maintained that an underlying pessimism informs his work. The reasons for this pessimism include, according to these critics, his personality, his inner turmoil, his view of sin, his idea of the past, among other culprits—all perfectly reasonable possibilities. Whatever the full range of probable sources, however, his inheritance of Humean skeptical empiricism is a mainstay of philosophical pessimism. Humean empiricism raises ontological and epistemological doubts identical to those in Hawthorne's writings.

Humean empiricism does not deny the probability that the world external to the perceiving mind is real; it refutes the possibility that the perceiving mind can ever "really" know that external world. This perspective seems to inform Hawthorne's comment to Sophia Peabody on 1 May 1841: "Every day of my life makes me feel more and more how seldom a fact is accurately stated," even "though the narrator be the most truth-telling person in existence"; "is truth a fantasy which we are to pursue forever and never grasp?"[6] The perceiving mind is confined to its subjective perceptions and cannot gain access to a world of objects that might exist independently of these perceptions. In the matter of causality, for instance, Hume indicates that the *experience* of a *seeming* constant conjunction leads the mind to *assert* a causal connection. But this conclusion is merely an idea (image), which in turn is merely the product of the *unreliable sensation* of contiguity and succession; and this subjective sensation (like any other) cannot be used to know an objective, *necessary* connection.[7] For Hume, that something in existence must have a cause is not demonstrable; the perceiving mind cannot "really" discover / dis-cover causal relations or necessary connections.

Such an approach to reality opens an abyss between the perceiving mind and its origins. This separation from origins—virtually an erasure of origins—is a characteristic of both some of the eighteenth-century writers (e.g., Charles Brockden Brown) *and* some of the nineteenth-century authors Hawthorne read.[8] This inability to verify ontologically what is real (the original) vexes any epistemological search for what is true. This feature of skeptical empiricism)provides a philosophical foundation for at least two of Hawthorne's recurrent artistic practices: ambiguously casting doubt on interpretations which at first seem clear[9] and equivocally depicting the world in his stories as constituted merely of the substance of dream.[10] In Hawthorne's fiction the reader circles and recircles some central "original" mystery that is the meaning of the story in hand, and of existence, as if to penetrate to some ontological core that might be something or nothing at all; but, as in Humean thought, that ontological center always seems to recede from the perceiving mind's ability to know it really.[11]

If the Humean tradition of skeptical empiricism discloses an unbridgeable gap between the external world of matter and the internal world of the registering mind, it also radically revises earlier comfortable notions of the mind itself as possessing a personal identity. Although some critics of Hawthorne's fiction have perceived an ontological chasm (albeit not its Humean analog) in his work, they have virtually evaded the issue of personal identity in Hawthorne's writings,[12] a problem similarly defined by Humean empiricism. Exploring this assault on the reality of personal identity in *The House of the Seven Gables* is perhaps especially appropriate because this romance has been read as a statement of Hawthorne's optimism (real or forced). So, if we succeed in finding in this work the sort of erasure that is typical of skeptical empiricism, then the case for a Humean reading of personal identity is easier to make for Hawthorne's other works, in which his pessimism is more overt. Our exploration of the nature of personal identity will begin with a discussion of Hume's concepts, then consider how the issue of personal identity relates to the characters, the narrator, the genre, and the author of *The House of the Seven Gables*.

## PERSONAL IDENTITY AND HUME

In *A Treatise of Human Nature* (I, 4:6) Hume attacks the concept of personal identity, the notion that there is a self, as a *fictitious* belief (p. 259). First, he demonstrates that no perceiving mind is constant or invariable. On the contrary, the mind is merely a collection of inconceivably rapid, different perceptions: "The mind is a kind of theatre, where several perceptions successively make their appearance" (p. 253). These various perceptions, including ideas (which are only faint images of phenomenal impressions), seem connected because the mind associates resemblance and contiguity with causation.

Second, this operation of perception, whether associating impressions of sensation or of reflection, is the product of two faculties: imagination and memory. *Imagination* particularly contributes to the fiction of a self by emphasizing perceptions of contiguity; *memory* primarily contributes to the fiction of a self by emphasizing perceptions of resemblance. Since "memory acquaints us with the continuance and extent of this succession of perceptions, 'tis to be consider'd . . . chiefly, as the source of personal identity" (p. 261). Memory raises up images of past perceptions; these images resemble their objects and thereby allow the imagination to associate them and make these perceptions seem continuous even though they are actually an interrupted succession of related impressions.

So radical is Hume's skeptical empiricism that the idea of a self is undercut from two directions. As we have seen, the senses of the body are unreliable as detectors of reality outside their subjective impressions. As we have also seen, the faculties of the mind are untrustworthy as detectors of reality because the mind (imagination and memory) is utterly dependent on unreliable sensation (whether physical or mental images). Hume has set out to destroy, among other notions, the valuation of reason advanced by such empiricists as John Locke—a valuation at the heart of at least the explicit ideology of America at its Revolutionary founding and a valuation Haw-thorne's work also challenges. Hume has also destroyed any sense of true human creativity, which he has reduced to a mere mechanical compounding, transposing, augmenting, or diminishing of the materials provided by the senses.

In dismissing personal identity Hume at one point offers a startling analogy: "When my perceptions are remov'd for any time, as by sound sleep; so long am I insensible of *myself*, and may truly be said not to exist. And, were all my perceptions remov'd by death, and cou'd I neither think, nor feel, nor see, nor love, nor hate, after the dissolution of my body, I shou'd be entirely annihilated, nor do I conceive what is farther requisite to make me a perfect non-entity" (p. 252). Here Hume says that without our body we are nobody, and that even with our body we are, in terms of having personal identity (self), still nobody. We are, Hume suggests, all nonentities, as if a form of living dead. We are, in Humean terms, merely animated corpses for whom the lack of a personal identity—which is equivalent to non-being (death)—is the paradoxical ground of our self-less (soul-less) animated bodies.

This bleak and chilling conclusion follows naturally from Hume's reasoning. It is, as well, an inevitable conclusion of Humean skeptical empiricism. And, interestingly, it provides a remarkable analog for several interrelated strange features of Hawthorne's *The House of the Seven Gables*.

## Personal Identity and Characterization

Hume's description of the lack of personal identity, as equivalent to non-being, parallels a description of Clifford in *The House of the Seven Gables*: "Continually . . . his mind and consciousness took their departure, leaving his wasted, gray, and melancholy figure—a substantial emptiness, a material ghost—to occupy his seat at table" (p. 105).[13] Clifford is substantial—has bodily substance—but is vacant within—has no identity of self; he is like a "material ghost" or, in terms similar to Hume's, a form of living dead.

Appropriately, Clifford is a creature completely dependent on sensation (p. 108). As if conforming to Hume's description of humanity as a production of physical life whose perceptions are merely the operation of imagination and memory, Clifford's feeble mind, dependent on unreliable sensation, is somewhat capable of these two functions. He evinces a dim capacity for the "play of imagination" and even for "remembrance" (pp. 109, 110), despite the fact that something "mysterious . . . had annihilated his memory" (p. 149).

But Clifford's lack of personal identity (an interior self) is not unique in the romance. His case merely represents an extreme example that actually reveals the fundamental nature of all of humanity. Clifford is "partly crazy, and partly imbecile; a ruin, a failure, *as almost everybody is*—though in less degree, or less perceptibly" (pp. 157–58; emphasis added). The word "almost" here is a narrative hedge to which we shall return, but the observation is clear: all of humanity seems to evince an inner instability of identity. Certainly the other characters in *The House of the Seven Gables* fare better than Clifford only in degree.

Holgrave, for example, makes what seems to be a radical inversion of his beliefs by the end of the romance. There is, in fact, a long history of critical debate about his sudden renunciation of his former positions. Some critics argue that the change has been anticipated and expresses Hawthorne's notions; others argue that the change indicates Hawthorne's loss of control or his concern with sales.[14] But Holgrave is like Clifford, differing only in degree. Holgrave's *fundamental* lack of stability in his viewpoint suggests that he too evinces a vacancy in personal identity.

This essential deficit, in spite of the narrator's one desperate assertion to the contrary (p. 177), seems implied in the description of Holgrave as someone readily given to "putting off one exterior, and snatching up another, to be soon shifted for a third" (p. 177). In Holgrave's instance, as for humanity in general, identifying oneself through alternating *external* guises not only suggests an instability of personal identity, but also the very absence of an *internal* center of self-definition. When Phoebe observes of Holgrave that "his humor changes without any reason that can be guessed at, just as a cloud comes over the sun" (p. 178), her unwitting simile displaces the idea that reason governs a self and suggests (in Humean terms) the phenomenal or sensorial basis for all acts of the mind. And just as Hume indicated how we mistakenly tend to believe that the mere collection of inconceivably rapid different perceptions of our mind (only connected through associational resemblance and contiguity, not necessary causation) are constant or invariable, so too Holgrave supposes that "all his past vicissitudes seem merely like a change of garments" (p. 180). The word "seem" certainly should problematize this belief for the wary reader, as should the simile, which (like Phoebe's analogy to the clouds) again intimates that whatever constitutes one's interior is grounded on, and perhaps entirely the product of, whatever constitutes one's exterior.

In this matter, moreover, Holgrave may be a descendent of the Maules, but he is very much like Judge Pyncheon. The Judge, like Holgrave, does not derive "his idea of himself" from "looking inward"; he looks outward to "the mirror of public opinion" (the exterior world) for "what purports to be his image" of himself (p. 232). The Judge's and Holgrave's sense of personal identity is only an insubstantial *image*. At the end of the romance, therefore, the sudden change in Holgrave's views (the word *views* coalesces the physical and the mental) seems to be little more than a continuation of his characteristic shifting about of externals as if in search for an ever-elusive internal core of self identity.

As for Phoebe's possession of a substantial personal identity, Clifford cannot locate it any better than she can Holgrave's. If the problem here is epistemological, the imagery of Clifford's thought, like that of Phoebe on Holgrave, conveys ontological implications. "He read Phoebe, as he would a sweet and simple story" (p. 142), which means that Clifford does with Phoebe what every character in the romance does with each other: try to read, to decipher, to interpret them—always to fail utterly in the attempt. "She was not an actual fact for him, but the interpretation of all that he had lacked on earth" (p. 142). If Phoebe is not a fact, then she is a fiction (a story, in Clifford's words) open to infinite interpretations; and her non-factuality, at least as she is experienced subjectively by Clifford, recalls Hume's idea about the role of the imagination in perpetuating the fiction of the self. Lapses in the continuity of this fictional self are inadmissible to Phoebe herself, who at a representative moment remains "unconscious of the crisis through which she had passed" when in fact she has entered some sort of mindless trance (mental absence) while Holgrave reads his narrative to her (p. 212).[15]

The inscrutability of the self, or personal identity—suggesting its ficti-tiousness, its non-reality—that is intimated in Clifford's, Phoebe's, and Holgrave's mutual inability to decipher others is also suggested by Clifford's appearance. His face evidences "furrows . . . so deeply written across his brow, and so compressed, as with the futile effort to crowd in all the tale, that the whole inscription was made illegible" (p. 139). Note that not only are these *lines* epistemologically unreadable, but they are ontologically associated with tales, fiction.

Hepzibah also tries "to read . . . the face" of Judge Pyncheon, who possesses a "capacity for varied expression," and the face of Uncle Venner "to discover what secret meaning, if any, might be lurking there" (pp. 57, 59, 64). Even worse, she cannot decipher her own face, which others puzzle over too (p. 47). "By often gazing at herself in a dim looking-glass, and perpetually encountering her own frown within its ghostly sphere," she tries "to interpret the expression" and "fancie[s] herself" to be just as miserably cross as the external world interprets her to be (p. 34). Her conclusion about her interior self or personal identity, like Judge Pyncheon's about himself, is the product of imagination and memory based on external perception. And ironically, her habitual scowl does in fact have at least one possible external cause, her nearsightedness, which she is too nearsighted in another sense to note because her mind has imaginatively, and mistakenly, connected other associations in ascertaining causality.[16] Not to be able to read one's own face, or one's own self, as is evident in Hepzibah's case, raises a Humean doubt about the reality of personal identity. Personal identity is apparently as ghostly as the impression of Hepzibah's face in her mirror, an image recalling Clifford as a material nonentity, as if a form of living dead.

Hepzibah's interpretations are generated by fancies, or "fantasies" (p. 59), or acts of imagination founded on external sensation. In more than one instance, "her very brain was impregnated with the dry-rot of [the] timbers" of the Pyncheon house (p.59), another instance of externality determining interiority. She is more like Clifford than she knows, and she is like entranced, de-spirited Phoebe during Holgrave's reading. Just as Clifford is substantial—has bodily substance—but is vacant within—has no identity of self—so also Hepzibah sometimes experiences life as if she were "a person in a dream, when the will always sleeps" (p.251). Sometimes she exists as if "walking in a dream" and as if her "spirit . . . flits away" and her "body remains to guide itself, as best it may, with little more than the mechanism of animal life" (pp. 66–67). As we are told later, everyone is like Clifford to some degree (pp. 157–58).

Clifford, somewhat improved in his use of memory and imagination at the end of the book, speculates about the relationship between matter and mind: "Is it a fact—or have I dreamt it—that, by means of electricity, the world of matter has become a great nerve . . . a vast head, a brain, instinct with intelligence! Or, shall we say, it is itself a thought, nothing but thought, and no longer the substance we deemed it?" (p. 264). The first idea, emphasizing matter as the ground for mind, is in the empirical tradition; the second idea, emphasizing mind as the ground for matter, is in the idealistic tradition. Both come together in Humean skeptical empiricism when it argues that all mind is grounded on matter, but that the perception of that matter by that mind constitutes an imaginative reading, or interpretation, that, in effect, renders the world (in terms of our experience) as insubstantial as a dream. This skeptical empirical view, in which personal identity is insubstantial and nonexistent, seems to define the characters of *The House of the Seven Gables*.

## Personal Identity and the Narrator

If a lack of personal identity seems to delimit the characters of Hawthorne's book, it also appears to characterize its narrator as well. That *The House of the Seven Gables* has a narrator who is distinct from Hawthorne has, surprisingly, gone unstudied. In fact, a conflation of narrative voice in this book and its author is commonplace in critical discussions.[17] The persistence of this habit is particularly odd given recent efforts to sensitize readers to Hawthorne's management of narration[18] and given several attempts to focus on a specific narrator in *The Scarlet Letter*.[19] The narrative voice of *The House of the Seven Gables* is just as complex a spokesman, and just as unreliable, as the narrator (Miles Coverdale) of *The Blithedale Romance*.

Unlike the speaker in *The Blithedale Romance*, the narrator of *The House of the Seven Gables* is never identified. Nevertheless, he registers his presence. Consider a curious feature in the first and second paragraphs of the romance. The narrator's sense of himself intrudes into these paragraphs in two ways. First, he draws attention to himself: "On my occasional visits to the town aforesaid, I seldom fail to turn down Pyncheon-street"; "the aspect of the vulnerable mansion has always affected me like a human countenance" (p. 5). Second, this is the only place in the romance where he uses the personal pronouns *I* and me, after which he resorts to the conventional (and expected) use of the editorial *we* and *us*.

This intrusion is peculiar and calls attention to itself. The narrator seems more than the (seemingly) mere self-effacing, disinterested voice of conventional third-person storytelling. Something more personal is intimated, but abandoned or retreated from as the conventional takes over. Who is this person, the teased reader cannot help at first wondering? Although the press of more conventional narrative proceeds to displace this very concern in the reader's mind, this bracketing of the reader's memory is never complete. The impression that the narrator is someone "there" is dimly recalled whenever the narrative specifically refers to "the writer" (e. g., pp. 20, 41, 124) and to "the reader" (e. g., pp. 10, 28, 37, 57, 150), or directly addresses the reader as "you" (e. g., pp. 57, 68, 149). The reader is left, like Hepzibah with Clifford, to play a game of "hide-and-seek" (p.35) with this elusive narrator, whom the reader is trying "to read" even as all of the characters in his story try to read each other.

The problem the reader has with a narrator who is there and not there (not identified by name or interest or role in the story) is another version of the problem of personal identity manifested in that narrator's depiction of the characters in his tale. To some extent the narrator is the conventional (seemingly) self-effacing presence of the conventional narrative of third-person novels, but this faintness of shadowy presence means more. The narrator is as fictional a creation as are the characters, and in this sense he is a nonentity, even as they are. Similarly, just as these characters represent "a substantial emptiness, a material ghost," so does the narrator. He admits at one point that he is "a disembodied listener" (p. 30), and he amounts to a disembodied voice. To have no body is to be nobody; he has no identity because he has no body, which (as the characters of his story reveal) is the source of the external sensation that comprises one's interior. Yet his voice is *embodied* textually, and so he exists as a substantial emptiness, a material ghost. He exists phenomenally as textual voice but he has no essential personal identity. In this philosophical sense, as in a literal sense, he is not real. He "reflects," like Hepzibah's ghostly representation in her mirror, the very vacuity at the center of the imaged presences and voices of the characters in his narrative.

Lacking definition as a self, the narrator is prone to the same vicissitudes dramatized in his characters, especially Holgrave (who, like the narrator, is an artist). These changes suggest a narrator who is as indefinite in his sense of identity and his beliefs as is Holgrave, and this problem within the narrator accounts for confusions which critics of *The House of the Seven Gables* have too readily attributed to Hawthorne. For instance, is this romance informed by the narrator's desire to succeed financially or to inculcate a moral? A virtual dialogue occurs in the book on this point, as on the question of the compatibility of art and commerce. Nowhere is the narrator's position clear—because his motives always recede before his (and our) ability to read or interpret them truly and because his self is unstable and insubstantial. Other gnarled questions arise, as well, only to be left open-ended in dialogic opposition. Does love conquer all? Does good come out of evil? Does death remedy wrongs (cf. pp, 133, 313)? Does humanity really progress?

Perhaps one of the most fundamental of the unresolved probes of the book is the narrator's vacillation between a Puritan and an Enlightenment reading of human nature. On the one hand, the narrator suspects that evil visits the progeny of successive generations, as if Adam's transgression passes on to all successive generations. At one point the narrator suspects that perhaps "the weakness and defects, the bad passions, the mean tendencies, and the moral diseases which lead to crime, are handed down from one generation to another, by a far surer process of transmission than human law has been able to establish" (p. 119).

The reference here to human law, however, alludes to another possible reading of humanity that the narrator entertains as well. In opposition to a Puritan concept of innate depravity, there is the Lockean notion that every human is a *tabula rasa* (a blank slate) with an innate rational capacity to make laws, social covenants, and thereby profitably progress. In this view humanity is like a garden, as Thomas Jefferson had typically argued. That "human" garden should not be allowed to exist "in a wilderness of neglect" that ("as is often the parallel case in human society") leads to the obstruction of "development"; it should be "scrupulously weeded" in order to bring it "to such perfection as [it is] capable of attaining" (pp. 73, 87). It is the momentary prevalence of this Enlightenment hope that informs the narrator's qualification of his extension of Clifford's dismal condition to all of humanity, when (as we saw) he indicates that Clifford is "partly crazy, and partly imbecile; a ruin, a failure, as almost everybody is—though in less degree, or less perceptibly." Such a statement intimates an unrelieved tension between Enlightenment and Puritan views in the narrator's interpretative acts.

Despite the extensive debate by literary critics, no one view can successfully be shown to prevail in *The House of the Seven Gables*. Both the Puritan and the Enlightenment concepts of human nature exist side-by-side in dialectic, as do all the other unresolved questions raised in the romance. These issues are allowed to proliferate in dialogic opposition without resolution, even as the narrator debates the pros and cons of a cynical response to human experience (p. 163). It is no surprise then that at one point the narrator, contemplating the mixture of "the mean and ludicrous," and of the joy and sorrow of life (p. 41), becomes peeved by "inexplicable Providence" (p. 149)—not only because of the inability of humanity to read or interpret or, specifically, trace back to origins, to causes. They are allowed to proliferate in opposition (and thereby make the book seem to be out of control) because the narrator of the romance is like the characters in his tale: a ghostly presence, without an ontologically stable self, who is trying "to read" or interpret his external observations (what he reports in the romance) and his own internal beliefs (what he also reports in the romance). The romance is for him (and for the reader) what Hepzibah's mirror is for her: a mere reflector of an indistinct ghostly presence. Insofar as he has a voice and his fictional story takes shape from that fictional voice, he is, like the fictional characters in his tale, "a substantial emptiness, a material ghost"; like those characters, his self is disembodied—it *is* nobody; it is void of essential being; it lacks reality as a personal identity.

## Personal Identity and Romance

The problem of personal identity that informs the characters and the narrator of Hawthorne's book also pertains to its definition as romance. Hawthorne's insistence on romance as a generic form urges a careful scrutiny of the appropriateness of this form, as Hawthorne explained it, to the concerns raised in his writings. Does romance possess a definitive identity for Hawthorne?

The Preface of *The House of the Seven Gables* equivocates about the identity of romance.[20] On the one hand, it is capable of delivering "a moral": in this particular book, "that the wrong-doing of one generation lives into the successive ones" (p. 2). On the other hand, this exterior feature of the form is not necessarily the truest, for "when romances do *really* teach anything or produce any effective operation, it is usually through a far more subtle process than the ostensible one" (p. 2; emphasis added). The truth about reality, such as it may be, lies more in the internal features of romance than in its external appearance—a separation reflecting the division between material body and apparent self in the characters and the division between a materialized (textualized) narrative voice which has no body and represents nobody. As the narrator remarks, the "charm of romance" lies in the fact that it is like nature, specifically moonlight and humanity (romance's phenomenal prototypes): it "hides . . . purpose by assuming [a] prevalent hue" (p. 213). Whatever constitutes the hidden interior of romance is finally no more definable or stable than whatever constitutes the destabilized vicissitudes of identity in the characters (subject to sudden alternation in viewpoint or belief) and in the narrator (subject to unresolved antithetical interpretations or convictions).

The breach between exterior appearance and interior impression mentioned in the Preface is manifest in several ways in *The House of the Seven Gables* as structured narrative. One noteworthy example involves the first chapter. This chapter is laden with the devices of Gothic fiction, and it is altogether likely that a reader in Hawthorne's time would have read the introduction as an ostensible promise that the work to follow would fulfill elicited expectations that this work is a Gothic novel.[21] It is a promise not kept, as the reader's encounter with the second chapter begins to indicate. A rupture occurs.

The first chapter is equivalent to the exterior of the seven-gabled house; it is a "ruinous portal" (Gothic tradition), like the "exterior face" of the Pyncheon house (p. 294), through which we enter the house of the romance. We try to read or interpret this "exterior face" (by way of expectation) even as the characters in the story try to read and interpret on the basis of the outward appearances of the faces they see. We pass through this face-like portal[22] of the first chapter and find our firm sense of material definition and of secure expectation of what is phenomenally real steadily eroded; we are increasingly exposed to the uncertainties of "perplexing mystery," which generate in the "scientific" (matter-oriented) reader a "bewilderment of mind" (p. 17). Passing through the external portal of the first chapter into the interior of the romance, the reader experiences what the characters in the romance experience when they enter the Pyncheon house: an incursion into an interior that raises questions about the reality of the external world.

Yet something curious happens. If the romance does not ostensibly fulfill the expectations it stimulates in its first chapter, it does after all *subtly* (as the Preface warned) make good on its promise of a Gothic novel. Although it fails to continue to use the weighty machinery of the Gothic novel and merges Gothic tradition with the domestic and sentimental tradition of the novel, it does, in Gothic tradition, potentially problematize and even destabilize the average reader's sense of the secure nature of phenomenal existence. And the horror here is not one of conventional ghosts; for as the narrator observes, "Ghost-stories are hardly to be treated seriously, any longer" (p. 279). The pause between *seriously* and *any longer* signals the narrator's attitude of irony; as his first chapter indicates, his prospective audience is still very interested in ghost stories, and so his remark is really a warrant, at one level, for the lacuna that occurs in his narrative between his implied promise to present a Gothic story and his actual production. But perhaps even beyond the narrator's knowledge, he has subtly delivered a ghost story, one much more frightening than the conventional ghost story of Gothic fiction.

After the portal-like first chapter, the romance steadily revises Gothic convention by substituting the fantasy of the materialization of some ghost with a still scarier notion that all material entities are already essentially ghosts. As we have seen, the characters and the narrator are each "a substantial emptiness, a material ghost." This revelation is, in accord with the Preface, one subtle message lurking, ghostlike, behind the ostensible Gothic features of the romance.[23] Because it is latent, hidden, like any apparent self, this revelation is itself there and not there—something seemingly substantial as a message, yet really an emptiness signifying the emptiness or absence of human personal identity.

Just how vexed is the identity of romance, so devoted in this instance to undercutting the sensible, is evident not only in the fracture (and revision) of expectations after the first chapter, but in the concluding paragraph as well. Critics, as we have noted, have debated the problems engendered by the ending of *The House of the Seven Gables* without finally resolving whether the conclusion represents forced or justified or qualified optimism. Something of this confusion, as we also noted, participates in the dramatization of the problem of personal identity in the characters and in the narrator, who suffer from the lack of a real and stable self. This confusion also participates in the vexation of the identity of the genre of romance, which coalesces phenomenal experience and dream experience without yielding concrete answers as to just what did "really" happen; and this confusion engages the reader in attempts to read and interpret that are as frustrating as are similar efforts by the characters and the narrator in the romance.

In the final paragraph the narrator's proclivity for a language of qualification, uncertainty, or evasion is manifested once more. This language is evident everywhere in the romance, but in Chapter Four alone, such words as *appeared to be*, *probably*, *seemed*, *fancied*, *perceived*, *might*, *perhaps*, *may*, *must have*, *would have*, and *as if* predominate in a way which underscores both his and romance's and, possibly, the world's lack of substance as a real identity which can be interpreted. The concluding paragraph uses this same sort of equivocation subtly to undercut its ostensible optimism and its own authority.[24] There we are told that "a gifted eye *might* have seen fore-shadowed the coming fortunes of Hepzibah . . . Clifford," Phoebe, and Holgrave (p.

319; emphasis added). Similarly, Uncle Venner "*seemed* to hear a strain of music, and *fancied* that sweet Alice Pyncheon . . . had given one farewell touch of a spirit's joy upon her harpsichord" (p. 319; emphasis added). The language here, a mere echo of its proliferation throughout the romance, distances reality, human perspective, and the nature of romance itself; for just what has the reader been told?

The reader is limited in the romance to mere words, which accrue (as if through a Humean type of association) rather than develop a plot sequentially.[25] These mere words are a peculiar embodiment as ultimately disembodied as is the narrator, and they are as unstable and vicissitudinal in meaning as are the characters' identities. Romance, in other words, is like the doctors in the first chapter and like the ominous September gale mentioned in the last paragraph; it only manages an *external substantial* "perplexing mystery of phrase" and *internal ghostly*, "whispered unintelligible prophesies" (pp. 17, 319). Similar to artwork mentioned in the book, romance blurs the "physical outline" of the seemingly substantive subject and hints at "indirect character," at the "truth" of a "secret character . . . no painter would ever venture upon [openly], even could he detect it" (pp. 58, 91). Romance (like the characters and the narrator) has an exterior (ostensible) substantial presence, but also an interior (attenuated) ghostly non-reality. It points not only to its own fictitiousness, but also to how its conjunction of phenomenal and dream experience (p. 140) represents the essential ficti-tiousness of the very identity that humanity readily attributes to the self and the expression of this alleged self in art. Like its characters and its narrator, romance is ostensibly a form, an *em-bodiment* as text or voice, but it remains essentially merely "a substantial emptiness, a material ghost."

## PERSONAL IDENTITY AND THE AUTHOR

This absence of personal identity in the characters, the narrator, and the generic form of *The House of the Seven Gables* includes the author. That Hawthorne's sense of himself involved many ambivalences has been exten-sively documented. Critics have scrutinized his life and art in terms of various kinds of self-division: for example, conflicts involving unreconciled allegorical and symbolic impulses, obsessive Oedipal themes, the polar de-mands of art and of commerce, and an ambiguous political and aesthetic allegiance to America and England.[26] Critical assessments of Hawthorne's pervasive ambivalence, including the fundamental one of his desire for public encounter and his counter-desire for privacy, finally imply a man who in some sense doubted the stability of his own identity. The portrait rendered by these critics suggests that Hawthorne sensed within himself antithetical and irresolvable impulses, as if his very self were little more than the dialogic encounter of these contrary, yet mutually constitutive forces. Even if, by some unlikely chance, Hawthorne were not actually self-consciously torn by such conflicts, few would deny that he has given a phenomenal impression of himself as a divided self in his work. And this impression of the author is worth consideration in terms of the Humean problem of personal identity evident in the characterization, narration, and generic form of *The House of the Seven Gables*.

The author in this work can be detected in the subtle ways the narrator is managed and at times subverted, as we have seen. The author can especially be vaguely perceived as a presence by exploring his management of the narrator's comments on three important concerns in the romance: the symbol of the house, the nature of death, and the function of Judge Pyncheon's demise.

We are told that the house "is like a great human heart" (p. 27),[27] a simile suggesting that whatever constitutes the human self is like the Pyncheon house. But, as some critics have also noticed in the Preface of the work, this house represents for the author the house of fiction, in which Hawthorne is apparently as uncomfortable as he was in the literal homes in which he lived.[28] The (a) house of fiction is like the (b) Pyncheon house and like the (c) house of the flesh (the heart): something physical, a seemingly substantial exterior *embodiment*, with a mysteriously elusive and unsubstantial essential interior, at least as humanly experienced. The house of fiction in effect becomes an embodiment of the author, its elusive center. This embodiment of the author's identity in the corpus of his work corresponds to the similar embodiment of his characters' personal identity in their bodies—the Humean tradition of skeptical empiricism that erodes the reality of personal identity by grounding it solely in unknowable external phenomena.

The Pyncheon house, the human heart, and the house of fiction are each a corresponding "stately edifice," "beneath [which] . . . may lie a corpse, half-decayed, and still decaying, and diffusing its death-scent all through the palace" (pp. 229–30). This suggestion of a decaying corpse at the core of every stately edifice, including every "man himself" (p. 229), images essential non-being, its lack of "real" personal identity, in Humean terms. People, however stately in their own or others' opinion, are fundamentally nonentities because they always remain "slaves . . . to Death" (p. 183), their ultimate past and future. In short, nonexistence (death) paradoxically defines the very core of our utterly mortal phenomenal being.

Mortality, death, is a metonymy for non-being in an ultimate philosophical sense; and this mortality at the center of our existence indicates our lack of enduring identity of self. In Humean terms, we are only bodies without a self (soul). In lieu of a self, we evince an essential vacancy. We are merely animated corpses for whom non-being (mortality) is the paradoxical ground of our self-less bodies. In short, "death is . . . a fact . . . a touch-stone" (p. 310) because death (absence) is the *real* core, or origin, of human identity.

Consider the function of death in Hawthorne's romance. Mortality is emphasized in the repetitive patterns of nature in the book. For instance, the second paragraph of the first chapter stresses that in nature (as in human affairs) whatever perishes becomes the seedlike germ for what follows (p. 6), and the last paragraph of the final chapter similarly intimates that in nature (as in human affairs) seasonal cycles of death and birth relentlessly prevail (p. 319). Likewise, throughout the book the Pyncheon garden is remarked. In that garden "the black, rich soil had fed itself with the decay of a long period of time; such as fallen leaves, the petals of flowers, and the stalks and seed-vessels of vagrant and lawless plants, more useful after their death, than ever while flaunting in the sun" (p. 87). This will be the fate as well of the seemingly regenerative blooming of Alice's Posies (p. 308). In nature all of life is fundamentally based on death. This fact includes human life, which (we are told) imitates the natural processes evident in the garden (p. 87) and which, therefore, is also enslaved by the ultimate past that is death (p. 310). Maule's malediction, haunting the Pyncheons from one generation to another, is merely the curse of death, and that curse (like the moldering in the garden) peculiarly provides a sort of rotting ground for the activities of the characters in the book.

Nor is artistic creation (of a self or an artifact) exempt from this curse of death. Hawthorne seems to see his own work as something that emerges into phenomenal existence out of his (gardenlike) moldering skeptical mind, so skeptical that it calls its own identity into question, considers itself to be essentially nothing. Just as the curse of mortality curiously serves as the origin of the plot of his story, and just as disintegration strangely serves as the source of generation in a garden, the deadly skepticism of his mind, itself the mere product of a body grounded on and subject to decay, engenders a representation, a kind of life (behind which there may be nothing). In Humean terms this means that the human mind derives from the material world, from matter (as Clifford speculates), and since all matter is an "outgrowth" of death, then the human mind, so grounded on mortality, is at heart *essentially* a nonentity. As a nonentity it lacks enduring or "real" personal identity.

This Humean skeptical empiricist reading of the unsubstantial self apparently informs one of the most bizarre scenes in Hawthorne's romance. In this episode, Judge Pyncheon is dead. However, just as the undetected death of Colonel Pyncheon, the Judge's ancestor, was once the "invisible" (13), or absent, center of celebratory activity in his time, now the corpse of the Judge himself, motionless in the dark interior of the house, causes remarkable actions and changes in everyone around him.[29] Even as the curse of death has driven him, his demise now motivates others. His corpse inspires

Clifford and Hepzibah to flee, which act in turn leads to seemingly regenerating transformations in their lives. His corpse also inspires Holgrave, suddenly, to renounce his former views and to propose to Phoebe in the very room containing Pyncheon's corpse. Such a scene apparently exceeds Gothic precedents.

In this grotesque episode Hawthorne emphasizes, through his unwitting narrator, the ultra-Gothic horror at the core of existence. He indicates that just as "the image of awful Death" is the material "situation [which] seemed to draw . . . together" Phoebe and Holgrave, and "held them united by his stiffened grasp," so humanity's experiences have always been dependent on how the "influences [of death] hastened the development of emotions" (p. 305). The experience of death (non-being) generates the insubstantial activities of the human mind (emotions, for example). Because its only ground of being is death, this mind manifests no ontologically verifiable personal identity any more than do the characters in a work of fiction.

This is the "fearful secret, hidden within the house" (p. 291)—within the Pyncheon house, the house of fiction, the house of the human heart—that the author of *The House of the Seven Gables* indirectly warns us he will disclose. This disclosure will not be ostensible (on the external surface), but subtle (at the internal level), like the artwork mentioned in his romance. In other words, the author speaks in a voice capable, like the Judge's, of two tones (p. 172). Hawthorne's entombment of this ultra-Gothic "fearful secret," deep within the interior of his house of fiction, potentially destabilizes his Victorian readers' conventional, secure sense of reality. This interment of his dreadful message beneath the surface might represent his personal psychological conflicts, which he can face only obliquely, or his fear of antagonizing his reading public, who might not purchase his book (p. 122); but finally it is a most appropriate gesture in terms of the Humean problem of personal identity that he explores through characterization, narration, and the genre of romance in his book. Just as an essential mystery, an essential absence, defines the core of the animated bodies of the protagonists, the narrative voice, and the embodiment of text, so now the essential fearful revelation buried within the heart (house) of the book concerns the nature of death. Death, absence, non-being, as the penetrating reader discovers, is the center of human existence; for "the current of human life mak[es a] small eddy . . . round and round [like nature's cycles], right over the black depth where a dead corpse lay unseen" (p. 291).

This image of the corpse at the center of things recalls a comment, which we noted earlier, indicating that beneath every "stately edifice" (house, heart, fiction) "may lie a corpse, half-decayed, and still decaying, and diffusing its death-scent all through the palace" (pp. 229–30). Just as the Judge's corpse inhabits the seven-gabled house,[30] the author is like an obscured decaying corpse within his house of fiction. Like the Judge, the author does not "mistak[e] a shadow for a substance" (p. 118), but unlike the Judge, he recognizes his own nonexistent personal identity, as a form of living death, to be such a shadow.[31] So he effaces himself and, as it were, lies very still within his romance, so still that the reader cannot easily detect him as a presence. The reader's attempt to interpret the author's face (to detect his identity as a self) is as difficult as is the characters' efforts to read each other and even themselves.

Yet, just as the Judge's corpse serves as the influencing center of the four protagonists' swirl of activity in the romance, the buried author produces effects. He represents himself indirectly through the embodiment of text,[32] which is animated through its narrator and characters. They eddy around him, but he remains hidden like an entombed fearful secret. The author is a ghostly, unreal (in ontological terms) identity secretly hidden or interred at the very center of his external manifestation of himself in the corpus of his book. Just as the center of all existence described in his romance is a mysterious non-being (death), so the very authorial center of the work itself is at once indirectly represented (as the animated corpse of the text) and directly absent (either as apparently present to the reader or as a real identity in any sense). Although the exterior phenomenal surface of his work testifies to his existence, the author lies buried within, a hidden secret or ghost or "substantial absence" or disembodied voice. The author, a non-identity, is a representational ghost haunting the emptiness of his house of fiction (romance).

At that intimated "dead" center the author imitates nature, as character-ized by the Pyncheon garden. He de-composes. Specifically he breaks down the illusion of the human mind as a real personal identity. Just as nature is founded on death, so too (the author suggests) mortality, as a metonymy for essential non-being, is the ground of human existence, particularly the human sense of self. This is the subversive hidden *internal* secret of nature, disguised by its *external* ceaseless regeneration (proliferation) of life, in gar-dens and in families; and this is the hidden internal secret of Hawthorne's romance, disguised by the external generation of narrative voice and character animation as well as the specific suggestion of a cyclic regeneration of life at the end of the book (which we already scrutinized).

Deluded by the surface of nature, of texts, and of their own corporality, people readily create external illusions of stability and permanence in their social structures. The idea of family lineage—another sort of stately edifice (the "house of" ancestors, descendants, and kindred) similar to a building, a fiction, and a human heart—provides a prime example. Through families humans try to quantify their internal non-substantiality through externally bonding together. The stately edifice of family lineage, suggesting continuity and some sense of a material immortality, is an illusion which permits people to continue to live; for even Hume admitted that he could not live his everyday life in terms of his bleak skeptically empiricist belief in the essential nonexistence of his own personal identity. To live we must live within the fiction of our reality, a fiction (as Hume noted) most manifest in the human need for society as a mirror for each individual mind.[33]

And so even if we are told by the narrator in his Puritan mode of thought in *The House of the Seven Gables* that the "absurd delusion of family importance," that the idea of the family may be "at the bottom of most of the wrong which men do" (pp., 19, 185), we are also shown by the unwitting narrator that the idea of family continuity and immortality (in the material world) is one of the fictions that people need in order to continue to live. As Hume himself noted, the family is utterly grounded on externals: "the natural appetite betwixt the sexes" (p. 486) and the preservation of material goods (p. 310); yet it is "the first and original principal of human society" (p. 486) whereby people associate through common concerns and achieve a temporal identity through various kinds of ancestral inheritances (as in a surname, for example). As the narrator of Hawthorne's romance speculates, the artist (who glimpses the inner vacancy of human life) *probably* (the uncertain narrator's usual word) finds that, outside of his art, he "needs . . . human intercourse" so as not to be "a stranger" (p. 141) to the necessary delusions of life. Through association with a family, one can, like Holgrave at the end of the romance, temporarily forget death (p. 307) and enjoy an external "impression of permanence" (pp. 314–15) as a self *incorporated* within a family lineage (objectified for Holgrave in the enduring Pyncheon house).[34] And this very illusion of social identity informs the buried author's indirect textual representation (embodiment) of himself, vis-a-vis certain (familylike) fictional conventions, to a society of readers.

But the generation of life in the family, as in nature and in *The House of the Seven Gables* by Hawthorne, is founded on de-composition: the reality of death, or non-being, as the blight at the center of all life (p. 71). Like everything else in the world—decaying nature, rotting houses, moldering hearts, subversive texts—a "downright plunge" into oblivion "sooner or later, is the destiny of all families, whether princely or plebeian" (p. 25). Just as the demise of ancestors in a family is the ground for lineage (and its illusion of a material immortality), families themselves decline and disappear to make room for other households. So, whatever is ostensibly, optimistically regenerative at the end of *The House of the Seven Gables* is, as the reference to autumnal September gales in the last paragraph suggests, inevitably subject to a fundamental autumnal decay and wintry dissolution.

Just as humanity, typifying nature, originates in this non-being, the protagonists and narrator and romance form of *The House of the Seven Gables* are composed (given external animation) by the author's internal *moldering*, decomposing theme about death (non-being) as the core of existence. Only obliquely represented as textual embodiment—a romance from defying specific definition—the author is in effect absent as an identity from his work; but like the body of dead Judge Pyncheon in the instance of Phoebe and Holgrave, the author's unsubstantial ghostly presence within his house of fiction engenders an illusory family: a disembodied narrator and animated self-less characters. Buried beneath these external phenomenal manifestations within his house of fiction is his own corpselike presence expressing in a nearly inaudible whisper an interior horrible (Gothic) secret at the center of his book. This (essentially Humean) secret about the nature of human existence is interred beneath the seemingly substantial stately edifice (house) not only of his fiction but of every family (house) and of every human heart (including the author's): that the cyclic sensible world of always decomposing matter comprises the entire composition of the human mind. Without our body we are nobody, and even with our body we are, in terms of having "real" personal identity, still nobody.[35]

*Notes*

1. Charles Feidelson, Jr., *Symbolism and American Literature* (Chicago: Univ. of Chicago Press. 1953), pp. 7–16.

2. Notable attempts to document certain features of this eighteenth-century influence include Leo B. Levy, "The Notebook Source and the 18th Century Context of Hawthorne's Theory of Romance," *Nathaniel Hawthorne Journal* 3 (1973): 120–29; Mona Scheuremann, "The American Novel of Seduction: An Exploration of the Omission of the Sex Act in *The Scarlet Letter*," *Nathaniel Hawthorne Journal* 8 (1978): 105–18; and O. M. Brack, Jr., "Hawthorne and Johnson at Uttoxeter," *American Bypaths: Essays in Honor of E. Hudson Long*, ed. Robert C. Collmer and Jack W. Herring (Waco: Baylor Univ. Press, 1980), pp. 1–18.

3. James Duban, "The Sceptical Context of Hawthorne's 'Mr. Higginbotham's Catastrophe,' " *American Literature* 48 (1976): 292–301.

4. See the letter of 5 August 1822, *The Centenary Edition of the Works of Nathaniel Hawthorne: The Letters, 1813–1843*, ed. Thomas Woodson, L. Neal Smith, and Norman Holmes Pearson (Columbus: Ohio State Univ. Press, 1984), pp. 174–75.

5. A recent study in fact has made an excellent case for the influence of Humean thought in English Romantic poetry: Andrew M. Cooper, *Doubt and Identity in Romantic Poetry* (New Haven: Yale Univ. Press, 1988). Germane is the fact that in the 1830s theologian Lyman Beecher specifically tried to refute the Humean attack on personal identity in a lecture delivered in Boston and printed in *Lectures on Scepticism* (Cincinnati: Corey and Fairbank, 1835), p. 65, and that Ralph Waldo Emerson also responded to Humean tradition in *Nature* (1836). On the tradition of skeptical empiricism and Humean tradition, see Karl R. Popper, *The Logic of Scientific Discovery* (New York: Basic Books, 1959).

6. Letter, p. 538.

7. David Hume, *A Treatise of Human Nature*, ed. L. A. Selby-Bigge (Oxford: Oxford Univ. Press, 1978), pp. 86–94 (1. 3:6). Subsequent references to the Treatise will refer to this edition and will be included parenthetically in the discussion. Hume's discussion of causation, however, might contain a dialogic component vexing the standard view of it: see Tom L. Beauchamp and Alexander Rosenberg, *Hume and the Problem of Causation* (New York: Oxford Univ. Press, 1981).

8. See William J. Scheick, "The Problem of Origination in Brown's *Ormond*," *Critical Essays on Charles Brockden Brown*, ed Bernard Rosenthal (Boston: G. K. Hall, 1981), pp. 126–41; Leslie Brisman, *Romantic Origins* (New Haven: Yale Univ. Press, 1978).

9. See, for example, Richard Harter Fogle, *Hawthorne's Fiction: The Light and the Dark* (Norman: Univ. of Oklahoma Press, 1952): and Michael J. Colacurcio, "A Better Mode

of Evidence—The Transcendental Problem of Faith and Spirit," *Emerson Society Quarterly* 54 (1969): 12–22.

10. See, among many others, James Folsom, *Man's Accidents and God's Purposes: Multiplicity in Hawthorne's Fiction* (New Haven: College and Univ. Press, 1963); Joseph C. Pattison, "Point of View in Hawthorne," *PMLA* 82 (1967): 363–69; David W. Pancost, "Hawthorne's Epistemology and Ontology." *Emerson Society Quarterly* 19 (1973): 8–13; Darrel Abel, "Hawthorne, Ghostland, and the Jurisdiction of Reality." *American Transcendental Quarterly* 24 (1975): 30–38; Rita K. Gollin, *Nathaniel Hawthorne and the Truth of Dream* (Baton Rouge: Louisiana State Univ. Press, 1979); and John E. Holsberry, "Hawthorne's 'The Haunted Mind,' The Psychology of Dreams, Coleridge, and Keats," *Texas Studies in Literature and Language* 21 (1979): 307–31.

11. William J. Scheick. "The Hieroglyphic Rock in Hawthorne's 'Roger Malvin's Burial,' " *Emerson Society Quarterly* 24 (1978): 72–76. In "Locke's Kinsman, William Molyneux: The Philosophical Context of Hawthorne's Early Tales," *Emerson Society Quarterly* 29 (1983): 1–15, John Franzosa cogently concludes that Hawthorne makes use of his readers' faith in perception and reason to discover and know the world, but he demonstrates that there is no ground for this faith: "the eye simply cannot see what it looks at; the mind cannot know what it thinks." Perhaps Herman Melville made a similar point when he commented to Hawthorne about *The House of the Seven Gables*: "There is a certain tragic phase of humanity which, in our opinion, was never more powerfully embodied than by Hawthorne. We mean the tragicalness of human thought in its down unbiased, native, and profounder workings . . . By visible truth, we mean the apprehension of the absolute condition of present things as they strike the eye of the man who fears them not . . . [He see that] Powers [may] choose to withhold certain secrets . . . And [that] perhaps, after all, there is *no* secret" *The Letters of Herman Melville*, ed. Merrell R. Davis and William H. Gilman (New Haven: Yale Univ. Press, 1960), pp. 124–25. In "Hawthorne, Heidegger, and the Holy: The Uses of Literature" (*Soundings* 64 [1981]: 17–96) Benita A. Moore pursues similar ontological concerns through Heideggerian philosophy, but she concludes that Hawthorne arrives at an affirmation.

12. Very recently, Richard H. Millington has expected the questions of authenticity of self and society in one of Hawthorne's novels: "American Anxiousness: Selfhood and Culture in Hawthorne's *The Blithedale Romance*," *New England Quarterly* 63 (1990); 558–83.

13. All quotations from this romance are taken from *The Centenary Edition of the Works of Nathaniel Hawthorne: The House of the Seven Gables*, ed. William Charvat, Roy Harvey Pearce, and Claude Simpson (Columbus: Ohio State Univ. Press, 1965) and page references are included parenthetically in the discussion. A few critics have made comments tangential to the problem of personal identity in Hawthorne's work: in *Form and Fable in American Fiction* (New York: Oxford Univ. Press, 1961), p. 201, Daniel G. Hoffman notes Hawthorne's concern over how identity can be erased in an egalitarian culture; in *The Corporeal Self: Allegories of the Body in Melville and Hawthorne* (Baltimore: Johns Hopkins Univ. Press, 1981), p. 82. Sharon Cameron indicates that Hawthorne tries to reduce the self to pure essence; and in "Hawthorne's House of Three Stories (*New England Quarterly* 57 [1984]: 163–183) [reprinted in this volume] Bruce Michelson claims that Hawthorne's ghost story warns about the loss of self in any excess of reality or imagination. Does the observation made by, among others, Donald Junkins ("Hawthorne's *House of the Seven Gables*: A Prototype of the Human Mind," *Literature and Psychology* 17 [1967]: 193–210) and Carl Dennis ("*The Blithedale Romance* and the Problem of Self-Integration," *Texas Studies in Literature and Language* 15 [1973]: 93–110), that Hawthorne's "fragmented" characters all represent parts of a whole self, reinforce his portrait of humanity as finally lacking any ideally integrated, or real, personal identity? Interest in the self as inconsistent and non-integrated can also be found in the writings of Poe and Melville: see, for example, Michael J. S. Williams, *A World of Words: Language and Displacement in the Fiction of Edgar Allan Poe* (Durham: Duke Univ. Press, 1988);

and Peter J. Bellis, "Melville's *Confidence-Man*: An Uncharitable Interpretation," *American Literature* 59 (1987): 548–69.

14. For a sample of this extensive debate, see *Hawthorne: A Critical Study* (Cambridge: Harvard Univ. Press, 1963), pp. 176–87, in which Hyatt H. Waggoner argues that the novel presents history as redemptive; "Hawthorne's Scarlet Bean Flowers," *University Review* 30 (1963): 65–71, in which Richard C. Carpenter shows that the novel indicates how good can grow out of evil; "*The House of the Seven Gables*: New Light on Old Problems," *PMLA* 82 (1967): 579–90, in which Joseph Battaglia shows how the final stress on love in the novel has been provided for by the plot; "Dramatic Structure in *The House of the Seven Gables*," *Studies in the Literary Imagination* 2 (1969): i:13–19, in which Arthur Waterman notes how the novel evades its ideological implications by falling into melodrama; "Hawthorne's Romance of Traditional Success," *Texas Studies in Literature and Language* 12 (1970): 443–54, in which Rex S. Burns stresses Hawthorne's deliberate rejection of the idea of material success; "In Defense of Holgrave," *Emerson Society Quarterly* 62 (1971): 4–8, in which Jerome F. Klinkowitz asserts that Holgrave is a free spirit and so can readily change his mind; "The Golden Stain of Time: Ruskinian Aesthetics and the Ending of *The House of the Seven Gables*," *Nathaniel Hawthorne Journal* 3 (1973): 143–53, in which Barton Levi St. Armand attributes the change at the conclusion of the novel to Hawthorne's mature acceptance of the past in all its complexity; *The Shape of Hawthorne's Career* (Ithaca: Cornell Univ. Press, 1976), pp. 167–71, in which Nina Baym construes the ending as a false gesture, even a pretense, obscuring pessimistic implications; and "Progress and Providence in *The House of the Seven Gables*," *American Literature* 50 (1978): 37–48, in which John Gatta discerns the work of providential design in a pattern of spiritual growth.

15. In "Romance and Real Estate" (*Raritan* 2 [1983]: 67, 87) Walter Benn Michaels notes that Alice, who has no "clear and unobstructed title" to a self, finds herself "ultimately betrayed . . . by the very claim to individual identity that made her imagine herself immune to betrayal."

16. Possibly here, with the specific application of the word "cross" to Hepzibah and the specific echo of *ecce homo* in reference to Clifford at the window "arch," Hawthorne alludes to questions about faith in miracles, such as the resurrection. For Hume such faith falls, like personal identity (which immortality in an after life would validate), before the pursuit of skeptical empiricism. On Hawthorne on the subject of Hume and miracles, see Duban, "The Sceptical Context"; on the religious meaning of the arch, see Duban, *Melville's Major Fiction: Politics, Theology, and Imagination* (Dekalb: Northern Illinois Univ. Press, 1983), pp. 41–44.

17. Five representative examples include Waggoner, *Hawthorne*, pp. 176–87; Alfred H. Marks. "Hawthorne's Daguerreotypist: Scientist, Artist, Reformer," *Ball State Teachers College Forum* 3 (1962): 61–74; Kenneth Dauber, *Rediscovering Hawthorne* (Princeton: Princeton Univ. Press, 1977), p. 133; John P. McWilliams, Jr. *Hawthorne, Melville, and the American Character: A Looking Glass Business* (Cambridge: Cambridge Univ. Press, 1984), pp. 110–111; and Evan Carton, *The Rhetoric of American Romance: Dialectic and Identity in Emerson, Dickinson, Poe, and Hawthorne* (Baltimore: Johns Hopkins Univ. Press, 1985), p. 221.

18. For example, Mary Gosselink De Jong's discussion of how Hawthorne narratively involves the reader in the search for meaning, in "The Making of the 'Gentle Reader': Narrator and Reader in Hawthorne's Romances," *Studies in the Novel* 16 (1984): 359–75. See also Mary M. Van Tassel, "Hawthorne, His Narrator, and His Readers in 'Little Annie's Ramble,' " *Emerson Society Quarterly* 33 (1987): 168–74.

19. Typically, David Stouck, "The Surveyor of the Custom-House: A Narrator for *The Scarlet Letter*," *Centennial Review* 15 (1971): 309–29; and Elaine Tuttleton Hansen, "Ambiguity and the Narrator in *The Scarlet Letter*," *Journal of Narrative Technique* 5 (1976): 147–63. In "Hester's Labyrinth: Transcendental Rhetoric in Puritan Boston" (*New Essays on the Scarlet Letter*, ed. Michael Colacurcio [Cambridge: Cambridge Univ. Press, 1985], pp.

57–100) David Van Leer focuses on an unreliable narrator who is as difficult to distinguish as are the nature of signs in Hawthorne's book.

20. Evan Carton reads romances such as *The House of the Seven Gables* (pp. 216–27) as an art form which paradoxically insists on its substantial real identity as a fiction yet also self-reflexively reveals itself to be only a fictional surface reflecting reality.

21. Modern critics register their discontent with the Gothic features, and some have tried to explain how the convention is fulfilled or modified: e.g., Daniel G. Hoffman, pp. 187–201; Maurice Charney, "Hawthorne and the Gothic Style," *New England Quarterly* 34 [1961]: 36–46; Ronald T. Curran, " 'Yankee Gothic': Hawthorne's 'Castle of Pyncheon,' " *Studies in the Novel* 8 (1976): 69–79; Jonathan Arac, "The House and the Railroad: *Dombey and Son* and *The House of the Seven Gables*," *New England Quarterly* 51 (1978): 3–22; Elizabeth MacAndrew, *The Gothic Tradition in Fiction* (New York: Columbia Univ. Press, 1979), pp. 171–79; and Donald Ringe, *American Gothic: Imagination and Reason in Nineteenth-Century Fiction* (Lexington: Univ. Press of Kentucky, 1983), pp. 156–59, 169–71.

22. Other important implications of the central image of the door in this novel are remarked in Richard H. Broadhead's *Hawthorne, Melville, and the Novel* (Chicago: Univ. of Chicago Press, 1976), pp. 69–90.

23. Consider in this regard Gordon Hunter's observation in *Secrets and Sympathy: Forms of Discourse in Hawthorne's Novels* (Athens: Univ. of Georgia Press, 1988), p. 101: "the secret that the novel demonstrates but cannot say is the disharmony underlying its sentimental vision of union and progress."

24. That Hawthorne equivocates the authority of his romance is noted by Brook Thomas in "*The House of the Seven Gables*: Reading the Romance of America, *PMLA* 97 (1983): 195–211. Thomas suggests that by problematizing the authority of his book Hawthorne hopes that his readers will reshape human history—a much too optimistic conclusion if my reading is correct. A too severe, politically-charged reading of Hawthorne's reservations about the possibility of social change appears in Caroline Borden's "Bourgeois Social Relations in Nathaniel Hawthorne" (*Language and Ideology* 10 [1971]: 21–28), which fails to focus on the ontological grounds of the novelist's doubt that any social change is *ultimately significant*.

25. Gordon Hutner notes the accretive pattern (p. 71).

26. Feidelson, *Symbolism and American Literature*, pp. 7–16; Frederick Crews, *The Sins of the Fathers: Hawthorne's Psychological Themes* (Oxford: Oxford Univ. Press, 1966); Michael T. Gilmore, *American Romanticism and the Marketplace* (Ithaca: Cornell Univ. Press, 1985), pp. 96–112; Frederick Newberry, *Hawthorne's Divided Loyalties: England and America in His Works* (Rutherford: Fairleigh Dickinson Univ. Press, 1987).

27. This symbol is explored by Claudia D. Johnson, *The Productive Tension of Hawthorne's Art* (University, Al.: Univ. of Alabama Press, 1981), pp. 70–72.

28. See, for example, Thomas H. Pauly, "Hawthorne's Houses of Fiction," *American Literature* 48 (1976): 271–91; Edgar A. Dryden, *Nathaniel Hawthorne and the Poetics of Enchantment* (Ithaca: Cornell Univ. Press, 1977), pp. 93–98.

29. Nina Baym appropriately equates Judge Pyncheon and death, but then argues that death gives life shape (p. 169). Equally problematically, in *Hypocrisy and Self-Deception in Hawthorne's Fiction* (Charlottesville: Univ. Press of Virginia, 1988) Kenneth Marc Harris asserts that "we end up, unconvincingly, in a sunshiny world from which death and darkness have been banished forever" (p. 90). Death is, in my argument, the one immutable reality of phenomenal existence and the factor that denies life any meaningful design whatsoever.

30. John P. McWilliams, Jr. briefly mentions a connection between the Judge's body and the decay of his house (*Hawthorne*, p. 110), and Kenneth Dauber briefly notes that Hawthorne identifies with Pyncheon (p. 135).

31. Pertinently, Clark Griffith suggests that the ironic transformations in this romance indicate that finally shadow dominates substance: "Substance and Shadow: Language and Meaning in *The House of the Seven Gables*," *Modern Philology* 51 (1954): 187–95.

32.   Eric Sundquist, in *Home as Found: Authority and Genealogy in Nineteenth-Century American Literature* (Baltimore: Johns Hopkins Univ. Press, 1979, pp. 122–38) notes that Hawthorne's atoning commemoration of the dead and simultaneous revengeful usurpation of their authority is like a sacramental totem meal whereby family debts are at once buried and kept alive at the heart of the romance; and that in the process the romance "cloaks and exposes its author's fantastic powers at the same time, lets the reader almost but not quite see, or see only at a *sideglance*, the manipulations that mobilize the drama before his eyes." This point is reinforced by Jeffrey L. Duncan's observation that Hawthorne is a dissembler who hides behind his fiction because he was uncomfortable with his own findings about ambiguous reality: "The Design of Hawthorne's Fabrications," *Yale Review* 71 (1981): 51–71. Mark R. Patterson's *Authority, Autonomy, and Representation in American Literature, 1776–1865* (Princeton: Princeton Univ. Press, 1988) provides an interesting study of various ways American authors, other than Hawthorne, have managed the paradoxical nature of representation.

33.   See Donald W. Livingston, *Hume's Philosophy of Common Life* (Chicago: Univ. of Chicago Press, 1984), pp. 210–46. Aptly, in *A Grammar of Motives* (New York: Prentice Hall, 1945) Kenneth Burke observes, in terms of a familial metaphor, that Hume's "dethronement of 'causality' is the rejection of a term essentially *ancestral* or *parental*, as is similarly the case with the dethronement of reason" (p. 183).

34.   Such a fiction corresponds to Hawthorne's method of making the reader apply an "as if" construction to everything in his work, as noted, among others, by Taylor Stoehr in " 'Young Goodman Brown' and Hawthorne's Theory of Mimesis," *Nineteenth-Century Fiction* 23 (1969): 393–412. On the necessity of communion with others, see William B. Dillingham, "Structure an Theme in *The House of the Seven Gables*," *Nineteenth-Century Fiction* 14 (1959): 59–70; and on the use of family as a remedy for isolation, a remedy with costs, see Allen Flint, "The Saving Grace of Marriage in Hawthorne's Fiction," *Emerson Society Quarterly* 19 (1973): 112–16. In this regard, relevant to my argument but unfortunately indicating only partial awareness on the part of Hawthorne, Michael Davitt Bell makes the following statement about *The House of the Seven Gables* in *The Development of American Romance: The Sacrifice of Relation* (Chicago: Univ. of Chicago Press, 1980): "Love does not renew society; it does change the social order. It simply provides a new, and highly contradictory, legitimacy for society as it already exists" (p. 184).

35.   Given the perils of writing at length about the non-reality of personal identity, I am especially indebted to James Duban and Catherine Rainwater for several instances of re-minding while this essay was in manuscript. A shorter version of this paper was read at a session of the Nathaniel Hawthorne Society, Modern Language Association, San Francisco, 28 December 1991.

# "That Look Beneath": Hawthorne's Portrait of Benevolence in *The House of the Seven Gables*

JOSEPH FLIBBERT*

The most common activity in *The House of the Seven Gables* is looking at faces. This should not be surprising. Among the most vivid impressions Nathaniel Hawthorne creates in the work are those associated with facial features. Like Dickens, Hawthorne displays a talent for using fixed physical features to reveal attributes of character. Thus, the dark, stern, and massive countenance of Colonel Pyncheon's portrait accurately reflects the "iron-hearted" character of "the grasping and strong-willed man."[1] But fixed features do not always mirror the inner attributes of the characters in the story. Hepzibah's near-sighted but fierce scowl creates the distorted impression that the "naturally tender, sensitive" woman is ill-tempered and as stern as her ancestor (p. 34). Facial features are also not always frozen—the liquid elusiveness of Judge Pyncheon's mien being the most striking example.

There is, however, an element of consistency in even the fluid aspect of Judge Pyncheon's face, which alternates between a natural expression of sternness that exhibits his true character—"sly, subtle, hard, imperious, and, withal, cold as ice"—and the grinning public posture "indicative of benevolence" (p. 92). Hawthorne reserves the term "benevolence" in order to fix in the reader's mind a definite impression of the smile as feigned and hollow. The devastatingly satirical effect of the benevolent smile has accurately been associated with Hawthorne's intention in this work to satirize the duplicity of a Charles Upham or the well-intentioned but heavy-handed paternal intrusions of the surrogate father, Robert Manning.[2] His antagonism, however, seems to be directed at least as venomously against the notion of benevolence itself.

*This essay was written specifically for this volume.

114

## I

The word "benevolence" may be used to signify a particular attitude displayed by one individual toward another in a specific situation or to denote an inherent disposition of character that tends to govern action. In the first kind—what I will call personal benevolence—the benevolent individual acts in a kindly and thoughtful manner, for example, toward a street beggar looking for a handout. In the latter the benevolent person is one who displays a cheerful good will (as the etymology of the word implies) toward that collective tag termed "humanity."

Judging from comments in *Our Old Home*, Hawthorne appears to have had a grudging affinity for the former—specific acts of benevolence. Unlike his English hosts who resisted "street-charity," they affirmed, because it "promotes idleness and vice," Hawthorne was an easy mark for English and Italian beggars while abroad in the 1850s. Although he occasionally resisted characters like the "sickly-looking wretch" of Assisi and the "phenomenon abridged of his lower half" of Liverpool, more often he bought a clear conscience and "the little luxury of beneficence at a cheap rate." Like Emerson, he succumbed and gave the wicked dollar. As consul, he was assaulted by "another class of beggarly depradators"—ministers, tradesmen, ladies, and authors—humbugs all, but successful supplicants for a cut of his valued emoluments.[3]

While instances of such instinctive acts of kindliness and generosity are relatively rare in Hawthorne's fiction, with its emphasis upon figures driven by self-centered goals, they do occur and are treated with favorable regard by their creator. The most conspicuous example is the role Hester assumes as a "Sister of Charity" in Boston. The depth, the spontaneity, and the sincerity of her impulse to help the poor, the sick, and the afflicted in the community is charitable in the truest sense, for she asks for nothing in return, not even acknowledgment. It is not "Christian" charity; Hester's thoughts have taken her well beyond the rigid confines of religious orthodoxy. Moreover, she is not motivated by some vague impulse of love for humanity. She merely responds to a community need in an area for which she seems uniquely and wholly suited.

Hawthorne's attitude toward humanitarian benevolence is quite different from that which he displayed toward personal acts of benevolence. Those who assume an attitude of love for humanity in Hawthorne's works are almost always posturing egotists who cultivate the sentiment as a form of self-aggrandizement. The individual whose benevolence extends to everyone usually steps on those closest to him. Rappaccini destroys his daughter to heal the world. Ethan Brand annihilates Esther in an experiment that originated in hillside musings prompted by love of mankind. Ironically, Rappaccini's benevolence is paternal; in an attempt to find a cure for all illness, he assumes the role of the benevolent Father of all, with providential power to alter the nature of things. Brand's benevolence is rooted in a conviction of brotherhood; but the lime-kiln tender who can feel no connection to former friends and even less to a fellow of his trade is "no longer a brother-man" to anyone. In Brand's case, and, we might reasonably assume, in Rappaccini's as well, the sentiment of benevolence—as a conviction of universal kinship—promotes a perception attuned to larger patterns but blind to proximate and tangible realities. In effect, they see the whole forest, but not the trees. While they delude themselves in believing that they embrace all of mankind, they separate themselves from all individuals. This isolation leads to obsessive fixation on some grand scheme, reflecting an inordinate sense of self-importance. Ultimately, the sentiment corrodes and distorts intellectual pursuits, for these individuals always fail grandly at the schemes they devise.

An alternative to intellectual pursuits for the man of humanitarian benevolence is philanthropic activity (*philos* + *anthropos* = loving mankind). The prototype of such activity is Hollingsworth in *The Blithedale Romance*. Consumed by a passion for criminal reform, Hollingsworth manipulates personal relationships in an effort to achieve his "overruling purpose," unaware of the debilitating effect his goals have on his "sympathies, and affections, and celestial spirit," unable to recognize the process "by which godlike benevolence has been debased into all-devouring egotism."[4] Ironically, Hollingsworth's recognition of the devastating effect of his posture begins with his confrontation of another man of humanitarian benevolence, Westervelt. This huckster of "mystic sensuality," envisions "one great, mutually conscious brotherhood" based upon a "universally pervasive fluid" that dissolves the limitations of time and space.[5]

Before exploring Judge Pyncheon's kinship with these putatively well-intentioned lovers of humanity, I want to comment on the source of Hawthorne's attack on humanitarian benevolence. An acute observer of human nature—as certainly Hawthorne was—will note in his personal relationships an occasional disparity between the outward display of humanitarian goodwill and an inner penury of actual benignity, and will conclude that such displays are fraudulent. Experiences like these undoubtedly influenced Hawthorne's attitudes, but if we stop there at least one problem arises. Underlying the sentiment of humanitarian benevolence is the assumption that all humans are linked—an assumption Hawthorne strongly advocated throughout his career. In attacking humanitarian benevolence, Hawthorne is not striking out at the notion of universal bonds; no one reminds us more often than he does of the great chain of humanity to which we all belong. Rather, he suggests that the truest experience of connectedness does not proceed from some vague affirmation of love for humanity but from sensitive and observant response to the needs of those closest to us. In the works of Hawthorne, that response is almost always one of sympathy.

## II

Hawthorne immersed himself in reading on the ethics of sympathy during a six-month period in 1827, beginning in March when he borrowed Adam Smith's *Theory of Moral Sentiments* (1759) from the Salem Athenaeum and ending in August with the withdrawal of Francis Hutcheson's *An Inquiry Into the Original of Our Ideas of Beauty and Virtue* (1725).[6] Best known today as a pioneer political economist, Smith, a professor of moral philosophy at the University of Glasgow in the 1750s, established an early reputation in the area of moral theory. Along with David Hume, Smith was the most influential proponent in his time of a theory of moral behavior that derives from feeling or emotion. A former student of Francis Hutcheson, Smith's ideas both derive from and respond to Hutcheson's theories, which are based on the notion that apprehension of virtue results from a faculty he calls the "moral sense."[7] When functioning properly, the moral sense guides one to approve of actions that appear to be benevolent, that is, "flowing from Good-will to others," because they appear morally good.[8] Benevolence is "the internal Spring of Virtue," the highest form being "a calm, extensive Af-fection, or Good-will toward all beings," the "humanitarian" benevolence I noted earlier. In Hutcheson's view, there is a "universal Determination to Benevolence in Mankind."[9]

Smith accepts the view of a nonrational moral faculty but rejects the vagaries of a "moral sense" by which we approve or censure the conduct of others. He advocates a specific and easily identifiable human sentiment he calls sympathy. In doing so, Smith separates himself from Hutcheson's view that virtue consists in benevolence, for the sentiment of sympathy is not directed toward all humans but is a response of fellow-feeling with the affections of a particular individual. Thus, although it is probably true, as one critic has suggested, that Hawthorne discarded most of Smith's theories, he appears to have been influenced by Smith's distinction between benevo-lence and sympathy.[10] As we shall see, Hawthorne consistently relies upon this distinction to differentiate the behavior of Judge Pyncheon from that of the other principal characters in *The House of the Seven Gables*. Smith also emphasizes the perceptual aspect of the relationship between the sympathizer and the subject of sympathy by describing the relationship as one between spectator and spectacle, suggesting that the mechanism of sympathy is acti-vated initially by the sense of sight. In this respect, Smith, like most of his contemporaries, reflects the influence of Locke's theory that knowledge has its origin in perceptions which arrive in the mind either through reflection or sensation. Sympathy becomes a "moral sentiment" when we develop an analogous feeling to the one we imagine the observed person to be experienc-ing and respond to the propriety and merit of that feeling. Sensitive observa-tion is also the key to sympathy as a moral faculty in *The House of the Seven Gables*.

Between his reading of Smith and Hutcheson, Hawthorne perused the works of two moral philosophers affiliated with the Scottish school of "common sense," Thomas Brown (*Lectures on the Philosophy of the Human Mind*, 1820) and Dugald Stewart (*Philosophical Essays*, 1811). Hawthorne had already become acquainted with Stewart in his last year at Bowdoin College, where two terms were devoted to the study of *Philosophy of the Human Mind* (1808).[11] Stewart was a disciple of Thomas Reid who succeeded Adam Smith as professor of moral philosophy at the University of Glasgow. Brown was a student of Stewart and was later to hold jointly the chair in moral philosophy with him at the University of Edinburgh. Like Smith, Stewart and Brown produce their own modulations on moral sentiment. The intuitional feature of "common sense" is reminiscent of Hutcheson's "moral sense" but is now part of a "Science of Mind"; that is, it has moved from the domain of philosophical speculation to the verges of empirical inquiry. Brown is especially forceful in his objections to Smith's doctrine of universal sympathy, arguing that to trace the moral sentiments to "occasional sympathies" is like deriving "the water of an ever-flowing stream from the sunshine or shade which may occasionally gleam over it."[12] While he acknowledges that "benevolent affections" are among the objects of "moral science," he distinguishes between benevolence as a desire for "the good of all" and as a "principle of moral feeling" that actually prompts us to promote the happiness of others.[13] Brown endorses this latter notion of benevolence as "the moral link which connects man with man" through "benefactions" that include "consolations, counsels, cares, friendships, protection."[14]

But for Brown, sympathy (as only one of the affections that involve moral feeling) has its basis in physiological mechanisms that have a direct bearing on human behavior. These mechanisms are activated by an "external sign" which, through the agency of suggestion, produces that state of mind by which we identify with the feelings of others. Brown's theory of suggestion was derived from the influence of David Hartley's doctrine of associationism. Hartley's chief work, *Observations on Man, His Frame, His Duty, and His Expectations* (1749), was withdrawn from the Salem Athenaeum about a month after Brown's *Lectures*.

In the first volume of his treatise—concerned with man's "frame" or physical constitution—Hartley, a physician, lays the groundwork for his notions in a theory of vibrations and association which posits a neurological basis for our sensations and thoughts. Sympathy is treated as the fourth of six classes of intellectual pleasures and pains but is distinguished from the moral sense—the sixth and the most elevated of the emanations from the mind. Here benevolence, in the sense of humanitarian goodwill, seems to have a modest place as one of four tendencies that arise from the first class of sympathetic affections by which we rejoice at the pleasure of others. But in the second volume of the treatise—concerned with human duty and expectations—the terms sympathy and benevolence are used interchangeably to identify a pivotal faculty that regulates the lower pleasures of sensation, imagination, ambition, and self-interest while it feeds into the higher pleasures of theopathy and the moral sense. In analyzing the dynamics of this faculty, Hartley emphasizes the personal outcomes and sources of satisfaction of the benevolent impulse (happiness, reciprocation, a feeling of unity, development of the moral sense, etc.) and thus affirms as "the grand design and purport of life" not some vague sentiment of good will toward humanity but a particular "benevolent act by A to B" based in part on self interest and resulting in the cultivation of the moral sentiment. [15]

Even a cursory glance at the moral concepts of these theorists reveals that Hawthorne did not accept their moral system but rather tested his own more sober contentions against theirs, harvesting some of their more lofty pronouncements, as we shall see, for ironic purposes. The element of high-minded meliorism in the works of all five of these authors is incompatible with the darker view of human potential presented in Hawthorne's fiction. These moral philosophers stand unanimously against the dark stain of innate depravity that blights the world of Hawthorne's characters and perverts even their nobler ambitions. The philosophers have, in effect, lifted the curse. For while there are occasional obligatory acknowledgments of the "consequences and marks of our fallen and degenerate nature," (Hartley's attempt to account for the difficulty in subordinating lower pleasures to higher ones) they are, to a man, committed to "the doctrine of the tendency of all beings to unlimited happiness through benevolence," a view Hartley uses to support the contention that malevolence is unnatural. [16]

Hawthorne may have been reading these authors (who acknowledge indebtedness to one another) one after the other to obtain as broad a view as possible of the nature and origin of moral knowledge and moral behavior at a time when he was also absorbing Puritan history and doctrine. While he may not have adopted their view of human nature, his works display a similarly strong commitment to the notion that feeling plays a crucial role in moral experience, that our apprehension of good and evil is triggered by a moral "sentiment." The consistent distinction in his works between a natural sentiment that bonds us to fellow humans and a parallel tendency that prompts us to exploit even those closest to us appears to have been influenced by the debate in these works concerning the nature of this sentiment. In *The House of the Seven Gables*, he portrays in the most vivid manner the differences between the sham of humanitarian benevolence and the sincerity of the human sentiment of sympathy.

## III

Our first view of Judge Pyncheon at the beginning of chapter 4, "A Day Behind the Counter," is suggestive and revealing. He arrives on Pyncheon Street, pauses across from the House of the Seven Gables, and "scrutinizes" the shopwindow. Hawthorne repeatedly presents Pyncheon as an observer of the scene before him ("His eye rested on the shop-window"; "he minutely surveyed Hepzibah's little arrangements"; "the elderly gentleman stood looking at the Pyncheon-house"; "The gentleman had paused in the street . . . still with his eyes fixed on the shop-window") (56–58). The face of this observer has a "capacity for varied expression" (57). While Pyncheon stares at the house, we are invited to observe him for he is "as well worth looking at as the house" (56). What we see is an elderly man with an outward appearance of respectability. We learn that this distinctive appearance—which sets him off in dignity, influence, and wealth from those around him—has been carefully cultivated. Every look, gesture, movement of the body, his clothing and his cane, his bearing—all are calculated to uphold the impression of a kindly gentleman of superior social position.

But we also see other things. His eyes are "too cold"; one of his most frequent expressions is a frown; his facial features are pinched and crabbed; his physical frame is obese; and his smile has an "acrid and disagreeable" quality to it (57). These externals seem to more accurately reflect the inner man when he manufactures a smile of "the sunniest complaisancy and benevolence" in response to Hepzibah's presence in the shop window (57). As he departs, she retreats to the parlor where she observes the portrait of Colonel Pyncheon. Like Jaffrey's, "the unlovely truth" of the Puritan's character surfaces with age. Despite her hesitancy to judge her ancestor, compelled by a "perception of the truth," Hepzibah reads the same decadent look on both faces (59).

In this scene, the posture of benevolence comes face to face with the sentiment of sympathy. Judge Pyncheon parades his smile and his vestments past the house in a deliberate display of concocted kindness. But the studied mannerisms, the self-absorbed smugness, the self-indulgent corpulence of the man hardly suggest genuine benevolence. Pyncheon rivets most of his attention on the shop window, barely gazing long enough at Hepzibah to modify his sagging smile, intent upon the implications for his own devices of the opening of a cent shop. Hawthorne strongly implies that his demeanor of benevolence is a front for greed and treachery—an ironic inversion of Hutcheson's conviction that displays of benevolence are, by their nature, displays of virtue.[17] Hepzibah, on the other hand, looks long and hard at the judge and then gazes as intensely at the portrait of Colonel Pyncheon. The look on Judge Pyncheon's face causes "a very bitter emotion" to arise in her; she tries to "drive it back into her heart" (57). She trembles under the stern look of Colonel Pyncheon but perseveres because it enables her to "read more accurately, and to a greater depth, the face which she had just seen in the street" (p. 59). Because she reads "with feeling" (*sym pathos*), she penetrates the deception, revealing the real man: "Let Jaffrey Pyncheon smile as he will, there is that look beneath!" (59). In later years, Hawthorne would observe, "There is a decorum which restrains you . . . from breaking through a crust of plausible respectability, even when you are certain that there is a knave beneath it."[18] Hepzibah maintains that decorum out of respect for the family patriarch until the face of her cousin prompts a moral judgment from her.

The sketch of Judge Pyncheon in chapter 4 is developed into a full-blown portrait in his next appearance in chapter 8. The most prominent features are those introduced in the first sketch—the judge's excessive attention to his physical appearance, his obesity, his artificial smile, and the general air of benevolence he exudes. Expansion of each of these features of the portrait is carefully calculated to reveal some facet of the judge's depravity. The shine on his boots seems too "conscientious," like his glowing smile. The "massive accumulation of animal substance" below his chin belies the "spiritual" posture he affects (116–17). A prominent aspect of his portliness is humorously associated with his posterior, described as "favored with a remarkable degree of fundamental developement, well adapting him for the judicial bench" (121). The smile, described merely as sunny in the earlier sketch, blazes forth with heated intensity, inspiring the extravagant hyperbole that it required "an extra passage of the water-carts . . . to lay the dust occasioned by so much extra sunshine!" (130) His look of "paternal benevolence" alternates with an appearance of "all-comprehensive benignity" (each term appears six times in the chapter) by which he gathers not only Hepzibah, Phoebe, and Clifford but "the whole world besides, into his immense heart" (130–31).

The observer of this bowing and smiling spectacle is Phoebe. Her observations quicken when she becomes the unwilling recipient of a kiss from the "unctuously-benevolent Judge" (118). The same instincts that prompt her to dodge the caress provoke a sudden recognition of a likeness between the dark-visaged face her embarrassed eyes now see and the stern face in the miniature that Holgrave had shown her earlier in the garden. Holgrave had captured the judge's true character when for a moment he dropped the "exceedingly pleasant countenance, indicative of benevolence" that he wears "to the world's eye" (92). Such a moment reccurs now, one of two flash revelations of the judge's true character in the chapter. In this instance, Phoebe instinctively sees a resemblance between Judge Pyncheon and Colonel Pyncheon, just as Hepzibah had done earlier.

Hawthorne reveals differences between the public posture the judge assumes and the private life he has lived. His consummate performance of the role of benevolence has enhanced his reputation with the public as a pillar of the community. He has "etherealized" the "rude benevolence" of his ancestor into a "broad benignity" displayed in each of his public persona—Christian, philanthropist, judge, and politician (122). His unblemished reputation in these public roles is a measure of the success of the spectacle. Hutcheson, Smith and their followers worked hard to offset the darker implications of the Hobbesian view that human behavior is motivated by grasping self-interest; in their scheme of things, virtuous behavior promotes private interest. For Judge Pyncheon, the appearance of virtuous behavior will do. But "private diurnal gossip" discloses a more intimate and less flattering view of his destructiveness in personal relationships. His exploitation of his wife, who died a few years after they married, is said to have given her a "death-blow in the honey-moon" from which she never recovered (122–23).

Phoebe's spontaneous repulsion at the prospect of being kissed by this man of animal substance arises from a suspicion of lecherous intent behind the "sultry, dog-day heat . . . of benevolence" (119). But her "sensible" nature prevents her from following her instincts. Moments later, she is inclined to grant him the withheld kiss, seduced by the sentiments of good will and kindliness he expresses toward Clifford and diffuses throughout the atmosphere of the room. The judge's display of compassion is, quite literally, a "spectacle"—not, as Adam Smith suggests, an observed scene of real and spontaneous feeling, but a staged performance put on for the spectator. Ironically, false feelings elicit true sentiments. Phoebe accepts what she sees at face value. At this point, she has retreated to the snug and superficial view that the judge's display of benevolence reflects his true character. Her "trim, orderly, limit-loving" mind refuses to acknowledge the darker truth under the veil of radiant deceit (131).

Not so with Hepzibah, whose resistance prompts the second and most startling glimpse of the real Jaffrey Pyncheon. Braced by "the moral force of a deeply grounded antipathy," she provokes a fierce and dark look on his face, expressive of "a certain hot fellness of purpose, which annihilated everything but itself" (127, 129). The profound disparity between this image of self-absorbed malevolence and the pretense of benevolent concern suggests the depth of Pyncheon's hypocrisy and the iron inflexibility of his purpose.[19] At the end of the chapter, Hawthorne implies that Pyncheon is the embodiment of a type, the public individual—"judges, clergymen, and other characters of that eminent stamp and respectability." While Phoebe remains perplexed by what has ensued, the observer capable of "a wider scope of view" and "deeper insight" would recognize that displays of humanitarian benevolence by public figures, cloaked in feigned sentiments of sympathetic identification with human misery, conveniently conceal the true motives of greed and ambition (131). In another ironic inversion—this time of an observation by Hartley—Jaffrey's "benevolence" regulates the higher pleasures of the moral sense while feeding the lower ones of ambition and self-interest.[20]

Judge Pyncheon succeeds in masking his intentions from Phoebe at this stage of the work. Her lack of astuteness is not surprising. Phoebe is not a Hester, a Zenobia, or a Miriam, women whose intellectual development and profound penetration into evil reflect their earlier experiences with the powers of darkness. Phoebe is Phoebe. She is the "other" woman—like the pursemaker Priscilla or the dovekeeper Hilda—a figure of virginal innocence. Judge Pyncheon's sunshine blazes forth with the blinding intensity of noon on the hottest summer day. Holgrave's is the angled ray that sharpens and clarifies the shadows of dusk on a clear autumn day. Phoebe's sunshine is the warming glow of an April morning. Her obtuseness is self-willed. She will go just so far. When Clifford exclaims, as he peers into Maule's Well, "the dark face gazes at me!" Phoebe "could see nothing of all this" because her "sphere lay so much in the Actual" (154). When Holgrave asks her if Clifford's disturbed state of mind is the result of dark thoughts, she replies, "I cannot see his thoughts!" and adds: "When he is cheerful—when the sun shines into his mind—then I venture to peep in, just as far as the light reaches, but no farther. It is holy ground where the shadow falls!" (178).

Phoebe misjudges Jaffrey's intentions because her perception is deflected by a moral sentiment that remains, at that moment, untested and undeveloped. Hutcheson notes that the moral sense prompts one to approve of actions that appear to be benevolent, regardless of their effect or utility.[21] Hawthorne implies that the spectator of such a display may not realize that she is witness to a performance. The difference in perspective is profound. Hutcheson assumes that such a display is an outward sign of virtue; Hawthorne presents it as a diversion from sinister goals. Phoebe will eventually do better, but the refinement of her sense of discernment will never be the result of intellectual growth. By nature, she is cautious and "limit-loving," just as she is naturally compassionate and generous. Her affection for and kindliness toward Clifford is grounded on "the simple appeal of a heart so forlorn as his, to one so full of genuine sympathy" (143).

Initially, she makes the same mistake with Holgrave. Even before she sees him, she has uneasy presentiments of his wild and lawless nature. When they first meet, she is "perplexed" by him. She does not "altogether like him" but is attracted by a "certain magnetic element" in him (94). Sympathy seeks affinities. The woman capable of sympathizing with the gaiety of the robins, and, "to such a depth as she could," with Hepzibah's "dark anxiety" and Clifford's "vague moan" will soon overcome her reticence about Holgrave (137). Hawthorne affirms a "spiritual force" in that kind of disposition which is rarely acknowledged (137). The "girlish" observer of feigned benevolence and apparent lawlessness overcomes her deficiencies of perception as the moral power of sympathetic association transforms her eyes into "larger, and darker, and deeper" recipients of her experience.

The same is true of Holgrave, but not because of any self-imposed limits. Whereas Phoebe will settle for the surface sunshine in Clifford's nature, Holgrave is intent on "fathoming Clifford to the full depth of his plummet-line" (178). At twenty-two, Holgrave is already a man of the world, a risk taker, one who ventures to ask and to answer the fundamental questions. Somewhat impetuous, rebellious, vaguely resentful of the oppression he senses, and given to strong preconceptions, like Phoebe he is not always accurate in his estimate of people. When he meets Phoebe, he is surprised by her simple, natural warmth and cheerfulness, having been predisposed to believe that all Pyncheons labor under the curse of his ancestors.

Also like Phoebe, Holgrave is sometimes bewildered by the "odd and incomprehensible world" he sees. Despite his readiness to probe the depths of humans, he reflects skeptically on the ability to "guess what they have been, from what he sees them to be, now." If Phoebe accepts limitations of intellectual curiosity, Holgrave acknowledges the constriction of perception that comes from being a "mere observer" (178–79).

Hawthorne's uneasiness with dispassionate observation is well known and best exemplified by his self-characterization in a letter to Longfellow as an owl peering out of the darkness at his prey, removed from "the main current of life."[22] Hawthorne projects this perspective into a host of characters: the narrator of "Sights From a Steeple" who "so coldly" describes the scene below him and who can but "guess" about "the interior of brick walls, or the mystery of human bosoms"; Wakefield, who aloofly observes the center of his social and emotional life for twenty years from the next street; the Rev. Mr. Hooper, who looks at his congregation through alienating shades of a dark veil; Heidegger and Aylmer, whose chilling detachment blind them to their deadly purposes; Ethan Brand, described as a "cold observer, looking on mankind as the subject of his experiment"; Chillingworth, peering into the soul of Dimmesdale; Coverdale, staring into Zenobia's and Priscilla's chamber with "that cold tendency . . . which made me pry with a speculative interest into people's passions and impulses." Recall the image of Jaffrey Pyncheon staring into the shop window. In a notebook entry, Hawthorne once commented that "men of cold passions have quick eyes." The consequences of such a way of seeing are devastating— for the observer (alienation, bitter recognition of failure, insanity, suicide, cynicism) and for the observed (guilt, loneliness, a sense of entrapment, heartache, and premature death).

Holgrave, on the verge of such an error, has set his mind on prying out Pyncheon secrets. Phoebe says he is "too calm and cool an observer." She "felt his eye, often; his heart, seldom or never." In his relationship with Hepzibah and Clifford, "he studied them attentively" (177). It is no accident that his current occupation is that of daguerreotypist. He is attempting to be an artist of the ugly. The brush and easel won't do; the painter invariably represents his own renditions of the scene before him, coloring them with the hues of his own subjective sentiments. With a camera, he can record merely what is visible to a mechanical eye. To be sure, some of his portraits penetrate character, notably the daguerreotype of Judge Pyncheon, which reveals the man in his true aspect. But the mechanical eye does not disclose the judge's nature. It is "the wonderful insight in heaven's broad and simple sunshine"—the warm "eye" of nature—whose beams penetrate the core of Judge Pyncheon's darkness (91). When Holgrave looks through the lens, his perception is as controlled by physical phenomena as is the eye of the camera and its chemical solutions. When he observes the Pyncheon world with studied detachment, he submits to the same mechanistic devices. But when he begins to look with sympathy, his observations become as acute as the rays of the sun.

By the time Holgrave and Phoebe discuss the regions of Clifford's mind, he has already begun to glimpse this truth. He observes that solving the "complex riddle" of human nature "requires intuitive sympathy" (179). What he does not appreciate is the extent to which he has already moved in that direction. Consciously, he is the embodiment of the probing mind. Unconsciously, he is the model of the quick heart. As early as chapter 3, as Hepzibah prepares to open her shop, she senses "genuine sympathy" in his voice and aspect when he offers to help, and she reveals her fears to him. When she comments that the genteel family tradition will tumble with the vulgar business of penny profits, Holgrave offers this advice: "Let it go! You are the better without it" (44). Holgrave needs to do the same thing, to let go of the past. The corrosive influence of vindictiveness and detached observation have not consumed him yet, as they do Chillingworth, perhaps because, unlike Chillingworth, his impulses to mesmeric inquiry have not yet become a life pattern.

Holgrave's moment of surrender and of triumph over the past comes as he finishes telling the story of Alice Pyncheon. As Phoebe hovers on the brink of a mesmeric trance, the "speculative" side of Holgrave's disposition tempts him to "acquire power over her human spirit." This is one of the rare instances in Hawthorne's fiction of a man with occult powers resisting the impulse to control the destiny of a woman, largely through the influence of another spellbinder on the scene, nature. The converging rays of a setting sun and a rising moon create an atmosphere of enchantment powerful enough to make Holgrave feel "sympathy with the eternal youth of nature" (213). In a moment of near animistic identification with nature, the other side of Holgrave's disposition—his inclination toward sympathetic association—prompts him to show "reverence for another's individuality" (212).

This scene, often disparaged by critics as maudlin mush, is the inescapable result of a subcurrent of forces as compelling as the "curse" of the story. It is not the "heart" alone, as we often vaguely assert, that prevails here. The specific disposition of sympathy, with its powerful moral promptings, pushes Holgrave past the temptations of manipulation and domination to see the need to respect each individual. Having released himself from the emotionally insulating influences of suspicion, acrimony, and resentment, and impassioned by an awakening of love, Holgrave the man rhapsodizes the beauty, goodness, and youthfulness of the world. Having sensitized his powers of observation by surrendering detachment for affective association, Holgrave the artist transforms the House of the Seven Gables into a "bower of Eden," achieving what Hawthorne refers to as "poetic insight": "the gift of discerning, in this sphere of strangely mingled elements, the beauty and the majesty which are compelled to assume a garb so sordid" (41).

Thus sympathy is not presented as a corollary to or a type of benevolence, as it is in the theorists Hawthorne read, but as a distinct sentiment operating in personal relationships, activating both the moral and emotional sensibilities of the individual, quickening the power of perception, and serving as a counteragent to specious benevolence. It diffuses its influence through the house principally through the agency of Hepzibah, Phoebe, and Holgrave, but also through the ruined Clifford—both as the object of the sentiment and as one who experiences it the most elementally in his identification with children, birds, and flowers. "The sympathy of this little circle of not un-kindly souls" breaks the curse (157). Their eventual retreat to the countryside is not the "bathetic turn" it has been made out to be.[23] They go not to the bower of Eden but from it, aware of the limitation that "man's best-directed effort accomplishes a kind of dream, while God is the sole worker of realities" (180).

But to return to our judge. His third and final visit to the House is his deepest and most threatening penetration of it. He is there to wrest the secret of the lost estate from Clifford. At first, he raises the facade of "a visage of composed benignity" enhanced by "the genial benevolence of his smile" (226). When he claims compassion for Clifford, cloaking these sentiments in professions of duty, conscience, and law, Hepzibah assaults "this loathsome pretense of affection," denying him the right "to stand in the ring of human sympathies" (228). The progress of the scene is arrested for a moment as Hawthorne deliberates upon the judge's public reputation as a man of respectability, acknowledged by church and state, "denied by nobody." In the next paragraph, Hawthorne expands his earlier portrait of the public man, detailing the methods and motives of "Judge Pyncheon's brotherhood." They are "men to whom forms are of paramount importance, . . . grasping, and arranging, and appropriating . . . landed estate . . . and public honors." Their good deeds are "done in the public eye" and out of this they build a glittering "palace." Only the "sadly gifted eye," such a one as Hepzibah's, can perceive the "secret abomination" within. Hawthorne then parades his public roles past the reader again—judge, public servant, political party faithful, Bible society officer, philanthropist—culminating in a sardonic reference to his "smile of broad benevolence" (229–31).

The most devastating portrait of the sham of public benevolence is saved for the last. As "Governor Pyncheon" sits quite dead in the ancestral chair in chapter 18, his watch ticking in his hand, the narrator reveals his schedule of activities for the morning, juxtaposing with trenchant irony the commitments of his private life with his public engagements. His assault on Clifford is to be followed by a visit to a broker to invest "a few loose thousands." Next, he will try to purchase former Pyncheon land before he attends the meeting of a charitable society, whose name he has forgotten, "in the multiplicity of his benevolence." The acquisition of fruit trees for his country estate is adjoined to the purchase of a tombstone to replace the broken one at his wife's grave site, which he will do "if he have time." The contribution of hundreds of dollars to a committee of his political party is measured against the "small bank-note" he might give to the destitute widow of a friend who he "partly intends" to call on (270–72). The Judge Pyncheon who is insensitive to the dignity of Clifford, his wife, and the widow of a friend is incapable of affective response to individuals. His lifelong pursuit of power and wealth has deadened him to truly sympathetic personal relationships. The final image of him is vaguely reminiscent of the opening scene where we find him staring intently at the house. Well before the fly that has "smelt out" the judge begins to crawl across his face to his "wide-open eyes," we sense that the man who has lost "that dog-day smile of elaborate benevolence" sees nothing and feels nothing (282–83).

*Notes*

1. *The House of the Seven Gables*, Ohio State Centenary Edition, vol. 2, ed. William Charvat et al. (Columbus, OH: Ohio State University Press, 1965), 15. All citations are from this edition and will be identified by page number within parentheses in the text.

2. Gloria C. Erlich, *Family Themes and Hawthorne's Fiction: The Tenacious Web* (New Brunswick, NJ: Rutgers University Press, 1984), 138–40; James R. Mellow, *Nathaniel Hawthorne in His Times* (Boston: Houghton Mifflin Co., 1980), 360–61.

3. *Our Old Home*, ed. Roy Harvey Pearce et al (Columbus: Ohio State University Press, 1970), 289–92.

4. *The Blithedale Romance*, Ohio State Centenary Edition, vol. 3, ed. William Charvat et al (Columbus, OH: Ohio State University Press, 1965), 70–71.

5. Hawthorne, *Blithedale*, 198–200.

6. Marion L. Kesselring, *Hawthorne's Reading, 1828–1850* (New York: New York Public Library, 1949), 53, 61. Although Hawthorne did not have borrower's privileges at the Salem Athenaeum at this time, it is likely that his aunt, Mary Manning purchased a share in October, 1826 to make the library's collection available to him and that most of the books borrowed while she owned the share were for Hawthorne. Kesselring presents evidence to support this view, especially pages 6–7. Mary's share was transferred to Nathaniel in May 1828.

7. Hutcheson derived his notion of the moral sense from the third earl of Shaftesbury's arguments for a moral faculty that balances the tendency toward self-interest and moves the individual toward virtuous behavior.

8. Francis Hutcheson, *An Inquiry Into the Original of Our Ideas of Beauty and Virtue*, 4th ed. (London: D. Midwinter, 1738), 166. I have used the edition of the Salem Athenaeum

which, according to Kesselring, Hawthorne borrowed, for this and all other works Hawthorne used during this period.

9. Hutcheson, 177, 218.

10. Lester H. Hunt's reading of *The Scarlet Letter* in the light of Smith's theories eventually concludes that Hawthorne's notion of sympathy in *The Scarlet Letter* discredits Smith's views. See especially page 86 in "*The Scarlet Letter*: Hawthorne's Theory of Moral Sentiments," *Philosophy and Literature* 8 (April 1984), 75–88. In an unpublished dissertation, Marie L. Foley argues that Hawthorne absorbed the influences of Smith's theories principally through his reading of Shelley, " 'The Key of Holy Sympathy': Hawthorne's Social Ideal," (Ph. D. diss., Tulane University, 1969). Roy R. Male had earlier argued that Hawthorne's concept of sympathy derived from organicism in " 'From the Innermost Germ': The Organic Principle in Hawthorne's Fiction," *English Literary History* 20 (1953), 218–36; "Hawthorne and the Concept of Sympathy," *PMLA* 68 (1953), 138–49; and "Sympathy—A Key Word in American Romanticism," *Emerson Society Quarterly* 35 (1964), 19–23.

11. Randall Stewart, *Nathaniel Hawthorne: A Biography* (New Haven: Yale University Press, 1948), 17.

12. Thomas Brown, *Lectures on the Philosophy of the Human Mind*, 3 vols. (Andover: Mark Newman, 1822), 3:246.

13. Brown, 1:150.

14. Brown, 3:340–42.

15. David Hartley, *Observations on Man, His Frame, His Duty, and His Expectations*, 4th ed., 2 vols. (London: W. Eyres, 1801), 2:285–88.

16. Hartley, 2:289–90.

17. Hutcheson, 166.

18. *Our Old Home*, 292.

19. Kenneth Harris argues that Hawthorne derived his notions of hypocrisy from Puritan theories in " 'Judge Pyncheon's Brotherhood': Puritan Theories of Hypocrisy in *The House of the Seven Gables*," *Nineteenth-Century Fiction* 39 (September 1984), 144–62. Harris's book, *Hypocrisy and Self-Deception in Hawthorne's Fiction* (Charlottesville: University of Virginia Press, 1988) treats the subject in other works by Hawthorne.

20. Hartley, 2:183.

21. Hutcheson, 166–67.

22. *The Letters, 1813–1843*, ed. Thomas Woodson et al. (Columbus, OH: Ohio State University Press: 1984), 251.

23. Leslie Fiedler, *Love and Death in the American Novel*, rev. ed. (New York: Dell, 1966), 444.

# Salem History and *The House of the Seven Gables*

## Allan Emery*

Despite its consistent use of historical names, intriguing references to historical events, and obvious preoccupation with historical continuities, *The House of the Seven Gables* (1851) has not received the careful attention devoted by historical critics to many of Hawthorne's other works.[1] One likely reason is that the plot of the novel is only peripherally historical. The central characters—Hepzibah, Phoebe, Clifford, and Jaffrey Pyncheon—are all present-day (that is, nineteenth-century) personages, despite their historical ancestry; the central narrative likewise concerns their present-day problems.[2] Another likely reason is that the circumstances surrounding the novel's creation cast doubt on its historical qualities. Hawthorne composed his account of the Pyncheons in the Berkshires, soon after permanently moving away from Salem; his departure from the place which had originally prompted and subsequently sustained his preoccupation with New England history may have encouraged him to abandon that preoccupation. Reviewers of *The Scarlet Letter* (1850) had complained that Hawthorne had "the shadow of the past over him" and asked to hear more from the cheerier author of "The Custom-House," the "Hawthorne of the present day in the sunshine."[3] Thus the predilections of his audience may also have tempted Hawthorne to discontinue his probings of the past. Given these facts and the novel's nineteenth-century focus, one can understand why historical critics have generally turned their attentions elsewhere.

Yet by doing so they have missed a rare interpretive opportunity. For upon reexamining *The House of the Seven Gables*, one discovers that Hawthorne's interest in "gloomy" history survived both his departure from Salem and the advice of reviewers. Though his novel is set mainly in the present and contains considerable "sunshine," it also continues his deeply serious investigation of the past, representing his most careful and perceptive treatment of local history—and one of his major achievements as a literary historian of New England. Commenting as cogently on historical figures and events as earlier Hawthorne works, *The House of the Seven Gables* goes

*This essay was written specifically for this volume.

beyond these works in its analysis of historical trends. Hawthorne took the occasion of his fictional step into the nineteenth century not to abandon history but to widen his historical focus. Similarly, he used his distance from Salem to obtain the power of perspective rather than the privilege of forgetting. Though he realized that one should attempt to escape the unhealthy social and psychological bonds of history, Hawthorne also realized that one must understand history in order to disentangle oneself from it. In writing his novel he enhanced both his own and his readers' understanding of New England history by providing a penetrating analysis of a representative period. Thus despite its being set mainly in the nineteenth century and having been written 150 miles from Salem, *The House of the Seven Gables* merits the same consideration by historical critics that Hawthorne's earlier historical works have received.

It is the history of Salem itself that the novel treats, and that critics need to consider when interpreting it. Hawthorne's interest in the history of his hometown was likely rekindled by his return to Salem in 1845, his famous employment in the Salem Custom-House from 1846 to 1849, and his angry departure from the city in 1850. It was probably also revived by the appearance between 1845 and 1849 of the second edition of Joseph Felt's *Annals of Salem*, the standard and only comprehensive history of the community in Hawthorne's day. Felt's first edition (1827), which Hawthorne is known to have consulted twice in the 1830s, was organized chronologically, providing the history of Salem from 1626 to 1783. The expanded second edition was organized thematically, carried Salem's history into the 1840s, and contained extensive discussions of Salem houses, religion, crimes, and business affairs.[4] Living in Salem in the late 1840s and curious about the history of his community, Hawthorne was undoubtedly familiar with both editions. Indeed, in writing *The House of the Seven Gables*, he appears not only to have relied on both for historical details but also to have woven thoughtful responses to Felt's primary emphases into the thematic fabric of his novel.

His most forceful response was to Felt's emphasis on the righteousness of Salem's founding and the uplifting effect of that righteousness on the city's later history. In the introduction to his second edition Felt explained:

> [Salem's] course of existence, having been planned and commenced on the noblest principles of human action, was kept from the baneful irregularities which have marked the way of all communities, begun and continued in motives of vicious ambition and debased selfishness.
>
> . . . . . . . . . . . . . . . . . . . . . . . . . . . . . . . . . . . . .
>
> A purpose to be free from the sufferings of persecution and to enjoy an undisturbed attendance on sanctuary duties, led our ancestors to forsake the endearments of native home, and to adopt this soil, fraught with perils and

afflictions, as the abode of themselves and their descendants. [Their second purpose] was to endow the aborigines around them with the teachings of Revelation, so that they too might be brought under its elevating, improving and saving efficacy.

Hence we discern that few communities can claim a nobler origin, as to the motives and character of their founders, than our own city. Her commencement was not in giving free scope to the baser passions of man, but in bringing them under dutiful subjection, and overcoming them by those of loftier aims and more blessed tendencies. . . . Let other codes of morals . . . cast reproach on such a beginning. But what can they avail? . . .

[Salem], comparatively viewed, has no cause to blush at her infancy. . . .[5]

Having presented this thesis, Felt went on to support it with an appropriately positive account of Salem's beginnings. The city was first settled in 1626 by a small band of planters sponsored by the Reverend John White of Dorchester, England. Fearing Indian attacks and lamenting the scarcity of supplies, several of these individuals soon became discouraged and decided to depart for Virginia—but were dissuaded by Roger Conant, the head of the settlement and the builder of the first house in Salem (a "cottage" with "thatched roof"), who believed that the colony could survive.[6] In 1628, however, White joined with a number of English gentry in obtaining a new grant in New England, and though "having reason to think highly of Roger Conant's integrity, as the Governor of their plantation," the new grantees "thought best to select one of their own number for such an office . . . [and] accordingly chose John Endicott." In other words, despite Conant's crucial role in the founding and saving of Salem, the new owners abruptly replaced him with Endicott, who soon after sailed for Salem and took control of the colony, building a "mansion" for himself out of materials taken from a house thought to have been Conant's.[7] Following Conant's ouster, there was, Felt confessed, "[a lack of] harmony between the first planters . . . and their successors," for "a part of the first settlers . . . considered themselves as injured by having the colony taken from their . . . control." Yet determined to erase any blot from his bright portrait of Salem's early history, Felt emphasized that the new planters were "careful to give the old planters the respect and favor which their seniority, as to the first occupancy of the soil, seemed to require." Aware of Endicott's reputation for rigidity, Felt also insisted that the new Governor exhibited "as few of [his imperfections] under his multiplied and trying duties, as the most excellent of men would in his situation." Endicott's "many exertions for the prosperity of Salem, and his ardent attachment to it, should," Felt declared, "impress his name and worth on the hearts of its inhabitants as long as its existence continues."[8]

That Hawthorne was familiar with Felt's account of Salem's beginnings is strongly suggested by chapter 1 of *The House of the Seven Gables* ("The Old Pyncheon Family"), in which Hawthorne launches his own history of Salem by describing the primordial conflict between the wealthy and powerful Colonel Pyncheon and the plebeian but defiant Matthew Maule over the rights to a certain piece of property claimed by Maule but desired (and eventually obtained) by Pyncheon.[9] The "original occupant of the soil," Maule built a "cottage," a "hut, shaggy with thatch," on the "sea-girt peninsula" which later became the site of the city (5–6). Yet "in the growth of the town . . . the site covered by [Maule's] rude hovel" became "exceedingly desirable in the eyes of [Colonel Pyncheon]," an individual known for his "iron energy of purpose" (7). To obtain the property, the Colonel arranged Maule's execution during the witchcraft episode of 1692. Yet at his death Maule warned his adversary—aristocratically situated "on horseback"—that "God would give him blood to drink" (8). And indeed, when the Colonel later claimed the contested land and hired Maule's son Thomas to build a "family-mansion" (9) on the former site of Maule's hut, he did not live to enjoy the spoils of victory. On the very day set aside for the celebration of the house's completion, Colonel Pyncheon was found dead in his study, the victim of either murder or an apoplectic attack.

The reader who encounters this narrative after reviewing Felt's *Annals* will inevitably conclude, I think, that Hawthorne intended it to serve in part as an allegory of Salem's founding. More precisely, he meant the dispossessed Matthew Maule to recall the ousted Roger Conant and his band of "old planters"—and Colonel Pyncheon to recall the stern sup-planter of Conant, John Endicott,[10] and his band of "new planters." The textual evidence is substantial. Hawthorne's narrative not only recapitulates the Conant-Endicott story in its general emphasis on the ancient conflict between a sturdy plebeian and a strong-willed aristocrat but also exploits the details of that story—Conant's original building of a thatch-roofed cottage, for instance, and Endicott's construction of a mansion out of materials taken from Conant. Yet "The Old Pyncheon Family" is more than a clever transcription of history into fiction. The themes of that introductory narrative suggest that Hawthorne sought to challenge Felt's positive interpretation of Salem's beginnings by portraying the Conant-Endicott conflict as the bitter struggle between two groups with different class affiliations and conflicting economic interests—rather than as Felt's mild dispute between like-minded parties, honorably respectful of each other's rights.[11] Hawthorne probably derived this interpretation from a reading of both Felt's *Annals* and Thomas Hutchinson's *History of New England* (1764, 1767, 1828), one of his favorite source books.[12] More than Felt, Hutchinson made explicit the socioeconomic reasons for Conant's ouster. "[Conant] is always spoken of, as a person of worth," he observed. "[But] the superior conditions of the persons who came over with the charter, cast a shade upon him, and he lived [henceforth] in obscurity." Hutchinson also went beyond Felt in specifying Endicott's "imperfections." Encouraging Hawthorne's depiction of Colonel Pyncheon as "iron-willed," he unflatteringly described Conant's successor as one of "the most zealous

undertakers [of the New England experiment], and the most rigid in principles."[13]

Yet Hawthorne's opening chapter does more than allegorize a single
episode in Salem's early history. For besides prompting him to challenge
Felt's interpretation of the Conant-Endicott conflict, Hawthorne's study of
Felt and Hutchinson also led him to question Felt's analyses of two other,
better-known episodes in Salem's early history: the persecution of Quakers
from 1656 to 1700 and the witchcraft trials of 1692. Felt granted that
the whippings and hangings administered to Quakers by Salem's religious
authorities were "hard measure indeed" but noted that these authorities
"believed that [their] treatment of [the Quakers] was essential to the preservation of the Commonwealth." He also blamed the Quaker persecution mainly
on the Quakers themselves, insisting that they were led into difficulty by
their "honest, but incorrect views of religious liberty." When interpreting
the story of the Quaker wife of Robert Wilson, who after "going through
Salem, without any clothes on, as a sign of spiritual nakedness in town and
colony," was "tied to a cart's tail, uncovered to her waist, and . . . whipped
from Mr. Gedney's gate to her own house, not exceeding thirty stripes,"
Felt commented, for example, only on the Quaker tendency to "show more
zeal than discretion," rather than on the severity of the Puritan authorities.
Felt also muted the darker aspects of the witchcraft episode, insisting, for
instance, that while "Cotton Mather and others of the clergy and laity, were
zealous for the enforcement of the law on those accused and condemned,
still there is no valid evidence, that they were actuated by any other motive
than what they believed to be right." Those executed were innocent, Felt
admitted, but they "fell . . . victims of well-intended . . . zeal."[14]

Hawthorne's interest in the Quaker and witchcraft episodes is clear
from the allusions to both that dot "The Old Pyncheon Family." As several
critics have observed, the name "Maule" directly invokes the Quaker persecution. According to Felt, Thomas Maule, a Salem Quaker, was ordered in
1669 "to be whipped for saying that Mr. Higginson preached lies, and that
his instruction was 'the doctrine of devils' "; in 1695, the General Court
likewise required that "all the copies of a book, entitled 'Truth Held Forth,'
and edited by Thomas Maule, be searched for and seized. This work contained
severe reflections on the government for their treatment of the Quakers."[15]
At the same time, Matthew Maule's execution for witchcraft clearly invokes
the witchcraft trials. So does Maule's famous "curse" of Colonel Pyncheon,
which derives from Thomas Hutchinson's account of an event which preceded
one of the hangings: "One of the women, being told at her execution by
the minister Mr. Noyes, that he knew she was a witch, and therefore advised
her to confess, she replied, that *he lied, and that she was no more a witch than
he was a wizard; and if he took away her life, God would give him blood to
drink.*"[16] Finally, Hawthorne deftly alludes to both the Quaker and witchcraft
episodes by twice referring (11, 17) to the Reverend John Higginson

(1616–1708), a rigorous persecutor of heterodoxy whose career spanned the period from 1656 to 1700—and who was both a leading antagonist of Thomas Maule and the senior pastor in Salem in 1692.[17]

In developing the historical thesis which lends significance to these allusions, Hawthorne probably relied first on Felt himself, whose descriptions of both the Quaker and witchcraft episodes contained, much evidence of Puritan bigotry and cruelty, despite his efforts to disguise it. Probably he also relied on Thomas Hutchinson, who declared that while "some [legal] provision was necessary against [the Quakers], so far as they were disturbers of civil peace and order," "such sanguinary laws [as those passed by the Puritans were] not to be defended."[18] When discussing the witchcraft episode, Hutchinson also noted that the property of convicted witches was regularly confiscated (see Colonel Pyncheon's easy appropriation of Matthew Maule's land) and anticipated Hawthorne's analysis of Matthew Maule's death as a product of class conflict when he noted that those executed in Salem were generally lower-class—and that Salem's social and religious elite quickly stopped the trials once they themselves began to be accused.[19] Finally, Hawthorne appears to have also relied on the Reverend Charles W. Upham's *Lectures on Witchcraft* (1831), which observed that, precisely like Colonel Pyncheon at Matthew Maule's hanging (8), Cotton Mather was aristocratically present, "mounted upon a horse," at George Burroughs' execution.[20] Upham's portrayal of Mather seems to have inspired Hawthorne's emphasis on Colonel Pyncheon's overweening ambition, personal use of the trials, disguise of his real motives and role in the witchcraft affair, and ultimate downfall, when Upham noted that there was "some ground for suspicion" that Mather "[had been] instrumental in causing the delusion in Salem" (though he later attempted "to escape the disgrace of having approved of the proceedings"); that he had "secretly and cunningly" promoted the delusion in order to "increase his own influence over an infatuated people"; and that, ironically, his promotion of the trials had eventually brought him into "disgrace" and had "broken down" his power.[21] Upham also appears to have inspired Hawthorne's portrayal of Maule's execution as both a proof of the Colonel's viciousness and a product of the Colonel's long-standing hostility toward Maule when Upham characterized the trials as an instance of "malignity and cruelty"—and when he blamed them on "theological bitterness, personal animosities, local controversies, private feuds, long cherished grudges, and professional jealousies."[22]

Having consulted Felt, Hutchinson, and Upham, Hawthorne evidently decided that, like the Conant-Endicott conflict, the Quaker and witchcraft episodes had resulted, not, as Felt suggested, from the natural desire of Salem's leaders to maintain a necessary social and political order, but from the manipulative efforts by a grasping social, political, religious, and economic elite to dominate their "inferiors." Felt's account of Thomas Maule's continuing skirmishes with the Salem establishment apparently suggested to Hawthorne that the Quakers were members of a frustrated underclass, denied access to political power because of their low socioeconomic status and unorthodox religious views.[23] Hutchinson's *History* likewise persuaded him that the Salem authorities had solved the Quaker problem in an overly peremptory and brutal way. Thus rejecting Felt's contention that the Quakers were undone by their own excesses, Hawthorne suggests in "The Old Pyncheon Family" that they were actually the victims of an authoritarian upper class, determined to stamp out lower-class presumption. His view of the witchcraft episode was equally dark. By raising the class issue, Hutchinson encouraged Hawthorne to conclude that other than spiritual factors had helped to precipitate the trials. So did Upham when he described the trials as an instance of self-interested scheming—and Cotton Mather as something other than an innocent bystander. Thus discarding Felt's theory that the trials were a manifestation of "well-intended zeal," Hawthorne portrayed them as a case of political imperiousness masquerading as religious fervor, as the work of a domineering and self-serving aristocracy, power-hungry to the point of murder.

Yet these provocative suggestions are subordinate to the main point of "The Old Pyncheon Family." For Hawthorne's primary purpose in writing that chapter was not to reinterpret the Conant-Endicott, Quaker, and witchcraft episodes but to demolish Felt's general thesis regarding the sanctity of Salem's early history. Whereas Felt claimed that Salem's founders had eschewed the "motives of vicious ambition and debased selfishness," Hawthorne forcefully implies—in both his characterization of Colonel Pyncheon and his allusions to specific events in Salem's past—that the city's earliest residents had regularly been influenced by these motives. And whereas Felt insisted that Salem's founders had avoided "giv[ing] scope to the baser passions of man," Hawthorne grimly reminds his readers that on several famous occasions Salem's seventeenth-century residents had very freely expressed such passions. To summarize the central argument of "The Old Pyncheon Family": if Salem examined her seventeenth-century history—with its power struggles, whippings, jailings, lies, curses, and killings—more closely than Felt had examined it, she would find ample cause to "blush" at her "infancy."

What of her subsequent history? Having argued that Salem could boast of her babyhood, Felt went on to insist that the city could feel equally proud of her "youth and maturity." Although a slight lapse from the high moral standard set by the founders had lately occurred, this problem could be remedied simply through recollection: "So far as [Salem] has departed from the righteous policy of her ancestors, may she return and sit undismayed and unharmed under the branches which were nurtured by their toils, and are still verdant and fruitful through the genial influence of their principles and examples."[24] In Felt's view, latter-day Salemites could be faulted, then, only for occasionally forgetting to model themselves after their city's founders. Yet after challenging Felt's portrait of these founders in "The Old Pyncheon Family," Hawthorne ironically suggests in later chapters of his novel that his fellow citizens had on the contrary been guilty of too frequently imitating their ancestors. He suggests, in other words, that rather than dying out with the seventeenth-century Puritans, the unfortunate attitudes and behavior patterns established at the outset of Salem's history had persisted into the eighteenth and nineteenth centuries.

This point is clearly made, for example, in the "Alice Pyncheon" chapter, Hawthorne's ingenious sketch of Salem in the eighteenth century. The author informs us here that the House of the Seven Gables eventually passed into the hands of Gervayse Pyncheon, a grandson of the Colonel, who "contracted a dislike to the house, in consequence of a shock to his sensibility, in early childhood, from the sudden death of his grandfather." "On arriving at manhood, [Gervayse] . . . visited England, where he married a lady of fortune, and . . . subsequently spent many years, partly in the mother-country, and partly in various cities, on the continent of Europe" (190). When Gervayse later returned to Massachusetts, accompanied by his daughter Alice and servants, he transformed the dark home of his Puritan ancestors into "a substantial, jolly-looking mansion" filled with fine furniture and imported works of art (191). Yet even this transformation failed to make New England attractive to him: having developed a refined aesthetic sensibility during his years abroad, Gervayse took no pleasure in "the New England modes of life, in which nothing beautiful had ever been developed" (192). Thus he again decided to leave New England. Before departing, however, he attempted to persuade Matthew Maule (grandson and namesake of Colonel Pyncheon's antagonist) to reveal the whereabouts of a document able to establish Gervayse's territorial rights to a feudal kingdom in America (195). So eager was he to possess this document that he let Maule place Alice under a mesmeric spell in exchange for information regarding its whereabouts. Yet Maule frustrated Gervayse's plan to become the next "Lord Pyncheon" by refusing, after he had hypnotized Alice, either to provide the information or to release the young lady from her trance. In so doing, he punished the Pyncheons and revenged his grandfather.

Hawthorne alerts us to the historical context of this story by noting three times that the events in "Alice Pyncheon" occurred precisely "seven-and-thirty years" (187, 191, 198) after the building of the House of the Seven Gables. If one locates the earlier event in 1693 (Hawthorne reports that construction of the house began shortly after Matthew Maule's execution for witchcraft), then one can place the Gervayse Pyncheon story in 1730, the precise year in which Jonathan Belcher (1682–1757), the probable model for Gervayse, became Governor of Massachusetts. Thomas Hutchinson provides the following sketch of Belcher:

Being the only son of a wealthy father, he had high views from the beginning of life. After an academical education in [America], he travelled to Europe, was twice at Hanover, and was introduced to the court there. . . . The novelty of a British American, added to the gracefulness of his person, caused distinguishing notice to be taken of him, which tended to increase that aspiring turn of mind which was very natural to him. . . . [His ambition] revived and was gratified to the utmost, by his appointment [in 1730] to the government of Massachusets-bay [*sic*] and New-Hampshire, and discovered itself in every part of his administration. . . .

He lived elegantly in his family, was hospitable, made great shew in dress, equipage, &c.[25]

Hawthorne's own knowledge of Belcher is apparent from *Grandfather's Chair* (1841), in which he describes, through his account of the redecoration of a symbolic armchair, Belcher's attempts to import European fashion and elegance into a hitherto unpolished New England:

In 1730, King George the Second appointed Jonathan Belcher to be governor of Massachusetts. . . . Mr. Belcher was a native of the province, but had spent much of his life in Europe. The new governor found Grandfather's chair in the Province House. He was struck with its noble and stately aspect, but was of opinion, that age and hard services had made it scarcely . . . fit for courtly company. . . . Wherefore, as Governor Belcher was fond of splendor, he employed a skilful artist to beautify the chair. This was done by polishing and varnishing it, and by gilding the carved work of the elbows, and likewise the oaken flowers of the back. The lion's head now shone like a veritable lamp of gold. Finally, Governor Belcher gave the chair a cushion of blue damask, with a rich golden fringe.

Aware, too, that Belcher's priorities and activities marked a major departure from the stark piety of seventeenth-century New England, Hawthorne carefully adds: "Our good old chair being thus glorified, it glittered with a great deal more splendor than it had exhibited just a century before, when the Lady Arbella brought it over from England." Elsewhere in *Grandfather's Chair* Hawthorne explains that during Belcher's administration most governmental offices "were filled by men who had lived in London, and had there contracted fashionable and luxurious habits of living, which they would not now lay aside. The wealthy people of the province imitated them; and thus began a general change in social life." "Balls and festivals" held during the Belcher era were, Hawthorne notes, "very magnificent." "Slaves in gorgeous liveries waited on the guests, and offered them wine in goblets of massive silver."[26]

That Hawthorne meant to link Gervayse Pyncheon with Belcher is clear not only from his dating of the "Alice Pyncheon" chapter but also from his description of Gervayse, who is Belcher's twin in his European education and travels, his return to America, his dislike for the "dark" House of the Seven Gables, his attempts to enliven and redecorate the house, his devotion to European elegance and refinement, and his personal ambition. That Hawthorne meant Gervayse's tastes to convey the flavor of the Belcher era is equally clear from Gervayse's ownership of a black servant, Scipio (187–88, 192, 194), his possession of "furniture, in an elegant and costly style, principally from Paris" (193), his sipping of French coffee, his wearing of both a coat of "blue velvet, with lace on the borders" and a waistcoat "flowered all over with gold" (193–94), and especially his territorial aspirations. For, according to Hutchinson, while lands in Massachusetts, New Hampshire, and Maine had, up until the late 1720s, been granted to individuals only "for the sake of settling them," during these years "plans [were] laid for grants of vast tracts of unimproved land." Hutchinson might have been describing the land-hungry Gervayse when he explained that "pretences were encouraged, and even sought after, to intitle persons to be grantees" and that "[the resulting] trade of land jobbing made many idle persons [and much] imaginary wealth," producing "mischievous effects."[27]

Since Belcher was not himself a resident of Salem, one wonders at first why Hawthorne so carefully included him in *The House of the Seven Gables*. Apparently Hawthorne felt that Belcher's priorities and proclivities nicely typified those of Salem during the period of Belcher's governorship. As Hawthorne paints the eighteenth-century scene, 1730 was a time when Salemites, tired of Puritan piety and gloom and eager to import the lively manners and secular ideals of Europe, sought to match Europeans in their appreciation for the arts, their fine dress and elegant establishments, their English "jollity," and, above all, their eager accumulation of land. Yet this last item underscores Hawthorne's potent historical point: while a culturally sophisticated, intellectually enlightened, and carefully Europeanized eighteenth-century Salem attempted to dissociate itself from its sternly pious and crudely "American" seventeenth-century predecessor, the most important (and least attractive) psychological traits and behavior patterns present in the earlier period survived into the later. As his willingness to risk his daughter's life proves, Gervayse Pyncheon—despite his servants, art collection, and European education—is every bit as avaricious as his unrefined grandfather; Hawthorne apparently saw an equally telling resemblance between eighteenth- and seventeenth-century Salem.

Concluding his account of the Belcher era in *Grandfather's Chair*, Hawthorne notes that, while the chair gilded by Belcher might have seemed to illustrate "the latest London fashion," it was nevertheless, beneath its new finish, the same old Puritan chair. "This may serve for an example," he says, "that there is almost always an old time-worn substance, under all the glittering show of new invention."[28] Precisely the same point is made—with more emphasis—in "Alice Pyncheon." For simultaneously concluding both his portrait of Gervayse's well-furnished parlor and his analysis of

Gervayse himself, Hawthorne insists: "Through all [its] variety of decoration, . . . the room showed its original characteristics; its low stud, its cross-beam, its chimney-piece, with the old-fashioned Dutch tiles; so that it was the emblem of a mind, industriously stored with foreign ideas, and elaborated into artificial refinement, but neither larger, nor, in its proper self, more elegant, than before." (193)

Only one further point need be made about "Alice Pyncheon": Hawthorne provides in that chapter not only a shrewd analysis of Salem's eighteenth-century aristocracy but also a valuable commentary on the city's eighteenth-century plebeians. In *Grandfather's Chair* Hawthorne notes that "the people" eventually "triumphed" over Belcher, first denying him a salary sufficient to support his lifestyle and then forcing him to resign;[29] and in "Alice Pyncheon" he reiterates this point through his account of Matthew Maule, who, in his refusal to enter Gervayse's house through the side entrance or to tolerate Gervayse's condescension (191–92, 194), and in his eventual triumph over Gervayse, embodies for Hawthorne the antiaristocratic sentiment which not only survived Belcher's attempts to remake New England society but permanently frustrated them. Yet Hawthorne's attitude toward this sentiment seems to have been as negative as his attitude toward Belcher: through Maule's bitterness toward the Pyncheons and indirect murder of Alice, he suggests that Salem's eighteenth-century plebeians were no more noble than their aristocratic opponents. Anticipating Hawthorne's depiction of Matthew Maule, Hutchinson insisted that Belcher's foes had behaved dishonestly and vindictively toward him,[30] and Hawthorne notes that they had also nullified Belcher's positive achievement—the helpful importation into a "darkly" Puritan Salem of European charm, gaiety, and beauty. Despite his rustic good looks and admirable determination to thwart the greedy schemes of Gervayse, the young Matthew Maule is finally (as his name and destruction of Alice imply) no working-class hero but the reincarnation of his vindictive grandfather, a man determined mainly to revenge himself on New England's upper class. "Spawn of the old wizard!" Gervayse calls him at a critical moment (206). Hawthorne seems to have attributed the frustrating of Belcher's aristocratic plans to the survival in New England of the sullenly retaliatory spirit of Roger Conant and Thomas Maule. Thus he saw Salem's eighteenth-century history as a disturbing reprise of the Conant-Endicott, Quaker, and witchcraft episodes, as a troubling reenactment of those earlier grim struggles between power-hungry aristocrats and vengeful plebeians.

If "Alice Pyncheon" draws highly instructive (and mainly negative) parallels between seventeenth- and eighteenth-century Salem, the rest of *The House of the Seven Gables* draws equally instructive parallels between early Salem and the Salem of Hawthorne's own day. These parallels are underscored, first, by the prevalence of seventeenth-century names in Hawthorne's nineteenth-century narrative: not only "Maule," "Holgrave," and "Pyncheon," but also "Dixey" and "Venner" are names taken from Salem's first century.[31] The individuals who bear these names also connect Salem's present to its past. The character of "Dixey," for example, a "laboring man" who comments on the aristocratic Pyncheons at several points in the novel (47, 290–91, 295–96, 318–19), is reminiscent of several plebeian seventeenth-century "Dixys" (all mentioned by Felt), among them "John Dixy," who, early in Salem's history, was "granted a ferry at North Point."[32] Hawthorne probably included Dixey in his novel in order to remind us that "laboring men" had lived in Salem throughout its history—and regularly provided an ironic commentary on Salem's aristocracy. Hawthorne's "Uncle Venner" serves a similar historical function. "The most ancient existence . . . in Pyncheon-street," a "miscellaneous old gentleman . . . patched together . . . of different epochs" (61–2), Venner embodies the survival of Salem past into Salem present. Yet his brief characterization—which emphasizes his deficiency of wits (61), his dream of retiring to a pleasant "farm" others know as the workhouse (62), and his "Fourierist" desire to eliminate private property (156)—also invokes one of his seventeenth-century forebears, described thus by Felt:

> Jan. 19th [1661]. Thomas Venner, made free 1638, and united to Salem Church, 1640, was hanged, drawn and quartered in London. He was a cooper by trade. He, while in this town, endeavoured to persuade others to leave Massachusetts and move to Providence, one of the Bahama Islands. In England, he was denominated a fifth monarchy man. After Charles II ascended the throne, Venner "persuaded his followers, that if they would take arms, Jesus would come to put himself at their head." They complied with his suggestion. . . . He, like many of various ages, was an unhappy example of the effects, which result from allowing the imagination to controul [sic] reason, conscience and revelation; and to put forth its distempered conclusions, in the violation of laws both human and divine.[33]

Uncle Venner (probably a sympathetic portrait of some nineteenth-century eccentric known to Hawthorne) likely underscores the continuing presence in Salem of "imaginative" but crackbrained idealists.

The more important personages in Hawthorne's novel highlight more important continuities in Salem history. With her advanced age, notorious scowl, and mental and behavioral quirks, Hepzibah Pyncheon, for example, evokes nineteenth-century stereotypes of the elderly women accused of witchcraft in seventeenth-century Salem. Dixey declares early in the novel that Hepzibah's scowl "is enough to frighten the Old Nick himself, if he had ever so great a mind to trade with her" (47). And later, fearing that foul play has occurred in the Pyncheon home, Dixey similarly remarks: "Well, I always said there was something devilish in that woman's scowl" (296). Yet Hepzibah is more than an ingenious allusion to Salem's most famous historical episode—and to the public suspicions which caused it. With her distinguished family name,[34] her "antique portraits, pedigrees, coats of arms, records, and traditions," and her grudging reluctance to open a cent-shop, she highlights the persistence of seventeenth- and eighteenth-century aristocratic pretensions in nineteenth-century Salem. Though financial reversals had destroyed the basis of these pretensions (as early as 1750 an indigent Pyncheon was forced to insert a shop-door into a wall of the family mansion (28)), they survive in the hauteur of Hepzibah, whom Hawthorne describes as "the final term of what called itself old gentility" (37). Despite her decrepitude, Hepzibah is, in fact, the direct spiritual descendant of the proud Colonel and supercilious Gervayse. Moreover, her pride is, as it was for these ancestors, a psychological liability: her nostalgia for the days before cent-shops prevents her from squarely facing an inevitably plebeian future.

Clifford Pyncheon is likewise linked in several important ways to Salem's past. "The most inveterate of conservatives" (161), he particularly enjoys observing "the antique fashions of the street": "He loved the old rumbling and jolting carts, the former track of which he still found in his long-buried remembrance, as the observer of to-day finds the wheel-tracks of ancient vehicles, in Herculaneum. . . . The baker's cart, with the harsh music of its bells, had a pleasant effect on Clifford, because, as few things else did, it jingled the very dissonance of yore" (161). Yet Clifford not only remembers the past: like Old Venner and Hepzibah, he embodies its survival into the present. In particular, his refined aesthetic sensibility, his overdeveloped "sense of beauty" (162), reminds us of the refined tastes of Gervayse and Alice Pyncheon, who filled the House of the Seven Gables with works of art. To be sure, the energetic connoisseurship of the eighteenth century has been reduced in the nineteenth to a feeble aestheticism: Clifford manifests his artistic tendencies partly by blowing soap bubbles (171–72). Yet like Hepzibah's hauteur, Clifford's aestheticism is clearly a family trait. It is also a dangerous one. For like Hepzibah's nostalgia, it imprisons its possessor in the past, denying him "the power to deal with unaccustomed things and to keep up with the swiftness of the passing moment" (161). Even more than Hepzibah, Clifford is an unattractive relic, selfish in his indulgence of his artistic whims, cruel in his treatment of his unbeautiful sister, and embodying (much like the Pyncheon chickens) the perpetuation in the nineteenth century of aristocratic attitudes and behaviors which Salem life can no longer sustain.

With her selflessness and sunny disposition, Phoebe Pyncheon might appear to be an exception to Hawthorne's rule that Salem present is a reflection of Salem past. Certainly she lacks the unattractive traits of the Colonel and Gervayse—and of Hepzibah and Clifford—and appears, with her optimism, kindness, domestic energy, and respect for the moral obligations of the present, to have escaped the bonds of history. Yet even Phoebe is, in one respect, an illustration of Hawthorne's theme, for she represents the reincarnation of Alice. Both women are beautiful and have an abiding appreciation for beauty. Both are linked by Hawthorne with flowers—particularly the posies, first planted by Alice, which have survived for years in an angle between two gables of the Pyncheon house. And most importantly, as their love for growing things implies, both embody for Hawthorne the human capacity for a rejuvenating love and sympathy, which, despite its being as endangered as Alice's posies at many points in Salem history, has never quite disappeared. Though Phoebe lacks the aristocratic birth, connections, and tastes of Alice (Hawthorne carefully underscores her "Plebeianism" [81]), she is, no less than Alice, an "example of feminine grace and availability" (80). Thus if Hawthorne had his wife Sophia in mind when creating the character of Phoebe (as seems likely),[35] his distaste for Salem did not prevent him either from identifying his wife's virtues as traditional to the women of the city—or from admitting that the persistence of these virtues proved that the spirit of Salem was not entirely unhealthy.

The resemblance between Phoebe's eventual husband Holgrave and his own ancestors is equally plain. Though in an important speech Holgrave decries society's adherence to "Dead Men's forms and creeds" (183), his sturdy independence and practical resourcefulness directly recall essential traits of both Matthew Maules. Yet it is Holgrave's attitude toward the Pyncheons that most clearly reveals his genealogical inheritance. In his brooding alienation from Salem society and ironic observations on Pyncheon pretensions (45, 185), he maintains the traditional blood feud between Salem's commonality and aristocracy. Indeed, those literary powers which enable him at one point to cast a spell over Phoebe (212) precisely recall not only the "wizardry" practiced by the first Matthew Maule upon Colonel Pyncheon but also the mesmerism employed by the younger Matthew upon Alice. As Holgrave notes in a climactic line: "In this long drama of wrong and retribution, I represent the old wizard, and am probably as much of a wizard as ever he was" (316). If Phoebe was meant to be, in part, a literary stand-in for Sophia Hawthorne, then the "artist" (178–79) Holgrave was probably meant to be a double for Hawthorne himself,[36] a writer discovering in himself both a creative "wizardry" and a "plebeian" bitterness toward Salem's elite— and thus able to cite himself as further proof of the persistence of Salem past in Salem present.

Such provocative instances of historical replication notwithstanding, the most crucial illustration of Hawthorne's theme is Judge Jaffrey Pyncheon, who more than any other present-day character in *The House of the Seven Gables* closely resembles his Salem ancestors.[37] Hawthorne regularly calls our attention to a portrait of Colonel Pyncheon which continues to hang in the room in which he died, one which not only pictures the "stern, immitigable features" of the Colonel (21) but also conveys the "hard, keen sense and practical energy" of the man (19). Yet significantly, this portrait is also an accurate likeness of Jaffrey, who, as Hawthorne repeatedly observes, is the Colonel's double in both appearance and personality (120–23). At one point

Phoebe is reminded of the pictured Colonel by the Judge (124); at another, the portrait recalls for Hepzibah the Judge's selfishness and victimization of Clifford (33). Meanwhile, the reader notes other parallels: the similarity, for instance, between Colonel Pyncheon's desire to be prominent in the community and to possess Matthew Maule's homestead and Jaffrey Pyncheon's determination to become "Governor Pyncheon" (274) and to obtain the Pyncheon inheritance. In manifesting the latter desire, the Judge clearly resembles both the Colonel and Gervayse.

Hawthorne drew precise parallels between the Judge and his ancestors partly in order to continue his assault on Felt, who insisted, as we have seen, that because of the saving influence of her founders' principles, Salem had been protected throughout her history from "vicious ambition and debased selfishness." By underscoring the Judge's disturbing resemblance to his undeniably vicious and debased forebears, Hawthorne forcefully suggests that the influence of Salem past on Salem present had been, on the contrary, mainly negative: that more than any other moral or psychological trait, "the hard and grasping spirit" (237) of the Puritans has survived into the Salem of his own day. Hawthorne did not rely solely on personal observation in reaching this conclusion. In his *Annals*, Felt himself attempted to counter the stereotype (apparently widespread in the 1840s) of Salemites as "avaricious and inhospitable"; he also admitted that many visitors found the residents of Salem to be calculating "men of business." Felt also included an account of the murder-for-an-anticipated-inheritance of Captain Joseph White by two residents of Salem (and an accomplice from neighboring Danvers) in 1830, a crime which probably inspired Hawthorne's account of Jaffrey Pyncheon's murder (likewise for an inheritance) of an "old bachelor" ancestor thirty years before the novel begins (22–23).[38] Undercutting Felt's claim regarding Salem's continued freedom from immorality, this episode also confirmed Hawthorne's sense of the malignant influence of Salem's seventeenth-century past on her present. And finally, Felt appears to have provided Hawthorne with his most memorable symbol of that influence when he included in the second volume of his second edition a portrait apparently intended to represent the "noble" spirit of the Puritans, that spirit which he believed to be presiding over the history of Salem. This portrait—of a grimly unsmiling John Endicott dressed in a skullcap and grasping a glove symbolizing his authority—might well have seemed to Hawthorne to depict the stern graspingness which, in his view, continued to dominate the history of his hometown. Thus it probably helped to inspire his portrait of Colonel Pyncheon, grimly presiding over the troubled history of the House of the Seven Gables.

Yet Hawthorne also had a more contemporary image of Salem viciousness in mind: the Reverend Charles Upham, the individual most responsible for Hawthorne's removal from office and apparently the real-life model for Jaffrey Pyncheon.[39] Hawthorne's savage caricature of Upham has been noted by many biographers and critics. Yet his primary point with regard to Upham has, I think, been overlooked. For Upham was not for Hawthorne merely an evil man or a personal foe but the nineteenth-century reincarnation of seventeenth-century iniquity, the perfect illustration of the persistence in Salem of "Puritan" avarice and hard-heartedness. Moreover, an important irony lies in Hawthorne's insistence upon this fact. For, as we have seen, Hawthorne almost certainly relied on Upham's *Lectures on Witchcraft* when creating "The Old Pyncheon Family"—and thus knew of Upham's emphasis on both the criminality of Salem's seventeenth-century aristocrats and the particular evils perpetrated by Cotton Mather. Thus Hawthorne hoisted Upham by his own petard when he cited Upham himself, caricatured as the vicious Jaffrey Pyncheon, in proving that the Matherian side of Puritanism, allegorized as the "iron-willed" and "grasping" spirit of Colonel Pyncheon, was alive and well in nineteenth-century Salem. Though Hawthorne insisted to Zachariah Burchmore in 1850 that he didn't plan "to make war on any of [his political] enemies" in his new novel, he added that "it must be a very excellent prospect of revenge that will bring them to my remembrance again."[40] In the case of Upham, *The House of the Seven Gables* seems to have provided such a prospect, for in this novel Hawthorne amply revenged himself on his enemy by accusing Upham of perpetuating—with his self-promoting political schemes and vindictive behavior toward his Democratic opponents—the very Puritan sins he had condemned in his *Lectures*.

Given his image of Salem as rife with such disturbing continuities (and such repulsive characters), it is scarcely surprising that Hawthorne fled Salem in 1850—or that he ended *The House of the Seven Gables*, his most extensive treatment of Salem history, by portraying Clifford and Hepzibah as bidding "a final, glad farewell to the abode of their forefathers, with hardly more emotion than if they had made it their arrangement to return thither at tea-time" (318). Yet by thus ending his novel Hawthorne also took further issue with Felt. For in the "Dedication" to his second edition, Felt emphasized both the special fondness felt by people for their hometowns and the value of this emotion:

> Among the endowments of our nature, are the affections and sympathies [we feel toward] the home of our birth or adoption. This is a wise provision of divine economy. . . . It is well that all should entertain a particular attachment to the place where their domestic ties exist and their civil rights are secured. The operation of this principle is mostly experienced by those who are called to distant sections of their own or other countries. . . . Justly has a departed genius doubted whether a man could be found, "Whose heart hath ne'er within him burned, / As home his footsteps he hath turned, / From wandering on a foreign strand."[41]

Yet upon moving to the "foreign" Berkshires in 1850, Hawthorne felt no very strong attachment to his home. Indeed, having been rewarded for his remarkable literary achievements and honorable public service by being falsely accused of political conniving and abruptly removed from office, having grown up in a town known for its avarice rather than its generosity, and having decided from examining Salem history that this trait had always been characteristic of the city, if anything, Hawthorne "cherished" only a disgust with Salem in 1850.[42] Thus when ending *The House of the Seven Gables* he forcefully (if indirectly) attacked Felt's claim that individuals invariably felt an abiding love for their "homes of birth or adoption." Moreover, by suggesting that Clifford and Hepzibah will be not only happier but healthier living somewhere other than the House of the Seven Gables, he also attacked Felt's related contention that the attachment of individuals to their hometowns was "a wise provision of divine economy." In "The Custom-House," he had insisted that his own attachment to Salem was "not love, but instinct"—and that, having become "unhealthy," that connection "should at last be severed."[43] In *The House of the Seven Gables* he more generally suggests that when the moral influence of anyone's hometown is as harmful as Salem's appeared to be, it is one's moral obligation not gratefully to succumb to that influence (as Felt suggested) but speedily to escape it.

Yet Hawthorne recognized that one could not fully escape the bonds of history simply by fleeing one's hometown: the cyclical pattern of human wrongdoing could end only if the tragic events, criminal motives and actions, and disturbing continuities of the past were discovered and understood.[44] Historians were vital, therefore, to any community. Able to discover the darker patterns of local history, they could help "liberate" their neighbors from the past—if they recognized their obligation to do so. Felt presented his view of the local historian's duty in his Dedication:

[The disposition to cherish our home towns] . . . is connected with appropriate responsibilities. Among these [are] the obligation to preserve the memorials of the community, which covers us with the shield of its protection. True, [the written history of a community] is no monument of marble or brass, rising in classic proportions and communing with the clouds, so as to command the admiration of every passenger. But it speaks to us in clearer tones and with greater instruction and effect. It takes deeper hold on the susceptibilities of our spirits and engraves more lasting mementoes on the tablets of our hearts.[45]

Felt insisted, in other words, on the moral value of celebratory history (particularly in the case of sanctified cities like Salem)—and on the historian's moral responsibility to provide such history. Yet in placing greater value on a different kind of history, Hawthorne also had a different sense of the historian's obligation. Overtly in "Alice Doane's Appeal" (1835), where he calls for the building of monuments to human "error" as well as heroism,[46] and covertly in a number of other works, he suggests that the responsible historian should commemorate human depravity as well as nobility. More-over, in works like *The House of the Seven Gables* he put this principle into brilliant literary practice. If the writing of this novel was partly motivated by Hawthorne's grudge against Salem, it was more usefully motivated by his objections to Felt's conception of the historian's role and his loyalty to his own very different conception. In *The House of the Seven Gables* Hawthorne preserved, precisely as Felt suggested, the "memorials" of his hometown; as Felt urged, he also let the past speak "with instruction and effect." But by emphasizing the ignoble continuities of Salem history, by making these the focus of his final historical study of New England, he also fulfilled—more fully than Felt, he thought—his responsibility to engrave the profoundest truths of past and present on the minds and hearts of his readers.

*Notes*

1. Two historical critics have paid such attention to the novel: Emily Budick, in *Fiction and Historical Consciousness* (New Haven: Yale University Press, 1989); and Charles Swann, in *Nathaniel Hawthorne: Tradition and Revolution* (Cambridge: Cambridge University Press, 1991). Yet their particular emphases—Budick focuses on the novel's treatment of historical "perception" (121–42), while Swann examines its depiction of nineteenth-century "modernity" (96–117)—lead these critics in very different directions from my own.

2. In an 1850 letter to his publisher J. T. Fields, Hawthorne himself noted that "all but thirty or forty pages" of the novel "refers to the present time." See *The Centenary Edition of the Works of Nathaniel Hawthorne*, vol. 16, *The Letters, 1843–1853*, ed. Thomas Woodson, L. Neal Smith, and Norman Holmes Pearson (Columbus: Ohio State University Press, 1985), 369.

3. See Arlin Turner, *Nathaniel Hawthorne: A Biography* (New York: Oxford University Press, 1980), 204.

4. See Joseph Felt, *The Annals of Salem, from Its First Settlement*, 1st edition (Salem: W. and S. B. Ives, 1827); Felt, *Annals of Salem*, 2nd edition, 2 vols. (Salem: W. and S. B. Ives, 1845, 1849); and Marion L. Kesselring, *Hawthorne's Reading, 1828–1850* (New York: New York Public Library, 1949), 50. According to the records of the Salem Athenaeum cited by Kesselring, Hawthorne charged out the first edition of Felt's "Annals of Salem" from September to October 1833 and from December 1834 to January 1835. He also charged out "Felt's Salem" from January to March 1849. Though Kesselring assumes that the latter notation refers to Felt's first edition, it might also refer to his second edition, the first volume of which had appeared in 1845. In either case, Hawthorne probably consulted Felt during the writing of "Main Street" (1849), a work which clearly demonstrates his interest in Salem history near the time *The House of the Seven Gables* was composed.

5. Felt, *Annals*, 2nd ed., 1:11, 35.

6. See Felt, *Annals*, 2nd ed., 1:38–39, 400–1. Hawthorne's familiarity with Conant's important role in Salem's early history is demonstrated by his reference to Conant in "Main Street." See *The Centenary Edition of the Works of Nathaniel Hawthorne*, vol. 11, *The Snow Image and Uncollected Tales*, ed. Roy Harvey Pearce, Claude M. Simpson, Fredson Bowers, L. Neal Smith, John Manning, and J. Donald Crowley (Columbus: Ohio State University Press, 1974), 53–56.

7. See Felt, *Annals*, 2nd ed., 1:42–43, 122.

8. See Felt, *Annals*, 1st ed., 223–24; and 2nd ed., 1:46, 77–78, 123.

9. In his first sentence, Hawthorne sets his novel in "one of our New England towns." See *The Centenary Edition of the Works of Nathaniel Hawthorne*, vol. 2, *The House of the Seven Gables*, ed. William Charvat, Roy Harvey Pearce, Claude M. Simpson, Fredson Bowers, Matthew J. Bruccoli, and L. Neal Smith (Columbus: Ohio State University Press, 1965), 5. Subsequent parenthetical citations are to this edition. In letters written in 1850 and 1851 to J. T. Fields and B. F. Browne, respectively, Hawthorne confirmed what the details of his novel make plain: that the "town" is Salem. See *Letters, 1843–1853*, pp. 369, 385.

10. Hawthorne's characterization of Colonel Pyncheon as "iron-willed" is highly reminiscent of his characterizations of Endicott in "The May-Pole of Merry Mount" (1836) and "Endicott and the Red Cross" (1838). In the former, he says of Endicott: "So stern was the energy of his aspect, that the whole man, visage, frame, and soul, seemed wrought of iron, gifted with life and thought, yet all of one substance with his head-piece and breast-plate" (63). In the latter, he refers to Endicott's "stern and resolute countenance" (434). See *The Centenary Edition of the Works of Nathaniel Hawthorne*, vol. 9, *Twice-Told Tales*, ed. Roy Harvey Pearce, Claude M. Simpson, Fredson Bowers, L. Neal Smith, John Manning, and J. Donald Crowley (Columbus: Ohio State University Press, 1974), 63, 434. Hawthorne's recollection of Endicott's role as military leader (a role emphasized in "Endicott and the Red Cross") might explain his decision to grant Pyncheon the title of "Colonel."

11. This interpretation of the Conant-Endicott affair is very different from that offered in Hawthorne's "Main-Street," where Roger Conant and his compatriots graciously welcome Endicott to Salem, tossing their hats in the air and saying, "The worshipful Court of Assistants have done wisely. . . . They have chosen for our governor a man out of a thousand" (56). Nor is any mention made in "Main-Street" of Endicott's rigidity. Perhaps Hawthorne changed his mind about Salem's early history between 1848 (when he wrote "Main-Street") and 1850 (when he wrote *The House of the Seven Gables*); he was after all, fired from the Salem Custom-House during this period and may quickly have developed a jaundiced view of all things connected with Salem. Or perhaps he simply suppressed certain unattractive aspects of Salem's history in the nonfictional "Main-Street," then slyly emphasized them in the fictional *House of the Seven Gables*.

12. See Kesselring, *Hawthorne's Reading*, 53.

13. See Thomas Hutchinson, *The History of the Colony and Province of Massachusetts-Bay*, 3 vols. (Cambridge: Harvard University Press, 1936), 1:8n, 9, 16n.

14. See Felt, *Annals*, 2nd ed., 2:483, 581–82, 584–85.

15. Felt, *Annals*, 2nd ed., 2:587, 590.

16. See Hutchinson, *History*, 2:41. Hutchinson's apparent source was Robert Calef, *More Wonders of the Invisible World* (1700).

17. See Felt, *Annals*, 2nd ed., 2:581–91, 626.

18. Hutchinson, *History*, 1:169. I note, however, that Hutchinson suggested that the measures taken by the Puritan authorities against the Quakers "proceeded not from personal hatred and malice . . . , nor from any private sinister views, . . . but merely from a false zeal and an erroneous judgement" (*History*, 1:175). Hawthorne's view of the Quaker episode as a manifestation of the private and sinister motives of Salem's ruling class does not, then, derive from Hutchinson.

19. See Hutchinson, *History*, 2:45, 47n.

20. See Charles W. Upham, *Lectures on Witchcraft, Comprising a History of The Delusion in Salem in 1692* (Boston: Carter, Hendee and Babcock, 1831), 103. Upham's source was probably Robert Calef; see *More Wonders of the Invisible World* (London: 1700; repr. Salem: William Carlton, 1796), 220–21. The episode reappears in Hawthorne's "Main-Street" (76–77). Hawthorne's knowledge of Upham's book is clear from his reference to the work in "Alice Doane's Appeal." See *The Snow Image and Uncollected Tales*, 267; and Michael J. Colacurcio, *The Province of Piety: Moral History in Hawthorne's Early Tales* (Cambridge: Harvard University Press, 1984), 88. To those familiar with Professor Colacurcio's work my method-

ological debt will be obvious. I take this occasion to thank him for the memorable seminars at Cornell (1973–1976) which paved the way for the present interpretation.

21. Upham, *Lectures*, 107, 110, 114.

22. Upham, *Lectures*, 115–16.

23. For a running account of Maule's dealings with the Salem establishment, see Felt, *Annals*, 1st ed., 236, 266–67, 290, 323, 325, 355, 363.

24. Felt, *Annals*, 2nd ed., 1:35–36.

25. Hutchinson, *History*, 2:280–81.

26. See *The Centenary Edition of the Works of Nathaniel Hawthorne*, vol. 6, *True Stories from History and Biography*, ed. Roy Harvey Pearce, Claude M. Simpson, Fredson Bowers, L. Neal Smith, and John Manning (Columbus: Ohio State University Press, 1972), 108–9, 110–11.

27. Hutchinson, *History*, 2:251–52.

28. *True Stories*, 111.

29. See *True Stories*, 111–12.

30. Hutchinson insisted that "the most unfair and indirect measures were used" to oust the governor, that incriminating letters were forged and "truth and right" were "violated" (*History*, 2:302).

31. For sample references to individuals with these names, see Felt, *Annals*, 2nd ed., 1:21 ("Dixy"), 1:55 ("Pinchion"), 2:528 ("Holgrave"), 2:577 ("Venner"), and 2:587 ("Maule").

32. See Felt, *Annals*, 1st ed., 126.

33. Felt, *Annals*, 1st ed., 209. See also 2nd ed., 1:173n.

34. William Pinchion, though never himself a resident of Salem, was one of the members of the London company that managed the city's founding. After living for a time in Roxbury, Massachusetts, he later settled in Springfield. For references to Pinchion, see Felt, *Annals*, 1st ed., 37, 182, 184, 525; 2nd ed., 1:55, 56, 127, 129, 130, 134, 139, 267, 349, 453; and Hutchinson, *History*, 16n, 87, 116.

35. Hawthorne called his wife "Phoebe" in many letters to her, especially during the mid-1840s. See *Letters, 1843–1853*, 29, 37, 42, 67, 70, etc.; and Turner, *Nathaniel Hawthorne*, 229.

36. At one point we learn that Holgrave is a successful writer as well as a daguerreotypist, having published stories in *Graham's* and *Godey's* (186).

37. By way of a meaningful chapter title, "The Pyncheon of To-Day" (115), Hawthorne underscores the Judge's possession of traditional family traits.

38. See Felt, *Annals*, 2nd ed., 2:68–74, 465–66. Seymour Gross was the first to discover Hawthorne's allusion to the White murder. See *The House of the Seven Gables*, ed. Gross (New York: Norton, 1967), 23n and 329n.

39. Hawthorne's wife and sister were convinced that Judge Pyncheon was a caricature of Upham; see *Letters, 1843–1853*, 403 n.5; and Turner, *Nathaniel Hawthorne*, 229. For sarcastic comments about Upham at the time when *The House of the Seven Gables* was being written, see *Letters, 1843–1853*, 365–66. For a summary of the biographical parallels linking Pyncheon with Upham, see *The House of the Seven Gables*, ed. Gross, 24–26 n. 7.

40. *Letters, 1843–1853*, 365.

41. Felt, *Annals*, 2nd ed., 1:iii.

42. For evidence of Hawthorne's distaste for Salem in 1850, see *Letters, 1843–1853*, 312, 329–30, 332, 335, 338, 346.

43. See "The Custom-House," in *The Centenary Edition of the Works of Nathaniel Hawthorne*, vol. 1, *The Scarlet Letter*, ed. William Charvat, Roy Harvey Pearce, Claude M. Simpson, Fredson Bowers, and Matthew J. Bruccoli (Columbus: Ohio State University Press, 1962), 11–12.

44. Hawthorne, for example, was able to "free" himself from Salem (in a psychological

sense) only by conducting the historical investigation which underlies *The House of the Seven Gables*. None of the works which Hawthorne wrote after 1850 manifests the gloomy preoccupation with Salem which permeates *The House of the Seven Gables*. With one exception, references to Salem in Hawthorne's letters also become far less negative after 1850. See *Letters, 1843–1853*, 383, 385, 386, 389, 392, 394, 397, 402, etc.; compare the references listed in note 42 above. The single exception is an 1860 reference, which, coming ten years after *The House of the Seven Gables*, presents no significant challenge to the idea that writing *The House of the Seven Gables* freed Hawthorne from Salem—at least for a considerable period of time. See *The Centenary Edition of the Works of Nathaniel Hawthorne*, vol. 18, *Letters, 1857–1864*, ed. Roy Harvey Pearce, Thomas Woodson, Fredson Bowers, James A. Rubino, L. Neal Smith, and Jamie Kayes (Columbus: Ohio State University Press, 1987), 311.

45. Felt, *Annals*, 2nd ed., 1:iv.

46. See *The Snow Image and Uncollected Tales*, 280.

# Salem in *The House of the Seven Gables*

## Thomas Woodson*

*The House of the Seven Gables* has become the focus of the debate over the American romance because of its brief preface, a text quoted by modern critics as often as any by Nathaniel Hawthorne, though still in need of biographical clarification. It ends with a suitably indirect—even coy—paragraph about Salem.

> The Reader may perhaps choose to assign an actual locality to the imaginary events of this narrative. If permitted by the historical connection, (which, though slight, was essential to his plan,) the Author would very willingly have avoided anything of this nature. Not to speak of other objections, it exposes the Romance to an inflexible and exceedingly dangerous species of criticism, by bringing his fancy-pictures almost into positive contact with the realities of the moment. It has been no part of his object, however, to describe local manners, nor in any way to meddle with the characteristics of a community for whom he cherishes a proper respect and a natural regard. He trusts not to be considered as unpardonably offending, by laying out a street that infringes upon nobody's private rights, and appropriating a lot of land which had no visible owner, and building a house, of materials long in use for constructing castles in the air. The personages of the Tale—though they give themselves out to be of ancient stability and considerable prominence—are really of the Author's own making, or, at all events, of his own mixing; their virtues can shed no lustre, nor their defects redound, in the remotest degree, to the discredit of the venerable town of which they profess to be inhabitants. He would be glad, therefore, if—especially in the quarter to which he alludes—the book may be read strictly as a Romance, having a great deal more to do with the clouds overhead, than with any portion of the actual soil of the County of Essex.[1]

The reader who has finished the story and returns to this preface may recall that none of the characters ever do "profess to be inhabitants" of Salem. The town's name and specific facts of its history and geography are never mentioned.

Further, what may surprise the reader who is familiar with both Haw-

---

*This essay was written specifically for this volume.

thorne's work and Salem's history of witchcraft in 1692, is the assertion in this passage that the connection is "slight" rather than "essential." For Hawthorne this historical moment dominates some of his best or most characteristic stories, notably "Young Goodman Brown" and "Alice Doane's Appeal." Is not the struggle of Maule and Pyncheon the essence of the story, as an earlier paragraph of the preface seems to suggest? Taking this cue, much criticism has assumed the centrality of this theme, though while Hawthorne was writing he warned his publisher James T. Fields, who might have expected another historical romance like *The Scarlet Letter*, that the story was to be "little less than two hundred years long; though all but thirty or forty pages of it refers to the present time."[2] Nevertheless, the public events of 1692, (rather than the events of the 1630s, that had figured in the direct portrait of William Hathorne and in the indirectly hinted one of Anne Hutchinson in "The Custom-House" and *The Scarlet Letter*), are the only ones in the history of the "venerable town" that are possibly so closely related to "the realities of the moment" in this story with which we make "almost . . . positive contact." Salem in 1850 had of course "local manners," but Hawthorne promises not to describe them here; further, he warns the reader not to expect another story like the "Tale of Salem Witchcraft" that his new literary friend G. P. R. James was inspired to write from his admiration of *The Scarlet Letter*.[3] But what else can he have to offer the reader, if not a story that will play with local history, with the present moment, and with the expectations shared by author and reader in historical fiction.

In "The Custom-House" Hawthorne describes Salem as he had lived in it while Surveyor of Customs, and his fantasy of meeting his ancestors there, including John Hathorne, judge of the witches. This personal fantasy, along with the description of the "neutral territory" he found in his moonlit study, has so fascinated modern readers as to obscure the reality "of the moment" most associated with him by his Salem friends and enemies, his expulsion from the Custom House in 1849. He cagily downplayed this moment in the essay, humorously dismissing it as only a routine, stock political "decapitation."

After his frantic effort to overcome his removal by the local Whigs from the Custom House, Hawthorne turned back to fiction and wrote *The Scarlet Letter*. "The Custom-House" projects his apparently Olympian acceptance, his seeming joy in his fortunate fall from office. But in Salem, where all the unnamed characters in "The Custom-House" were well known, it was read as an act of impudence, as Benjamin Lease has shown. These local readers would come to the paragraph I have quoted above with the close of "The Custom-House" fresh in their memories:

> Soon . . . my old native town will loom upon me through the haze of memory, a mist brooding over and around it; as if it were not portion of the real earth, but an overgrown village in cloud-land, with only imaginary inhabitants to

people its wooden houses, and walk its homely lanes, and the unpicturesque prolixity of its main street. Henceforth, it ceases to be a reality of my life. I am a citizen of somewhere else. My good townspeople will not much regret me; for—though it has been as dear an object as any, in my literary efforts, to be of some importance in their eyes, and to win myself a pleasant memory in this abode and burial-place of so many of my forefathers—there has never been, for me, the genial atmosphere which a literary man requires, in order to ripen the best harvest of his mind. I shall do better amongst other faces; and these familiar ones, it need hardly be said, will do just as well without me.[4]

As the insulting description of "an overgrown village in cloud-land" is echoed in the new preface by "the clouds overhead . . . the actual soil of the County of Essex," the anxious Salem reader would likely become increasingly apprehensive about the new book's real intention.

Hawthorne wrote "The Custom-House" in Salem, some time before he finished *The Scarlet Letter*, perhaps even before he got far into it, if we can believe his first letter to Fields of 15 January 1850.[5] Early in "The Custom-House" he tells of walking "its long and lazy street . . . for a little while" longer (*Letter*, 8). *The Scarlet Letter* was published on 16 March 1850. On April 13 Hawthorne wrote to Horatio Bridge that he would soon move to Lenox, and of the "infinite contempt" he felt for "the Salem people," which he admitted to expressing more openly than he intended, "for my preliminary chapter has caused the greatest uproar that ever happened here since witch-times. If I escape from town without being tarred-and-feathered, I shall consider it good luck. I wish they *would* tar and feather me—it would be such an entirely novel kind of distinction for a literary man! and from such judges as my fellow-citizens, I should look upon it as a higher honor than a laurel-crown."[6] Here he says much more directly than in "The Custom-House" that Salem did not provide "the genial atmosphere which a literary man requires." A few days later Hawthorne had left for good. He soon remarked sarcastically in a letter from Boston to his Custom-House friend Zack Burchmore: "Please to present my best regards to the Salem people generally. I presume it to be merely an oversight that they did not invite me to a public dinner."[7] The Hawthornes arrived in the Berkshires on 23 May; he wrote on 17 June to his old crony Horace Conolly, who had turned against him to support the Salem Whigs in displacing him: "Forgive your enemies, and leave that wretched old town of Salem, the moment you are your own man."[8]

The record shows that Hawthorne did not mellow his opinion of Salem. He stayed in the hotel there for three days in September 1851, in the course of moving from Lenox to West Newton, and spent an hour in August 1852, to attend his sister Louisa's funeral. By the time he left England for the Continent he could walk London's busiest streets, "with a kind of enjoyment as great as I ever felt in a wood-path at home; and I have come to know these streets as well, I believe, as I ever knew Washington-street, in Boston, or even Essex-street in my stupid old native-town."[9] After his return from Europe in 1860 he explained to his sister Elizabeth that he retained "a terrible repugnance against spending any time in Salem, or even passing through the wretched old town."[10] The closest he ever came was when visiting her in nearby Beverly in August 1861, a few months into the Civil War: he could "hear the noise of drums, over the water, from Marblehead or Salem, and very often the thunder of cannon."[11] It is ironically appropriate that his last impression of his own town, like the first he published, in "Sights from a Steeple" in 1830, should be of the scene of preparation for war, even though his distance, now as in the early sketch, allowed for a humorous contempt for "a proud array of voluntary soldiers in bright uniform, resembling, from the height whence I look down, the painted veterans that garrison the windows of a toy-shop."[12]

During his first few weeks in Lenox Hawthorne began serious thinking about writing the *Seven Gables*, his first long fiction about the contemporary world, and which, in spite of his coy vagueness in the preface about its "actual locality," was as firmly placed in Salem as "Sights from a Steeple" itself had been. He had only half-exaggerated his situation as a "literary man," writing to Bridge that the Salem people "certainly do not deserve good usage at my hands, after permitting me—(their most distinguished citizen; for they have no other that was ever heard of beyond the limits of the Congressional district)—after permitting me to be deliberately lied down . . . without hardly a voice being raised in my behalf."[13] Salem and his recent political experiences there were prominent in his mind as he approached this new writing. Sophia Hawthorne wrote to her mother on 1 August: "He says that he cannot write deeply during midsummer at any rate. He can only seize the skirts of ideas and pin them down for further investigation. Besides he had not recovered his pristine vigor. The year ending in June was the trying year of his life, as well as of mine . . . Mr Hawthorne thinks it is Salem which he is dragging at his ankles still."[14] His letter of 17 September 1850, to Zack Burchmore, his closest friend and admirer in the Custom House, and among the Democratic politicians of Salem, gives a special insight into his literary intentions:

> I have had a good many visitors, who come to ask for a sight of the Scarlet Letter; and as it is impossible to produce that article, I endeavor to satisfy them in the best way I can. . . .
>
> You say nothing in your last of Conolly. . . . I am rather sorry for our reconciliation, because I would have used him up to good advantage in my next book, and now I feel as if it would be hardly fair to do it unless he should commit some new offence.
>
> I have had a glorious time here this summer, but have been rather lazy, and am just taking hold of my work in earnest now. I hope to have a volume

ready for the press by the end of the year. . . . I don't think I shall make war on any of my enemies in the new volume; the time is past now, and the public would not uphold me in it. Besides, being of a very forgiving disposition, I have forgotten my enmities, and it must be a very excellent prospect of revenge that will bring them to my remembrance again. If I had remained in Salem I should doubtless have felt differently. But I must confess I have enjoyed our reverend friend's defeat, and hope he will have a worse whipping at the next trial. [15]

The last reference is to Charles Wentworth Upham, formerly Unitarian minister in Salem, now Whig candidate for Congress, whose ambitions had just been thwarted in a local runoff election. He was Hawthorne's most active local tormentor, author of the letter to Washington that led to Hawthorne's dismissal, and he was to be "used . . . up to good advantage in my next book," as the principal model for Judge Pyncheon, whom Hawthorne's sisters recognized immediately when they read the book. As "an active political intriguer" and "artful agent," Burchmore had contributed to and shared Hawthorne's fate, making Hawthorne his "abused instrument," in the Whigs's words. [16] He lost his lifelong job as manager of the Custom House (being, in Hawthorne's words, "the Custom House in himself"), and knew as well as his literary friend that Conolly would be a much smaller target in a story about contemporary Salem than Upham.

Given that he could not resist portraying Upham as Judge Pyncheon, does the book show Hawthorne to have "forgotten [his] enmities," and given up any "excellent prospect of revenge"? Not at all, though the preface does display very good manners. It promises no frontal attack, no attempt "to meddle with the characteristics of [the] community," presumably through caricature and parody of actions by the Silsbees, Saltonstalls, and Chapmans who, with Upham, effected the Whig plot. Instead, the author proposes to "appropriate" only a street, a lot of land, and a house. The reader finds for most of the book no more than this much of Salem present, as if the author, in controlling his righteous anger at the actions of Salem's political leaders, needs to remind himself and them of his "proper respect and . . . natural regard" for the communal reputation, as a member of a family that had lived there for more than 200 years. Hawthorne's apparently eccentric and harmless reportorial intention is consistent with those of the fictional predecessors he would honor (as far back as Chaucer and Cervantes), such as Washington Irving (with Diedrich Knickerbocker) and Sir Walter Scott (with Jedediah Cleishbotham and Peter Pattieson), who never exult in their creations, posing as harmless drudging retellers of twice-told tales.

Hawthorne was a natural dweller in a city like Salem, a "man of letters" whose literary "productions" appeared over a number of years in newspapers, periodicals, and annuals, even though with such minor success as to make him persevere "without much danger of being overheard by the public at large."[17] In the *Seven Gables* part of what he proposes for Salem then, is no "cloud-land" but the same minuteness of observation Henry Thoreau used in the woods of Concord, with the same aspiration of revealing the truth that citified and materialistic man has not allowed himself to see. As narrator he begins chapter 1 in the manner of Scott's regional antiquarians, introducing "a by-street of one of our New England towns. . . . On my occasional visits to the town aforesaid, I seldom fail to turn down Pyncheon-street, for the sake of passing through the shadow of these two antiquities; the great elm-tree, and the weather-beaten edifice" (*Gables*, 5). But after the historical narration of the first chapter he abandons this distance without explanation, to become for the rest of the book a "disembodied listener," "an attendant spirit." (*Gables*, 30, 277–78), who stays within the House itself, fussily partaking in Hepzibah's frenzied hopes and fears, venturing only as far as the tree, the well, the garden, leaning with Clifford from the arched window far enough to "catch a glimpse of the trains of cars, flashing a brief transit across the extremity of the street" (*Gables*, 160). This narrator often merges into his characters. But he does not share Phoebe's ride on the "steam-devil," nor do we know more of Holgrave than Hepzibah knows, that he is "an artist in the daguerreotype line, who, for about three months back, had been a lodger in a remote gable" (*Gables*, 30). He takes walks "to the seashore, before going to my rooms, where I misuse Heaven's blessed sunshine by tracing out human features, through its agency" (*Gables*, 46). He tells Phoebe that these "public rooms" are "in Central-street" a thin disguise for Essex-street (*Gables*, 94). Hawthorne shows in his notebooks and in other fictions his interest in artists' studios, and long acquaintance with Salem's hotels and restaurants (having dined with Longfellow in one that the poet found more "mean" than any "German village with a dozen houses in it could have furnished").[18] But he chose to put none of this knowledge into the *Seven Gables*.

His previous fictions about Salem, taken all together, provide rather little in the way of realistic detail. Some of his Boston acquaintances, and even his personal friend the attorney and essayist George Hillard, had long proposed that Salem could have the same historical and social density as the popular British novelists' settings in Bath and Chester, and had recently urged him to become its novelist: rather than writing another *Scarlet Letter*, "I could wish that you would dwell more in the sun, . . . and expand into a story the spirit of the Town Pump."[19] *The House of the Seven Gables* is Hawthorne's answer. But Hawthorne's short fiction gave only brief glimpses of the town, usually from the margins of Salem, under titles like "Night Sketches: Beneath an Umbrella" or "Foot-prints on the Sea-shore" (echoed in Holgrave's choice of recreation) or "Sunday at Home" or "Sights from a Steeple." "A Rill from the Town-Pump," written in 1835, begins, however, with a rhetorical engagement with the whole community like Thoreau's and the preface to the *Gables*:

Truly, we public characters have a tough time of it! And, among all the town-officers, chosen at March meeting, where is he that sustains, for a single year, the burthen of such manifold duties as are imposed, in perpetuity, upon the Town-Pump? The title of "town-treasurer" is rightfully mine, as guardian of the best treasure, that the town has. The overseers of the poor ought to make me their chairman, since I provide bountifully for the pauper, without expense to him that pays taxes. . . . As keeper of the peace, all water-drinkers will confess me equal to the constable. I perform some of the duties of the town clerk, by promulgating public notices, when they are posted on my front. To speak within bounds, I am the chief person of the municipality, and exhibit, moreover, an admirable pattern to my brother officers, by the cool, steady, upright, downright, and impartial discharge of my business, and constancy with which I stand to my post. (*Tales*, 141–42)

It is not hard to see hiding under this comic surface the opinion that Hawthorne allowed himself to express to his closest friend outside of Salem, Horatio Bridge, after he had finished *The Scarlet Letter* and was about to leave Salem for good: he, the writer, was "their most distinguished citizen; for they have no other that was ever heard of beyond the limits of the Congressional district." Of course this sketch, its tongue-in-cheek qualities ignored, was taken as a temperance tract, and reprinted far and wide for nonliterary reasons. Hawthorne, predicting the strains and antagonisms his posthumous relation to Salem would undergo, concluded "The Custom-House" with a genial joke about his most famous sketch, and the actual pump's importance to "the great-grandchildren of the present race" as an antiquarian memorial to "the scribbler of bygone days" (*Letter*, 27). And long after the *Seven Gables* had been written, providing immortality for its House, as *The Scarlet Letter* had for the Custom House, Hawthorne brooded over the relationship of this early sketch to his fame. He was in Italy in June 1858, where he found an old well in Arezzo

whence Petrarch had drunk, around which he had played in his boyhood, and which Boccaccio has made famous . . . As I lingered round it, I thought of my own Town Pump, in old Salem, and wondered whether my townspeople would ever point it out to strangers, and whether the stranger would gaze at it with any degree of such interest as I felt in Boccaccio's well. Oh, certainly not; but yet I made that humble Town-Pump the most celebrated structure in the good town; a thousand and a thousand people had pumped there, merely to water oxen or fill their tea-kettles, but when once I grasped the handle, a rill gushed forth that meandered as far as England, as far as India, besides tasting pleasantly in every town and village of our own country. I like to think of this, so long after I did it, and so far from home, and am not without hopes of some kindly local remembrance on this score.[20]

The pump is nothing in itself; it is the artist's celebration of this structure that makes it the "best treasure that the town has," as the sketch claimed.

Another sketch that illuminates the relation of the narrative voice to the setting of Salem in the *Seven Gables* is "Main-street," an account of the development of Essex Street, written only a few months before his expulsion from the Custom House, and not long after Hawthorne wrote to Longfellow: "I am trying to resume my pen, but the influences of my situation and customary associates are so anti-literary, that I know not whether I shall succeed. Whenever I sit alone, or walk alone, I find myself dreaming about stories, as of old; but these forenoons in the Custom House undo all that the afternoons and evenings have done."[21] In "Main-street" an unusual narrative method is abruptly presented, calling attention to its own artifice:

A respectable-looking individual makes his bow and addresses the public. In my daily walks along the principal street of my native town, it has often occurred to me, that, if its growth from infancy upward, and the vicissitude of characteristic scenes that have passed along this thoroughfare, during the more than two centuries of its existence, could be presented to the eye in a shifting panorama, it would be an exceedingly effective method of illustrating the march of time. Acting on this idea, I have contrived a certain pictorial exhibition, somewhat in the nature of a puppet-show, by means of which I propose to call up the multiform and many-colored Past before the spectator, and show him the ghosts of his forefathers, amid a succession of historic incidents, with no greater trouble than the turning of a crank. Be pleased, therefore, my indulgent patrons, to walk into the showroom, and take your seats before yonder mysterious curtain. The little wheels and springs of my machinery have been well oiled; a multitude of puppets are dressed in character, representing all varieties of fashion, from the Puritan cloak and jerkin to the latest Oak Hall coat. . . . (*Snow*, 49)

This dramatic presentation features interplay between Hawthorne as showman and his customers, including two local critics, one "an acidulous-looking gentleman in blue glasses," who demands an exact realism in the pictures and scorns the intent of the whole performance as "manifest catchpenny" (*Snow*, 52), much as the Whig politicians were to demand a conventional deference from the "Loco-foco Surveyor" of "The Custom-House." The second, another "gentlemanly person," heatedly challenges the accuracy of the scenes that the showman presents: "These historical personages could not possibly have met together in the Main-street. They might, and probably did, all visit our old town, at one time or another, but not simultaneously; and you have fallen into anachronisms that I positively shudder to think of!" (*Snow*, 62). Hawthorne seems to have modeled him on Charles Upham, who in addition to his careers as clergyman and politician had written a history of Salem witchcraft, where he had insisted on the value of the facts of history, and had used the Delusion of 1692 as an example of the dangers of creative imagination.[22]

In the *Seven Gables*, the omniscient, God-like "author" appears only as a "disembodied listener," never as someone who might be "invited to a public dinner," either to receive a laurel wreath or to be tarred and feathered, as he wrote to Bridge and Burchmore. Nor does he grasp the handle of a pump, nor demonstrate his puppets literally. Rather, this narrator is more like Thoreau, in the form of the unglamorous Uncle Venner, who performs outdoor menial but "essential offices" and has "seen a great deal of the world, not only in people's kitchens and backyards, but at the street-corners, and on the wharves, and in other places where my business calls me" (*Gables*, 60–61, 82), much as Thoreau claims to have "travelled a good deal in Concord."[23] This poor man's world is the essential Salem of this book, beyond the house on Turner Street itself. In his survey of the architectural symbolism of the *Seven Gables*, Curtis Dahl points to the "actual Salem prototypes" of only two other buildings that are described, realistically or at any length: the railroad station through which Hepzibah and Clifford pass, and the Almshouse, which Uncle Venner calls his "farm."[24] This latter, Dahl notes, "ironically resembles" the great mansions designed and built early in the century by Samuel McIntire on Chestnut Street. By a further irony, in 1846 the Hawthornes temporarily rented the small Pickering House at 18 Chestnut Street. Sophia Hawthorne proudly described their location to Bridge as the "most stately street in Salem,"[25] but it had no room for her husband's study, and he never gave the place the literary attention that she presumably would have liked.

One location distinguished Salem from all other New England towns— Gallows Hill, where the infamous executions of 1692 had been carried out. Another place, the wharves, with the shipping activities connected with them, had given Salem in the half-century following the Revolution a prominence that Hawthorne celebrated for a moment in "The Custom-House" as "the old town's brighter aspect, when India was a new region, and only Salem knew the way thither" (*Letter*, 29). He had prominently mentioned Gallows Hill—a name usually discreetly suppressed rather than advertised to sightseers—in "Alice Doane's Appeal" (*Snow*, 267, 278) and in "Main-street" (*Snow*, 74), and incidentally in "The Custom-House" (*Letter*, 8). It appears for a crucial moment in the first chapter of the *Seven Gables*, in the account of Matthew Maule's martyrdom to the "terrible delusion" of Colonel Pyncheon's aristocratic tyranny, named only as "the hill of execution" (*Gables*, 8).[26]

The wharves of Salem were prominent in "Sights from a Steeple," as might be expected in a sketch by an innocent young writer: "I see vessels unlading at the wharf, and precious merchandise strewn upon the ground, abundantly as at the bottom of the sea, that market whence no goods return, and where there is no captain nor supercargo to render an account of sales." The narrator goes on to register his apparent pride in a leading shipowner: "Grave seniors be they, and I would wager—if it were safe, in these times, to be responsible, for any one—that the least eminent among them, might vie with old Vincentio, that incomparable trafficker of Pisa. I can even select the wealthiest of the company. It is the elderly personage in somewhat rusty black, with powdered hair, the superfluous whiteness of which is visible upon the cape of his coat" (*Tales*, 195). Shakespeare's merchant in *The Taming of the Shrew* might be a fit partner to Salem's "magnates," including Hawthorne's uncle Simon Forrester in "The Custom-House," but there Hawthorne reminds us that this "powdered head, . . . was scarcely in the tomb, before his mountain-pile of wealth began to dwindle" (*Letter*, 28), and the writer-surveyor after leaving the Custom House feels "disconnect[ed] . . . from all these men of traffic, who seemed to occupy so important a position in the world" (*Letter*, 44). In the world of the *Seven Gables*, there are no "princely merchants," but only Jaffrey Pyncheon, the modern politician, and his hoarded, ill-gotten gains.

Matthew Maule built his original hut by a spring on a "sea-girt peninsula" (*Gables*, 6), a clear indication of Salem's geography to those who lived there, much as Isaac Johnson's lot in Boston is honored at the beginning of the *Scarlet Letter* as the site of the first prison there (*Letter*, 47). The Maules, "always plebeian and obscure," labored "on the wharves, or following the sea as sailors before the mast" (*Gables*, 25). Salem's maritime nature does not return to the story until the crisis of Judge Pyncheon's arrival at the House to confront Clifford and extract his secret; Hepzibah begins to worry that the judge's "fiendish scheme" may have succeeded. She

> reflected that the town was almost completely water-girdled. The wharves stretched out towards the centre of the harbor, and, in this inclement weather, were deserted by the ordinary throng of merchants, laborers, and sea-faring men; each wharf a solitude, with the vessels moored stem and stern, along its misty length. Should her brother's aimless footsteps stray thitherward, and he but bend, one movement over the deep, black tide, would he not bethink himself that here was the sure refuge within his reach, and that, with a single step, or the slightest overbalance of his body, he might be forever beyond his kinsman's gripe? Oh, the temptation! To make of his ponderous sorrow a security! To sink, with its leaden weight upon him, and never rise again! (*Gables*, 248)

Though more than twenty years separates these texts, the thought of "Sights from a Steeple" that the bottom of the sea is "a market whence no goods return," seems echoed in the suicidal mind of Clifford, or, more exactly, in Hepzibah's imagination of that mind. Judge Pyncheon resembles the complacent merchant of the sketch, and Clifford the gloomy observer upon the steeple. The next twist of the romance's plot will reverse this position, and restore the intent of the sketch's subtly implied moral. "The bottom of the sea, that market whence no goods return," suggests the Chaucerian moral that avarice is the root of evil, and the cause of premature death in the greedy man. It is Jaffrey Pyncheon, to whom this moral points, who already sits dead in his chair, while Clifford, whose sensitive, even morbid, self-doubt might rightly worry his sister, is about to experience in his railway journey his most manic pleasure in life. The same point is echoed in the joking reference to suicide in "The Custom-House" by the writer-surveyor, apparent victim of Whig pride and greed: "My fortune somewhat resembled that of a person who should entertain an idea of committing suicide, and, altogether beyond his hopes, meet with the good hap to be murdered" (*Letter*, 42).

Hawthorne's fiction, particularly the *Seven Gables*, gave contemporary readers who did not know Salem personally a quite narrow perspective on it. British readers came to assume it a much smaller and quieter town than it was.[27] Both "The Custom-House" and the story of the Pyncheons would not show any of the leading or even active people of the town at work on the wharves, or in the banks and offices of Essex Street. In these works very little is seen outside of the decaying buildings that give them their titles.

Observing this fact, and combining it with a reading of *The American Notebooks*, Henry James concluded in his biography of the author that "Hawthorne seems to have ignored the good society of his native place almost completely." He found the *Seven Gables* "nearer [to] being a picture of contemporary American life than either" *The Scarlet Letter* or *The Blithedale Romance*, but that to find even the "spirit" if not the letter of American life in it "the reader must look . . . between the lines of his writing and in the *indirect* testimony of his tone, his accent, his temper, of his very omissions and suppressions." Perhaps we should notice his decision not to name Salem in so many of the pieces that are so intimately concerned with it as an overt suggestion of this indirectness. James goes on to describe the four main characters of the *Seven Gables* (excluding the Judge) as "all types, to the author's mind, of something general . . . each of them is the centre of a cluster of those ingenious and meditative musings . . . which melt into the current and texture of the story and give it a kind of moral richness." He describes the characters as "a grotesque old spinster . . . an amiable bachelor . . . a sweet-natured and bright-faced young girl . . . a young man still more modern."[28] This is, I think, to take them too much on the terms of "Sights from a Steeple"; but they do, with the exception of Clifford, seem to repeat the stock characters there. Hawthorne's four characters give the reader (in an almost late-Jamesian sense) "centers" of consciousness that do "melt" together: each one is an extension of the narrator's controlling consciousness, rather than a novelistic "character." As Hawthorne put it in the preface: "The personages of the Tale—though they give themselves out to be of ancient stability and considerable prominence—are really of the Author's own making, or, at all events, of his own mixing; their virtues can shed no lustre, nor their defects redound, in the remotest degree, to the discredit of the venerable town of which they profess to be inhabitants." He would seem to include here Judge Pyncheon, who certainly does "redound

. . . to the discredit" of Salem, precisely through his "stability" and "prominence." Marcus Cunliffe's comment is apt here: "Jaffrey Pyncheon is a more solid, more memorable portrait, belonging firmly to the province of the novelist, where Clifford and Hepzibah suggest the essayist side of Hawthorne."[29] Clifford and Hepzibah, and Phoebe and Holgrave (in a modified gesture toward the "modern") speak for the narrator's personal hopes and fears: his love of observation and harmless fun, his devotion to imagination, and his sense of inadequacy before the grasping common sense and materialism of the Salem businessman.

Hawthorne wrote to Bridge, soon after publication: "The House of the Seven Gables, in my opinion, is better than the Scarlet Letter; but I should not wonder if I had refined upon the principal character a little too much for popular appreciation, nor if the romance of the book should be found somewhat at odds with the humble and familiar scenery in which I invest it."[30] Clifford *is* the central character of the romance, though Cunliffe is right to called the Judge "the most fully realized of all Hawthorne's characters,"[31] if we take "realization" to be the novelistic property of specific detail. Hawthorne's perverse twist is to give most of the detail after the character is dead, taunting him, as he sits in a barely disguised Grandfather's Chair, for his inability to extricate himself from the romance. Clifford's triumph over Jaffrey (which parallels that of the narrator), or at least his survival of him, has been seen by many readers as unearned and gratuitous, a happy ending imposed by an exhausted or inept author. Hepzibah finally reveals that Clifford's real "crime" against his cousin was his telling a story to a person incapable of appreciating it: " 'When they were young together, Clifford probably made a kind of fairy-tale of this discovery. He was always dreaming hither and thither about the house, and lighting up its dark corners with beautiful stories. And poor Jaffrey, who took hold of everything as if it were real, thought my brother had found out his uncle's wealth. He died with this delusion in his mind!' " (*Gables*, 316). Thus, as Cunliffe remarks, the ostensible treasure of a land claim turns out to be "a comical anachronism;[32] the moral of this extended fable about American history is to trust your imagination, not the people around you. The narrator, as so frequently in this book, has made a comment that explains Hepzibah's idea. The following passage occurs during his extended description of the dead man in the chair.

A man of sturdy understanding, like Judge Pyncheon, cares no more for twelve o'clock at night, than for the corresponding hour of noon. However just the parallel, drawn in some of the preceding pages, between his Puritan ancestor and himself, it fails in this point. The Pyncheon of two centuries ago, in common with most of his contemporaries, professed his full belief in spiritual ministrations, although reckoning them chiefly of a malignant character. The Pyncheon of tonight, who sits in yonder chair, believes in no such nonsense. Such, at least, was his creed, some few hours since. His hair will not bristle, therefore, at the stories which—in times when chimney-corners had benches in them, where old people sat poking into the ashes of the past, and raking out traditions, like live coals—used to be told about this very room of his ancestral house. In fact, these tales are too absurd to bristle even childhood's hair. What sense, meaning, or moral, for example, such as even ghost-stories should be susceptible of, can be traced in the ridiculous legend, that, at midnight, all the dead Pyncheons are bound to assemble in this parlor! (*Gables*, 278–79)

The Judge, like the modern politician and historian Upham, and like so many important people in Salem society, requires all literature to provide a firmly grounded moral. And so this "Author," in his preface to the *Seven Gables*, has provided one for him, that "fails" as much as the parallel with the Colonel.

Not to be deficient, in this particular, the Author has provided himself with a moral;—the truth, namely, that the wrong-doing of one generation lives into the successive ones, and, divesting itself of every temporary advantage, becomes a pure and uncontrollable mischief;—and he would feel it a singular gratification, if this Romance might effectually convince mankind (or, indeed, any one man) of the folly of tumbling down an avalanche of ill-gotten gold, or real estate, on the heads of an unfortunate posterity, thereby to maim and crush them, until the accumulated mass shall be scattered abroad in its original atoms. In good faith, however, he is not sufficiently imaginative to flatter himself with the slightest hope of this kind. When romances do really teach anything, or produce any effective operation, it is usually through a far more subtle process than the ostensible one. The Author has considered it hardly worth his while, therefore, relentlessly to impale the story with its moral, as with an iron rod—or rather, as by sticking a pin through a butterfly—thus at once depriving it of life, and causing it to stiffen in an ungainly and unnatural attitude. A high truth, indeed, fairly, finely, and skilfully wrought out, brightening at every step, and crowning the final development of a work of fiction, may add an artistic glory, but is never any truer, and seldom any more evident, at the last page than at the first. (*Gables*, 2–3)

This may be paraphrased: "Not to be deficient, I have scraped up a moral that may be a high truth, but is here hardy worthwhile, and will prove deficient." Such flippancy undermines the dominance, if not the very existence, of the historical message. Cunliffe speaks perhaps for many thoughtful readers in asking, "Why, then, all the bother about Evil and Lineage?"[33] Colonel Pyncheon's greedy crime is oddly, impatiently described here as "tumbling down an avalanche of ill-gotten gold, or real estate, on the heads of an unfortunate posterity, thereby to maim and crush them." This grotesque, allegorically toned image recalls better Thoreau's "poor immortal soul . . . well nigh crushed and smothered under its load, creeping down the road of life, pushing before it a barn,"[34] than any laments for the past voiced by characters in the *Seven Gables*, and it says nothing about the Judge's difference from the Colonel.

After chastising the Judge for his failure to appreciate "spiritual ministrations," the narrator proceeds to practice them himself: "We are tempted to make a little sport with the idea. Ghost-stories are hardly to be treated seriously, any longer"[35] (*Gables*, 279). He depicts a wild scene of "half-a-dozen generations, jostling and elbowing one another," another parody of his historical moral, till he seems to catch and sober himself: "Indulging our fancy in this freak, we have partly lost the power of restraint and guidance," but goes on, till he ends with mock-horror: "Is it the Judge, or no? How can it be Judge Pyncheon? We discern his figure, as plainly as the flickering moonbeams can show us anything, still seated in the oaken chair! Be the apparition whose it may, it advances to the picture, seems to seize the frame, tries to peep behind it, and turns away, with a frown as black as the ancestral one" (*Gables*, 280–81). Here Hawthorne seems to recall an image that may have begun his idea of the character of Judge Pyncheon. In his "Lost Notebook," between August and October 1837, he recorded a visit to see old portraits in the cabinet of the Essex Historical Society: "Peter Oliver, who was crazy, used to fight with these family pictures, in the old mansion-house, and the face and breast of one lady bears cuts and stabs inflicted by him."[36] Peter Oliver, last royalist chief justice of Massachusetts, was related to a "Judge" Pyncheon from Salem, who was also a royalist; a descendant objected to Hawthorne's use of the name.[37] Charles Upham's grandfather was also a royalist who sat out the Revolution in Halifax.

We have been well prepared for the narrator's gloating over Judge Pyncheon's inability to imagine things: this "Pyncheon of to-night, who sits in yonder chair, believes in no such nonsense" as ghost stories. His antithesis, Clifford, on the other hand, experiences his own difficulties. Phoebe reads to him from "works of fiction, in pamphlet-form," popular domestic fiction which "interested her strange auditor very little, or not at all. Pictures of life, scenes of passion or sentiment, wit, humor, and pathos, were all thrown away, or worse than thrown away, on Clifford; either because he lacked an experience by which to test their truth, or because his own griefs were a touch-stone of reality that few feigned emotions could withstand" (*Gables*, 145–46). To what extent does Clifford's blindness to "life" and his deeper emotional appreciation of its mysteries reflect the narrator's and even the author's personality? Holgrave provided Phoebe with these books, and we know that Hawthorne particularly enjoyed realistic fiction, by Paul de Kock or Anthony Trollope among many others, for relaxation between his own efforts at composition.

Clifford is the person before whom the action of this book is played, whose arched window serves as the steeple did in the sketch; Clifford enjoys the puppet show played in front of him on Pyncheon-street. Meanwhile Phoebe lives happily "in reality" without suffering its deprivations, as Sophia

Hawthorne did, and Holgrave has enough of Zack Burchmore's adaptation to the world while retaining his integrity. As potential author, Clifford is to Holgrave as Hawthorne is to Stephen Burchmore, Zack's father, and the "story teller" of the Custom-House:

> Could I have preserved the picturesque force of his style, and the humorous coloring which nature taught him how to throw over his descriptions, the result, I honestly believe, would have been something new in literature. Or I might readily have found a more serious task. It was a folly, with the materiality of this daily life pressing so intrusively upon me, to attempt to fling myself back into another age; or to insist on creating the semblance of a world out of airy matter, when, at every moment, the impalpable beauty of my soap-bubble was broken by the contact of some actual circumstance. (*Letter*, 37)

This was written before *The Scarlet Letter*'s success, and perhaps before Hawthorne believed he would have a success. It is of course his public voice, and it would be foolish to identify what he calls a "soap-bubble" here with Clifford's bubbles, those "airy spheres . . . with the big world depicted, in hues bright as imagination, on the nothing of their surface" (*Gables*, 171).

But "when romances do really teach anything, or produce any effective operation, it is usually through a far more subtle process than the ostensible one," writes the author of the *Seven Gables*. Hawthorne needed Clifford and his bubbles as much as any of the observers and commenters on Salem of his earlier career. It was this aspect of the book he must have had in mind when he wrote to Fields while in the midst of its composition: "Sometimes, when tired of it, it strikes me that the whole is an absurdity, from beginning to end; but the fact is, in writing a romance, a man is always—or always ought to be—careering on the utmost verge of a precipitous absurdity, and the skill lies in coming as close as possible, without actually tumbling over."[38]

*Notes*

1.  *The House of the Seven Gables*, ed. William Charvat et al. (Columbus: Ohio State University Press, 1965), 3. Subsequent parenthetical references will refer to this edition as *Gables*.
2.  *The Letters, 1843–1853*, ed. Thomas Woodson et al. (Columbus: Ohio State University Press, 1985), letter #452. Subsequent references to this, volume 16, and to *The Letters, 1857–1864*, ed. Thomas Woodson et al. (Columbus: Ohio State University Press, 1987), volume 18 of *The Centenary Edition of the Works of Nathaniel Hawthorne*, are by letter number, preceded by the number symbol and *Letters*.
3.  *Letters*, #493.
4.  *The Scarlet Letter*, ed. William Charvat et. al. (Columbus: Ohio State University Press, 1962), 44–45. Subsequent parenthetical references refer to this edition as *Letter*.

5. *Letters*, #427.

6. *Letters*, #437.

7. *Letters*, #438.

8. *Letters*, #443.

9. *The English Notebooks*, ed. Randall Stewart (New York: Modern Language Association, 1941), 618.

10. *Letters*, #1116.

11. *Letters*, #1170.

12. *Twice-told Tales*, ed. J. Donald Crowley (Columbus: Ohio State University Press, 1974), 195. Subsequent parenthetical references refer to this edition as *Tales*.

13. *Letters*, #437.

14. Manuscript, Berg Collection, New York Public Library.

15. *Letters*, #449.

16. *Letters*, #420 n 3; #421n3.

17. *The Snow-Image and Uncollected Tales*, ed. J. Donald Crowley (Columbus: Ohio State University Press, 1974), 3. Subsequent parenthetical references refer to this edition as *Snow*.

18. *Letters*, #358 n1.

19. *The Letters, 1813–1843*, ed. Thomas Woodson et al. (Columbus: Ohio State University Press, 1984), 77–79.

20. *The French and Italian Notebooks*, ed. Thomas Woodson (Columbus: Ohio State University Press, 1980), 269–70.

21. *Letters*, #377.

22. By this time Hawthorne had written two criticisms of theatrical performances in Salem, for the Salem *Advertiser*, in May 1848. In the second of these he wrote "the highest estimate that our conscience will allow us to place upon the company's aggregate and individual merits, which we heartily wish were ten times as great and as numerous—in which case, it would give us more than ten times the pleasure to acknowledge them. But, it is hardly possible that a city of the size of Salem should support a theatre worthy of the name."

23. Henry D. Thoreau, *Walden*, ed. J. Lyndon Shanley (Princeton: Princeton University Press, 1971), 4.

24. Curtis Dahl, "The Architecture of Society and the Architecture of the Soul: Hawthorne's *The House of the Seven Gables* and Melville's *Pierre*," in *University of Mississippi Studies in English* 5 (1984–87): 3–6.

25. *Letters*, #364.

26. Later, in "Alice Pyncheon," Holgrave's more unbuttoned version of the story, the name "Gallows-Hill" appears in his retelling of Hawthorne's familiar charges against the handling of the Witchcraft Delusion by Cotton Mather and Sir William Phips (*Gables*, 188). For an account of antiquarian attempts by later generations to locate the infamous (and concealed) spot of the executions, see Sidney Perley, "Where the Salem 'Witches' Were Hanged," *Essex Institute Historical Collections*, LVII (1921): 1–18.

27. For instance, Henry Chorley in *the Athenæum*, 3 December 1853: "Mr. Hawthorne is now at Liverpool, observing customs on a scale somewhat larger than those so wonderfully daguerreotyped by him at Salem, 'the place of rest.' " This was reprinted in the *Times* of London, 4 January 1854.

28. Henry James, *Hawthorne* (1879; reprinted, Ithaca: Cornell University Press, 1956), 37, 98–99.

29. Marcus Cunliffe, "The House of the Seven Gables," *Hawthorne Centenary Essays*, ed. Roy Harvey Pearce (Columbus: Ohio State University Press, 1964), 88.

30. *Letters*, #474.

31. *Hawthorne Centenary Essays*, 101.

32. *Hawthorne Centenary Essays*, 99.

33. *Hawthorne Centenary Essays*, 100.

34. *Walden*, 5.

35. This statement, and the other references in the *Seven Gables* to "chimney-corner legends" are glossed by Hawthorne's review of John Greenleaf Whittier's *Supernaturalism of New England* in the *Literary World*, I: 11 (17 April 1847): 247–48. There he faults Whittier for some of the failings of imagination here imputed to Judge Pyncheon:

> The proper tone for these legends is, of course, that of the fireside narrative, refined and clarified to whatever degree the writer pleases, but still as simple as the Bible— as simple as the babble of an old woman to her grandchild, as they sit in the smoky glow of a deep chimney-corner. Above all, the narrator should have faith, for the time being. If he cannot believe his ghost-story while he is telling it, he had better leave the task to somebody else. Now, Mr. Whittier never fails to express his incredulity either before or after the narrative, and often in the midst of it. It is a matter of conscience with him to do so. (MS, Duyckinck Collection, New York Public Library)

36. Manuscript, Morgan Library, New York, 41–42; see *The American Notebooks*, ed. Claude M. Simpson (Columbus: Ohio State University Press, 1972), 154–55.

37. *Letters*, #494.

38. *Letters*, #453.

# An Annotated Select Bibliography
## of *The House of the Seven Gables*

### DAVID CALLAWAY*

This bibliography is intended as a guide for the general reader or Hawthorne specialist to criticism of *The House of the Seven Gables*, from the early reviews and notices in 1851 to more recent criticism up to 1989. The bibliography is divided into three sections for convenience: 1851 to 1899, which represents the early reviews and notices and much of the Hawthornalia or "cottage industry" of the late nineteenth century; 1900 to 1949, which represents a lull in Hawthorne studies; and 1950 to 1989, which Buford Jones, speaking of the period between 1951 and 1966, but whose words still apply today, called the "Golden Age of Hawthorne Criticism." Within sections the entries are arranged alphabetically and then chronologically, if there is more than one entry per writer or title.

The bibliography is selective, although it is the result of a comprehensive search of criticism on *The House of the Seven Gables*. I do not include dissertations and include only English-language entries and entries that I consider of sufficient scope to be of interest—that is, I include only essays or chapters in books which deal specifically with *The House of the Seven Gables*, or essays and chapters which may focus on another topic, but discuss *The House of the Seven Gables* in significant enough terms to warrant inclusion. I also include essays which I consider important as historical documents, though they only briefly discuss *The House of the Seven Gables*; for example, short essays by influential writers such as Trollope, Howells, and James, and early British opinions of Hawthorne.

The annotations are brief and descriptive rather than evaluative, and are meant to give a general impression of the entry in the author's own words rather than a complete summary. All entries have been verified; however, the essays themselves have not been checked for critical or historical accuracy.

There are several helpful bibliographies of Hawthorne that I have used in compiling my own: Nina E. Browne's *A Bibliography of Nathaniel Hawthorne* (New York: 1905. Reprint, Burt Franklin, 1968), which includes a chronological list of Hawthorne's works; Maurice Beebe and Jack Hardie's

---

*This essay was written specifically for this volume.

*Criticism of Nathaniel Hawthorne: A Selected Checklist* (*Studies in the Novel* 2 [1970]: 519–87); Beatrice Ricks, Joseph D. Adams, and Jack O. Hazlerig's *Nathaniel Hawthorne: A Reference Bibliography 1900–1971* (Boston: G. K. Hall, 1972), which although a bit dated gives a list of Hawthorne's works, including complete collections, partial collections, and individual works, and the various editions of *The House of the Seven Gables* before 1970; Jeannetta Boswell's *Nathaniel Hawthorne and the Critics: A Checklist of Criticism 1900–1978* (Metuchen, NJ: Scarecrow, 1982); and Gary Scharnhorst's *Nathaniel Hawthorne: An Annotated Bibliography of Comment and Criticism before 1900* (Metuchen, NJ: Scarecrow, 1988), which contains 2,586 entries, including some reviews of *The House of the Seven Gables* that I have omitted because I was unable to verify them. Other sources include the *MLA* index, *Studies in the American Renaissance* (edited by Joel Myerson), and bibliographies in *American Literature* and *American Literary Scholarship*.

The current standard edition of *The House of the Seven Gables* is the second volume of the Ohio State Centenary Edition, William Charvat, Roy Harvey Pearce, Claude M. Simpson, general editors; Fredson Bowers, Matthew J. Bruccoli, L. Neal Smith, textual editors (Columbus: Ohio State University Press, 1965).

## 1851–1899

"American Novels." *North British Review* 20, no. 39 (November 1853): 44–53. *House* contains "redundance of description" and suffers from two main defects— Hawthorne uses the supernatural and his moral subserves his art. Language described as being "for an American extraordinarily accurate," although "always light and free."

"American Romance." Review of *The House of the Seven Gables*. *London Leader*, 21 June 1851, 587–88. Discovers in *House* a "quaintness, a wildness, an imagination, and a sort of weird sombreness." Concludes that "there is a want of skill in the denouement; indeed throughout the romance we miss constructive power; but its originality and vividness are unquestionable."

Benson, Eugene. "Poe and Hawthorne." *Galaxy* 6 (December 1868): 742–48. Clifford and Donatello are "remarkable creations," Clifford an example of "portrait art." Finds that "in all Hawthorne's works the remarkable and characteristic thing is the incessant action of the moral faculty." Portrait of Clifford in "The Guest" chapter "uncommon and impressive piece of work."

"The Book World." Notice of *The House of the Seven Gables*. *North American Miscellany*, 12 April 1851, 528. *House* "now printed." "A wider circulation and thorough appreciation, we think, can safely be predicted, for this new work by one of the first masters of American fiction."

"The Book World." *North American Miscellany*, 10 May 1851, 95. *House* is "trenchant in its wit, playful in humor, and delicate to a hair's breadth in description."

Bradfield, Thomas. "The Romances of Nathaniel Hawthorne." *Westminster Review* 142, no. 2 (August 1894): 203–14. *House* a "lovelier and more fascinating story" than *Scarlet*. There are "indications of a freer and healthier impulse" in *House*. It "belongs to a higher region of imaginative art."

[Chorley, Henry Fothergill.] Review of *The House of the Seven Gables*. *Athenaeum*, 24 May 1851, 545–47. Exceeds *Scarlet* in "artistic ingenuity—if less powerful, less painful also—rich in humours and characters." Details in Judge's death scene "fret the reader with their prosy and tantalizing ingenuity" and are "frivolous and vexatious."

Courtney, William Leonard. "Hawthorne's Romances." *Fortnightly Review* 46 (1 October 1886): 511–22. Discusses Judge's death scene; finds "female characters more actual" in *House*.

————. "Hawthorne's Romances." In *Studies New and Old*, 77–99. London: Chapman and Hall, 1888. After *Scarlet*, Hawthorne "added to the concreteness of his personages" in *House*. Clifford, however, "remains as the representative of the shadows, and there is a half-intimated background of ancestral feud and mesmeric influence to keep the story within the limits prescribed by the author's peculiar genius."

[Duyckinck, Evert Augustus.] Review of *The House of the Seven Gables*. *Literary World* 8, no. 17 (26 April 1851): 334–36. [Reprinted in this volume.] "The chief, perhaps, of the dramatis personae is the house itself."

"Fiction." Review of *The House of the Seven Gables*. *London Critic*, July 1851, 312. Hawthorne a "thoroughly original writer; his humour and pathos are his own; there is no affected refinement." He has "keen eye to detect the nice traits of character."

[Griswold, Rufus Wilmot.] "Nathaniel Hawthorne." *International Magazine of Literature, Art, and Science* 3 (May 1851): 156–60. [Reprinted in this volume.] *House*, "the longest and in some respects the most remarkable of his works." Finds it "not less original, not less striking, not less powerful" than *Scarlet*. "[P]urest piece of imagination in our prose literature."

Hale, Charles. "Nathaniel Hawthorne." *Today* 2 (18 September 1852): 177–81. Hawthorne "stands at the head of all the living writers of fiction in this country." Who but Hawthorne "would be able to invest with such a mysterious interest, the miserable fouls that lived in the garden?" Thinks death of Judge Pyncheon is a scene "unsurpassed in fiction."

Harper, G. M. "Hawthorne's Subjective Characters." *Nassau Literary Magazine* 38, no. 1 (May 1882): 22–27. Holgrave, like Coverdale, is a "subjective character"; "he brings the active force, the practical energy of modern times, into that dim mansion. . . ." Sees contrast between Holgrave and Hepzibah. When Hepzibah enters his attic it is as if she is "emerging from death into life."

"Hawthorne's New Romance." Review of *The House of the Seven Gables*. *Boston Daily Evening Transcript*, 8 April 1851, 1. *House* "will be welcomed all over the country as another evidence of Hawthorne's marked and brilliant genius." It "will give greater satisfaction" than *Scarlet*. It has more "glowing sunlight" and is "interspersed [with] a lively humor. Characters "all vividly rise at the author's bidding."

Hillard, Katharine. "Hawthorne as an Interpreter of New England." *New England Magazine* 12 (August 1895): 732–36. *House* is "picture *par excellence* of New England in the minds of most people." Characters, however, are romance characters when compared to "real" characters like Howells's Silas Lapham or Stowe's Sam Lawton.

Howells, William Dean. "George Eliot, Hawthorne, Goethe, Heine." In *My Literary Passions*, 137–42. New York: Harper Brothers, 1895. Howells admits he "never cared much" for *House*.

Hutton, Richard Holt. "Nathaniel Hawthorne." *National Review* 11 (October 1860): 453–81. Partially reprinted in *Littel's Living Age* 68 (26 January 1861): 217–32. Discusses Judge's death scene. Finds Hawthorne's moral shortcomings "painfully evident" in the political world.

———. "Nathaniel Hawthorne." In *Literary Essays*, 437–90. London: Macmillan, 1871. Holgrave shrewd, cold, inquisitive hero. Judge's death scene "most striking chapter." *House* "nearly a perfect work of art, is yet composed of altogether thinner materials" than *Scarlet*.

James, Henry. "The Three American Novels." In *Hawthorne*, 102–41. New York: Harper, 1879. [Reprinted in part in this volume.] Reprinted. Ithaca, NY: Cornell Univ. Press, 1967. *House* "has always seemed to me more like a prologue to a great novel than a great novel itself. . . . Evidently, . . . what Hawthorne designed to represent was not the struggle between an old society and a new, for in this case he would have given the old one a better chance, but simply . . . the shrinkage and extinction of a family."

Kimball, A. L. "Hawthorne." *Nassau Literary Magazine* 36, no. 1 (May 1880): 9–13. *House* most characteristic of Hawthorne's writings. Hepzibah "seems more a relic of the grey past than a figure of the present"; Judge is a "*subjective representation*" of evil; Clifford an "objective emblem" and "exquisite study." Hawthorne writes of Hepzibah in "the true spirit of chivalry."

Lang, Andrew. "Nathaniel Hawthorne." *Independent* 41 (26 September 1889): 1237–38. Judge's death scene reminiscent of Dickens. *House* "always appeared the most beautiful and attractive of Hawthorne's novels. . . . He . . . gives us a love story and condescends to a pretty heroine." More of a "lightness and of a cobwebby, dusty humor in Hepzibah Pyncheon . . . than Hawthorne commonly cares to display."

Lathrop, George Parsons. "Lenox and Concord: Productive Period." In *A Study of Hawthorne*, 226–48. Boston: Houghton, Mifflin and Co., 1893. Philip English house model for house of seven gables. In *House* "Hawthorne attained a connection of parts and a masterly gradation of tones which did not belong, in the same fulness, to 'The Scarlet Letter.'" Includes larger range of characters: "Hepzibah is a painting on ivory"; Judge an "almost unqualified discomfort to the reader." Regrets that Hawthorne "did not give freer scope to his delicious faculty for the humorous, exemplified in the 'Seven Gables.'"

Lawton, William Cranston. "'The Scarlet Letter' and its Successors." *New England Magazine* 18 (August 1898): 697–700. *House* "indicative of a happier and less brooding mood."

"Literary Gossip." *Boston Daily Evening Transcript*, 11 June 1851, 1. Discussion of "flattering notice" in London *Athenaeum*. *House* "a story widely differing from its predecessor,—exceeding it perhaps, in artistic ingenuity—if less powerful, less painful also—rich in humors and characters."

"The Literary Guild." *North American Miscellany*, 28 June 1851, 432. *House* "has met with rich and deserved success in England, and has been issued by Mr.

Bohn, for one shilling and sixpence a copy. The *Athenaeum* commends it highly."

Mayo, Amory Dwight. "The Works of Hawthorne." *Universalist Quarterly* 8 (July 1851): 273–93. [Reprinted in this volume.] *House* "inferior to the 'Scarlet Letter' in artistic proportion, compactness and sustained power." But better because "nearer actual life, and more comprehensively true to human nature, than any former work of its author." *House* "well represents the old order in the process of vexatious adjustment to the new." Hepzibah and Clifford represent "phases of a decaying order" while Phoebe "is its point of contact with the new incarnated in Holgrave."

"Modern Novelists—Great and Small." *Blackwood's Edinburgh Magazine* 77, no. 475 (May 1855): 554–68. [Reprinted in part in this volume.] Finds that "The affectation of extreme homeliness and commonplace in the external circumstances, and the mystery and secret of the family . . . is very effective in its own way; and if it were not that its horrors and its wonders are protracted into tedious long-windedness, we would be disposed to admire the power with which these figures were posed and these situations made." In Judge Pyncheon's death scene, "we are wearied and worried out of all the horror and impressiveness which might have been in it, had its author only known when to stop. Perhaps there is scarcely such another piece of over-description in the language. The situation is fairly worn to pieces."

Moore, Herbert Hill. "Hawthorne's *House of the Seven Gables*." *Nassau Literary Magazine* 54, no. 5 (December 1898): 253–57. *House* the "longest, the most elaborate, and in some phases perhaps the most perfect" of Hawthorne's novels. "Expansive" like a photograph rather than an impressionistic painting. "[W]eirdly beautiful in its fantasies and symbolical imaginings." Although not realistic, Hawthorne's novels reproduce the atmosphere of the New England town. Characters are types: Holgrave a democrat; Clifford and Hepzibah aristocrats. Hepzibah "ludicrously yet pathetically dignified."

"Nataaniel [*sic*] Hawthorne." *Tait's Edinburgh Magazine* 23 (December 1856): 756–57. "Struck" by Judge's death scene. Holgrave "well drawn"; Phoebe "a refreshing little picture of humanity." Although "it is not generally known that Hawthorne is a Unitarian . . . more than one passage in 'House of Seven Gables' will prove this to any who understand the tenets of that sect."

"Nathaniel Hawthorne." *New Monthly Magazine* 94 (February 1852): 202–7. *House* is "less powerful and pathetic" than *Scarlet*, but it "gives unusual scope . . . to its author's humour."

"Nathaniel Hawthorne." *Dublin University Magazine* 46 (October 1855): 463–69. Reprinted in *Eclectic Magazine* 36, no. 3 (November 1855): 996–1001. *House* the "most pleasing and complete of Hawthorne's tales."

"Nathaniel Hawthorne." *Atlantic Monthly* 5, no. 31 (May 1860): 614–22. Discusses Hawthorne's misanthropy: "a blandly cynical distrust of human nature was the result of his most piercing glances into the human soul." Nevertheless, finds "more humor" in *House*.

"Nathaniel Hawthorne." *North British Review* 49 (September 1868): 93–113. Hawthorne's humor reflected in Hepzibah's aristocratic hens and Judge's "overflowing benevolence." *House* "is in some respects the most elaborate and finished, if neither the most pleasing nor the most profound, of his writings." Holgrave "the least satisfying character."

"New Books." Review of *The House of the Seven Gables. Worcester Palladium*, 16 April 1851, 2. *House* "will take precedence of all he has yet written." Has "earnestness of manner" and "as strong an individualism of character and scenery" as *Scarlet*, but is "pervaded by a better humanity." Hepzibah as a "decayed gentlewoman opening a cent-shop . . . is an exquisite portraiture."

"New Publications." Review of *The House of the Seven Gables. Hartford Daily Courant*, 10 April 1851, 2. *House* a "work of great genius and decidedly singular and original in its character. Most persons will be pleased with it, though the concealed satire will not gratify those it may hit."

"New Publications." *Boston Daily Evening Transcript*, 11 April 1851, 2. Hawthorne's "popularity seems to increase with every work he writes." *House* "published on Monday morning, and the 6th thousand is now being printed. . . . [T]he striking genius of a great romance is appreciated even in this work-day period of the world."

"New Publications." Review of *The House of the Seven Gables. New York Daily Tribune*, 26 April 1851, 6. Hawthorne has "produced a story which in point of mystic intensity of conception, vivid portraiture of character, and quaint originality of expression, is not unworthy of the noble creations of his characteristic genius." *House* has a "refined comic humor."

Notice of *The House of the Seven Gables. Harper's New Monthly Magazine* 2, no. 12 (May 1851): 855–56. [Reprinted in this volume.] *House* "Destitute of the high-wrought manifestations of passion which distinguished the *Scarlet Letter*, . . . more terrific in its conception, and not less intense in its execution, but exquisitely relieved by charming portraitures of character, and quaint and comic descriptions of social eccentricities." The "frequent dashes of humor . . . blend with the monotone of the story."

Notice of *The House of the Seven Gables. Knickerbocker* 37, no. 5 (May 1851): 455–57. Includes an excerpt describing Hepzibah.

Notice of *The House of the Seven Gables. Southern Quarterly Review* n.s., 4, no. 7 (July 1851): 265–66. *House* "will prove less attractive to the general reader" than *Scarlet*. "[B]ut it is a more truthful book, and, if less ambitious in plan and manner, is not less earnest of purpose, nor less efficient in the varieties of character."

"Notices of New Books." Review of *The House of the Seven Gables. United States Magazine and Democratic Review* 28 (May 1851): 478. Hawthorne's reputation "sufficiently established and widely known." His "delineations of New England manners" governed by good taste. Works will convey to succeeding generations "a truthful picture of the manners of our time."

"Notices of New Works." Review of *The House of the Seven Gables. Albion*, 26 April 1851, 201. *House* a "charming tale" with "common characters well developed, and the minor incidents of life graphically described." Hawthorne's merits "widely recognized." Hawthorne's style combines "great breath of general effect with a singular delicacy of touch in detail."

"Notices of New Works." Review of *The House of the Seven Gables. Southern Literary Messenger* 17 (June 1851): 391. [Reprinted in this volume.] Finds romance "really charming, not, perhaps, as strongly marked as 'The Scarlet Letter,' but full to overflowing of rare and peculiar beauties. There is . . . error in the author's predisposition to represent wealth as always vicious and poverty always virtuous, which is not the case, but his genial, receptive, loving spirit is attuned to all that is good and beautiful in man and nature."

"Notices of Recent Publications." Review of *Twice-Told Tales* and *The House of the Seven Gables*. *Christian Examiner* 50 (May 1851): 508–9. Romance "is a production of great power, though inferior" to *Scarlet*. Plot "more complex, the characterization more exaggerated, and the artistic execution less perfect. . . . There is too much disquisition, and too little of narrative and dialogue."

"Notices of Recent Publications." Review of *The Scarlet Letter* and *The House of the Seven Gables*. *English Review* 16 (October 1851): 179–82. Likes *House* less than *Scarlet*. "It errs by a finical indulgence in details which is here and there tedious, as well as by exhibiting an exultation in the death of an unhappy man, 'Judge Pyncheon.' " Death scene of judge is "brutal."

Pollock, (Lady) Juliet. "Imaginative Literature of America." *Contemporary Review* 22 (August 1873): 358–63. *House* "inferior in constructive skill to the 'Scarlet Letter,' and much narrower in its range than 'Transformation,' yet contains some of Hawthorne's most beautiful ideas and most remarkable descriptive paragraphs."

"Reading Raids. I.—American Literature: Poe; Hawthorne." *Tait's Edinburgh Magazine* 22 (January 1855): 33–41. Hawthorne not ranked high among men of genius, "but a man of genius he is." There is a "mystic horror" in *House* which appeals to "general sensibilities." Criticizes Hawthorne for saying that "existence is always a blank without sexual attachment." Gives readings of allegorical characters: Maules are Labour and Invention; Pyncheons are Wicked Might; Hepzibah is Aristocracy; Clifford is the Gentle and Beautiful; Holgrave is Wronged Industry; Venner is Poverty; and Phoebe is Middle Classes of Society.

Review of *The House of the Seven Gables*. *Boston Daily Mail*, 14 April 1851, 3. Finds "a moral in every chapter, and a *thought* upon every page." Although Hawthorne is the writer's favorite author, he sometimes draws too freely from "the darker abodes and frailty in human nature." "If at times his descriptions are wild and startling, they are blended with morals . . . healthful, and reasonings . . . sublime."

Review of *The House of the Seven Gables*. *Essex County Freeman* (Salem), 16 April 1851, 2. *House* "having a great run with the literary public." Evidence of immediate popularity is "that within five days after its first publication, the sixth thousand of copies passed through the press and off the bookseller's counter." "It receives the highest praise of the critics."

Review of *The House of the Seven Gables*. *Peterson's* 19 (June 1851): 282–83. [Reprinted in this volume.] Though superior to *Scarlet* in "some of its details, the romance, as a whole, is not equal to its predecessor." Fault of romance is the moral aspect; "the sombre coloring" which pervades it and "leaves an effect more or less morbid on even healthy minds." "The only really loveable character" is Phoebe."

Review of *The House of the Seven Gables*. *North American Review* 76, no. 158 (January 1853): 227–48. Review of *House* and *Blithedale*. *House* "deserves to be the most successful with the public." Describes Hepzibah's shop opening as "pathos, streaked and veined by the richest humor." Successive scenes of *House* "are portrayed with a vividness and power unsurpassed, and rarely equalled. . . . [N]arrative is sprightly, quaint, and droll, the dialogues seldom otherwise than natural and well managed, (though the daguerreotypist talks more than anybody but Phoebe could care to hear,) and the *denouement* free, for the most part, from abruptness and improbability."

Trollope, Anthony. "The Genius of Nathaniel Hawthorne." *North American Review* 129, no. 274 (September 1879): 203–22. [Reprinted in part in this volume.] Hepzibah best character, however, *House* "very inferior" to *Scarlet* and Hawthorne "labored over his plot." "In no American writer is to be found the same predominance of weird imagination as in Hawthorne."

Tuckerman, Henry Theodore. "Nathaniel Hawthorne." *Southern Literary Messenger* 17 (June 1851): 344–49. [Reprinted in this volume.] In use of detail in *House* Hawthorne is "like a Flemish painter." Clifford represents "the man of fine organization and true sentiments environed by the material realities of New England life"; Judge is "type of New England selfishness"; Phoebe is the "ideal of genuine, efficient, yet loving female character"; Uncle Venner "most fresh, yet familiar" portrait; Holgrave "embodies Yankee acuteness and hardihood redeemed by integrity and enthusiasm."

[Whipple, Edwin Percy.] Review of *The House of the Seven Gables*. *Graham's Magazine* 38 (June 1851): 467–68. [Reprinted in this volume.] Unlike *Scarlet*, *House* has "humor and . . . pathos combined." It is "Hawthorne's greatest work," although first hundred pages are strongest. Hepzibah and Phoebe are "masterpieces of characterization," whereas Holgrave "appears to us a failure."

Whipple, Edwin Percy. "Nathaniel Hawthorne." *Atlantic Monthly* 5 (May 1860): 614–22. Clifford "marvellously subtile delineation of enfeebled manhood"; Phoebe "cheerful, blooming, practical, affectionate, efficient, full of innocence and happiness, with all the 'hardness' and native sagacity of her class, and so true and close to Nature that the process by which she is slightly idealized is completely hidden." Pyncheon poultry are a "sort of parody of his own doctrine of the heredity transmission of family qualities."

# 1900–1949

Blair, Walter. "Color, Light, and Shadow in Hawthorne's Fiction." *New England Quarterly* 15 (March 1942): 74–94. Holgrave and Phoebe "agencies of light"; Judge is "black shadow."

Brooks, Van Wyck. "Introduction." Nathaniel Hawthorne's *The House of the Seven Gables*, vii–xiii. New York: Heritage, 1935. Book is "Salem itself, as Hawthorne saw it in these eighteen-forties." Salem "old in spirit," has a past "much in common with the past of the ancient ports of northern Europe." Salem still "Gothic in its frame of mind."

Chandler, Elizabeth Lathrop. "A Study of the Sources of the Tales and Romances Written by Nathaniel Hawthorne before 1853." *Smith College Studies in Modern Language* 7, no. 4 (July 1926): 1–64. Reprint. Darby, PA: Arden Library, 1978. Sources include: Hathorne, the witch-judge, cursed by Rebecca Nurse's

husband; Philip English's son's marriage to his persecutor's daughter; Ingersoll
house on Turner street source for house; Phoebe pet name for Sophia Hawthorne;
reference to Pyncheon name in notebooks; Maule Quaker sympathizer; and
Knox estate land claims and Hawthorne family land claim in Raymond, Maine,
as sources for Pyncheon claims.

Doubleday, Neal Frank. "Hawthorne's Criticism of New England Life." *College English* 2 (April 1941): 639–53. *House* "more significant piece of social criticism" than *Blithedale*.

———. "Hawthorne's Use of Three Gothic Patterns." *College English* 7 (January 1946): 258–59. Use of mysterious portrait is a "gothic pattern" used in *House*.

Drake, Samuel Adams. "Salem Legends." In *A Book of New England Legends and Folk Lore in Prose and Poetry*, 167–201. Boston: Little Brown, 1901. Reprint. Detroit: Singing Tree, 1969. *House* in relation to witchcraft and Salem legends.

Erskine, John. "Nathaniel Hawthorne." In *Leading American Novelists*, 179–273. New York: Henry Holt, 1910. *House* "less powerful and less unique" than *Scarlet* but a "truer picture of New England." Romance resembles *The Tempest* in its treatment of punishment of sin. Characters are "strangely solitary figures."

Ferguson, J. D. "The Earliest Translation of Hawthorne." *Nation* 100 (1915): 14–15. Earliest translations into German of *House* and *Scarlet*.

Gates, Lewis E. "Hawthorne." In *Studies and Appreciations*, 92–109. New York: Macmillan, 1900. Reprint. Freeport, NY: Books for Libraries, 1970. *House* as "Romance of Heredity."

Gorman, Herbert. "Chapter Two." In *Hawthorne: A Study in Solitude*, 55–111. New York, 1927. Reprint. New York: Biblo and Tannen, 1966. *House* "falls to pieces and the reader is confronted with varying ingredients that do not, by any manner of reasoning, form a unified ensemble."

Griffiths, Thomas Morgan. " 'Montpelier' and 'Seven Gables': Knox's Estate and Hawthorne's Novel." *New England Quarterly* 16 (September 1943): 432–43. Hawthorne's 1837 visit to Montpelier may have been source for *House* since two houses are similar. Similar shadowy land claim connected to the Knox estate.

———. *Maine Sources in The House of the Seven Gables*. Waterville, ME: 1945. Result of study of "documents relating to the Waldo patent in Maine and its succession of proprietors in the Waldo, Flucker, and Knox families." Suggests "some of the historical and biographical facts in their family records for which parallels may be found in the imaginary Pyncheons and their estate."

Hall, Lawrence Sargent. "Hawthorne: Critic of Society: The Making of an American Philosophy." *Saturday Review of Literature* 26 (1943): 28, 30, 32. *House* is Hawthorne's "most obvious use of American democratic philosophy as a basis for social ethic."

Herron, Ima Honaker. "The New England Village in Literature." In *The Small Town in American Literature*, 28–69. Durham, N C: 1939. Reprint. New York: Pageant, 1959. *House* reveals "minutiae of speech, manners, and appearances of the exemplary and conventional society of provincial and later Salem."

Lathrop, George Parsons. "Introductory Note." Nathaniel Hawthorne's *The House of the Seven Gables*, 7–12. Boston: Houghton Mifflin, 1924. Discussion of the history of curse, the land claims, and the house itself. *House* better than *Scarlet*.

Lewisohn, Ludwig. "The Troubled Romancers." In *The Story of American Literature*,

153–93. New York: Modern Library, 1932. Trouble with *House* is it's "all texture, quite without bone or muscle, that is, acceptable intellectual or moral content." Maule-Pyncheon curse is "puerile machinery."

Lovecraft, H. P. "The Weird Tradition in America." In *Supernatural Horror in Literature*, 60–75. New York: Ben Abramson, 1945. *House* is "New England's greatest contribution to weird literature." Compares it to Poe's "House of Usher."

Matthiessen, Francis Otto. "Hawthorne's Politics, with the Economic Structure of *The Seven Gables*." In *The American Renaissance*, 316–37. New York: Oxford Univ. Press, 1941. Hepzibah "the embodiment of decayed gentility." Hawthorne deliberately contrasted "the Pyncheon family, and rising democracy." Maule's curse illustrates "how economic motives could enter even into the charge of witchcraft." Main theme "not the original curse on the house, but the curse that the Pyncheons have continued to bring upon themselves." "Hawthorne could conceive evil in the world but not an evil world." The "final pages drift away into unreal complacence." Characterization not really successful: "Although he could see his characters in a definite environment, he could not give the sense of their being in continuous contact with that larger outside world."

More, Paul Elmer. "The Solitude of Nathaniel Hawthorne." *Atlantic Monthly* 88 (November 1901): 588–99. Discusses the seclusion of Hepzibah.

Reed, Amy Louis. "Self-Portraiture in the Work of Nathaniel Hawthorne." *Studies in Philology* 23, no. 1 (January 1926): 40–54. Compares Holgrave to Kenyon.

Stewart, Randall, ed. *The American Notebooks by Nathaniel Hawthorne, Based upon the Original Manuscripts in the Pierpont Morgan Library*. New Haven, CT: Yale Univ. Press, 1932. "Recurrent themes in Hawthorne's Fiction." Introduction considers *House*.

Turner, Arlin. "Hawthorne's Literary Borrowings." *PMLA* 51 (June 1936): 543–62. Hawthorne took names Maule and Pyncheon from New England histories and moving of Colonel Pyncheon's portrait from Walpole's *Castle of Otranto*.

Van Doren, Carl. "Nathaniel Hawthorne." In *The American Novel 1789–1939*, 58–83. New York: Macmillan, 1940. Characters and action "suffer a little from the perfection of the background." The "picture is the memorable aspect of the book."

Warren, Austin. "Nathaniel Hawthorne." In *Rage for Order: Essays in Criticism*, 84–103. Chicago: Univ. of Chicago Press, 1948. Reprint. Ann Arbor: Univ. of Michigan Press, 1959. Strength of *House* "lies in its delicate realism." Romance damaged by the presence—or handling—of Judge Pyncheon.

Winters, Yvor. "Maule's Curse, or Hawthorne and the Problem of Allegory." In *Maule's Curse: Seven Studies in the History of American Obscurantism*, 3–22. Norfolk, CT: New Directions, 1938. (First published as "Maule's Curse: Hawthorne and the Problem of Allegory" in *American Review* 9 [September 1937]: 339–61.) *House* an "impure novel" and "failure." In *House* "the moral understanding of the action . . . is corrupted by a provincial sentimentalism ethically far inferior to the Manicheism of the Puritans, which was plain and comprehensive, however brutal."

# 1950–1989

Abel, Darrel. "Hawthorne's House of Tradition." *South Atlantic Quarterly* 52 (October 1953): 561–78. *House* "an allegory of love versus self-love, of human tradition versus personal ambition and family pride, of imagination versus preoccupation with present fact."

Adams, John F. "Hawthorne's Symbolic Gardens." *Texas Studies in Language and Literature* 5, no. 2 (Summer 1963): 242–54. Garden settings "constitute a separate reality." Discusses "significant aspect" of garden scenes below trees, including scenes below the Pyncheon elm. Comments on Hawthorne's use of pools and their symbolic pollution.

Albertini, Virgil. "Hepzibah and Prayer." *American Notes and Queries* 12 (November 1973): 35. Points out that Hepzibah prays the morning she opens shop. Critics argue that Hepzibah cannot pray in house.

Arac, Jonathan. "The House and the Railroad: *Dombey and Son* and *The House of the Seven Gables.*" In *Commissioned Spirits: The Shaping of Social Motion in Dickens, Carlyle, Melville, and Hawthorne*, 94–113. New Brunswick, NJ: Rutgers Univ. Press, 1979. (First appeared in *New England Quarterly* 51 [March 1978]: 3–22.) Both works "build up novelistic wholes from the materials typical of the periodical literature of the 1830s," particularly the Gothic tale and the sketch of contemporary life. Both are "social fables" with a "proud established family" that must change in a society in transition. "Family" and "Society" in each novel is represented respectively by an ancestral house and the new railroad.

Barnes, Daniel R. "Orestes Brownson and Hawthorne's Holgrave." *American Literature* 45 (May 1973): 271–78. Holgrave satire of Brownson, which explains Holgrave's reversal (similar to Brownson's and the "comic resolution" of the plot.

Bassan, Maurice. "The English Years." In *Hawthorne's Son: The Life and Literary Career of Julian Hawthorne*, 102–42. Columbus: Ohio State Univ. Press, 1970. Thematic comparison of Julian Hawthorne's *Garth* and *House*.

Battaglia, Francis Joseph. "*The House of the Seven Gables*: New Light on Old Problems." *PMLA* 82 (December 1967): 579–90. Defense of romance against critics who find the plot episodic and the ending forced.

———. "The (Unmeretricious) *House of the Seven Gables.*" *Studies in the Novel* 2 (Winter 1970): 468–73. Hawthorne did not yield to public taste in writing the novel.

Baym, Nina. "Hawthorne's Holgrave: The Failure of the Artist-Hero." *JEGP* 69, no. 4 (October 1970): 584–98. [Reprinted in this volume.] Holgrave is "dispossessed hero" who is "most unequivocally heroic of Hawthorne's generally weak male characters." Holgrave not intellectual—which is positive. Hawthorne demonstrates "the sexual power of art and its near relation to witchcraft" in the Holgrave-Phoebe scene when he reads the legend. Holgrave not happy after conversion: "By asserting that the ending, in which a romantic self dies and is reborn as a solid social citizen, is happy, Hawthorne undermines his own romanticism and identifies the narrative voice with the conservative side of the Pyncheon-Maule conflict."

————. "Hawthorne's Women: The Tyranny of Social Myths." *The Centennial Review* 15 (Summer 1971): 250–72. *House* "Hawthorne's most savage indictment of the patriarchy."

————. "The Major Phase II: 1851." In *The Shape of Hawthorne's Career*, 152–83. Ithaca, N Y: Cornell Univ. Press, 1976. "[E]rotic response" in both Alice Pyncheon and Phoebe when controlled by Maules.

Beebe, Maurice. "The Fall of the House of Pyncheon." *Nineteenth-Century Fiction* 11, no. 1 (June 1956): 1–17. Compares Poe's "House of Usher" and Hawthorne's *House*. Similarities include: house symbol; exiled brother and sister; stories within stories; "conflict between physical and psychological elements"; and climactic storms.

Bell, Michael Davitt. "Past and Present." In *Hawthorne and the Historical Romance of New England*, 193–242. Chicago: Univ. of Chicago Press, 1980. *House* "most sustained attempt to establish connections between Puritan past and nineteenth-century present." Witchcraft has modern equivalent in mesmerism. Ending least satisfying part of romance: "the emphasis on progress . . . ignores his earlier insistence on historical repetition."

Bell, Millicent. "The Artists of the Novels: Coverdale, Holgrave, Kenyon." In *Hawthorne's View of the Artist*, 151–72. New York: State Univ. of New York, 1962. In *House*, "Hawthorne turns uncritically to the great conventional symbol of progress—the triumph of light over darkness."

Benardete, Jane. "Holgrave's Legend of Alice Pyncheon as a *Godey's* Story." *Studies in American Fiction* 7, no. 2 (Autumn 1979): 229–33. Legend can be identified with women's magazine: "The tale Holgrave tells . . . should be read as an example of literary imitation, pastiche, or, perhaps, parody." Gives a brief history of "women's publications" in the period. "*Godey's* fiction reads like 'moralized fashionplates.' "

Bewley, Marius. "Hawthorne's Novels." In *The Eccentric Design: Form in the Classic American Novel*, 147–86. New York: Columbia Univ. Press, 1959. Holgrave's sudden transition in final chapter "fails to the point of appearing grotesque." Clifford an unusual Hawthorne character because he "is the only one who is perfectly innocent, and entirely the victim."

Birdsall, Virginia Ogden. "Hawthorne's Fair-Haired Maidens: The Fading Light." *PMLA* 75 (June 1960): 250–56. Argues that with "changes from Phoebe to Priscilla, and from Priscilla to Hilda, the optimistic light shed by Hawthorne's faith in redeeming human love has begun perceptibly to fade."

Brodhead, Richard H. "Double Exposure: *The House of the Seven Gables*." In *Hawthorne, Melville, and the Novel*, 69–90. Chicago: Univ. of Chicago Press, 1976. Discusses realism of *House*, the alternation between "close-ups and long views," and the modulation between mimetic and symbolic.

Bruccoli, Matthew J. "A Sophisticated Copy of *The House of the Seven Gables*." *Papers of the Bibliographic Society of America* 59 (Fourth Quarter 1965): 438–39. Discovery of 1853 sixth printing with an 1851 title page.

Buell, Lawrence. "Provincial Gothic: Hawthorne, Stoddard, and Others." In *New England Literary Culture*, 351–70. Cambridge: Cambridge Univ. Press, 1986. Compares Elizabeth Barstow Stoddard's *The Morgeson's* to *House*. "Provincial gothic . . . takes impetus from the awareness of social change but is grounded in the premise that institutions and values resist change." Both novels use witchcraft, and both novels present "the anticlimactic nature of disenchantment."

Burns, Rex S. "Hawthorne's Romance of Traditional Success." *Texas Studies in Literature and Language* 12 (Fall 1970): 443–55. Defines "traditional success" as "competence, an independence, and the respect of fellow men for his morality." *House* defends traditional success against competitive materialism.

Bush, Sargent, Jr. " 'Peter Goldthwaite's Treasure' and *The House of the Seven Gables*." *Emerson Society Quarterly* 62 (Winter 1971): 35–38. "Treasure" is "trial run" for *House*.

Byers, John R., Jr. *"The House of the Seven Gables* and 'The Daughters of Dr. Byles': A Probable Source." *PMLA* 89 (January 1974): 174–77. Eliza Leslie's "The Daughters of Dr. Byles" published in *Graham's* in 1842 as source for *House*. Themes of both are similar—"the isolation of [the] individual" and the "baneful influence of past." Also "suggestive" is the treatment of the two houses, spinsterhood, and the conclusions.

————. "The Possible Background of 3 Dickinson Poems." *Dickinson Studies* 57 (1986): 35–38. Finds that "Hawthorne's notorious scene of the dead Judge Jaffrey Pyncheon may very well have given rise to Dickinson's 'I heard a Fly buzz—when I died—' " (Poem 465).

Caldwell, Wayne Troy. "The Emblem Tradition and the Symbolic Mode: Clothing Imagery in *The House of the Seven Gables*." *ESQ* 19 (1973): 34–42. Finds a total of 429 clothing and "emblematic decoration" metaphors. Compares Clifford's dressing gown to his soul. Analyzes Hepzibah's turban. Clifford and Hepzibah put on new clothing to go to church.

Carlson, Constance H. "Wit and Irony in Hawthorne's *The House of the Seven Gables*." In *A Handful of Spice: A Miscellany of Maine Literature and History*, edited by Richard S. Sprague, 159–68. Orono: Univ. of Maine Press, 1968. Hawthorne's wit and irony reveal his values and artistic designs.

Carpenter, Richard C. "Hawthorne's Scarlet Bean Flowers." *The University Review* (*Kansas City Review*) 30 (Autumn 1963): 65–71. Analysis of "horticultural symbols and images." Sterility of elder Pyncheons versus the promise of the young couple, as seen by images of fruitfulness, means optimistic ending inevitable. Defends "happy ending."

Carter, Everett. "Varieties of Rejection." In *The American Idea: The Literary Response to American Optimism*, 134–95. Chapel Hill: Univ. of North Carolina Press, 1977. *House* the "most dramatic statement of the permanence of the past and the futility of the American attempt to ignore it." Uncle Venner personifies Franklinesque American optimism. The train image Hawthorne's "most brilliant description of the pervasive powers of the past [and] . . . his rejection of the faith in material progress toward a better future."

Carton, Evan. "The Prison Door." In *The Rhetoric of American Romance: Dialectic and Identity in Emerson, Dickinson, Poe, and Hawthorne*, 191–227. Baltimore: Johns Hopkins Univ. Press, 1985. "A striking feature of Hawthorne's language, in this initial differentiation of Pyncheons and Maules, is its tendency to align the two families with masculine and feminine properties, respectively."

Chai, Leon. "Hawthorne." In *The Romantic Foundations of the American Renaissance*, 257–70. Ithaca, N.Y.: Cornell Univ. Press, 1987. "The guilt" obsession of Pyncheons "is not for Hawthorne, one of conscience, in the sense of moral awareness. It refers rather to a psychological force that those whose rights are violated have over their oppressors." Argues that Pyncheons lose "self"—for example, Alice loses her "self" to Matthew Maule.

Charvat, William. "Introduction." Nathaniel Hawthorne's *The House of the Seven Gables*, xv–xxviii. Columbus: Ohio State Univ. Press, 1965. Provides chronology of Hawthorne's writing of *House* and statistics of book sales compared to *Scarlet*. Discusses the denouement as "professional problem" and finds that "in all Hawthorne's work there is no other such unmitigated villain" as Judge. Discussion of history and notebooks as "raw materials."

Clark, Robert. "*The House of the Seven Gables* and the Taking of Naboth's Vineyard." In *History, Ideology and Myth in American Fiction, 1823–1852*, 124–31. London: Macmillan, 1984. A reason *House* "now judged a lesser novel than *Scarlet* may be that it is the more direct and therefore more contradictory expression of Hawthorne's ambivalent relationship to the 'aristocratic' past and the Democratic present." Holgrave and Clifford represent the opposition "between the radical Democrat and aristocratic Whig." By associating with Holgrave, "Hawthorne adopts a Democratic discourse that blames the Whig élite for the failure of America to fulfil its promise of regeneration."

Cohn, Jan. "The American House in the Early Republic." In *The Palace or the Poorhouse: The American House as a Cultural Symbol*, 29–61. East Lansing: Michigan State Univ. Press, 1980. House "symbol for property." Through Clifford, Hawthorne "articulated the novel's attack on the house as property, especially as inherited property."

Cox, Clara B. " 'Who Killed Judge Pyncheon?' The Scene of the Crime Revisited." *Studies in American Fiction* 16, no. 1 (Spring 1988): 99–103. Response to Marks's "Who Killed Judge Pyncheon?. . . ." Argues it was Holgrave rather than Clifford. "Holgrave could have mesmerized the Judge to confront him not only with the sins of his ancestors but also with those of Jaffrey himself, a revelation that upset the Judge to the point of death."

Crews, Frederick. "Homely Witchcraft." In *The Sins of the Fathers: Hawthorne's Psychological Themes*, 171–93. New York: Oxford Univ. Press, 1966. When "aesthetic order" is sought "something fundamentally contradictory" is found in *House*. "The ending, which strikes the modern reader as morally complacent, is in fact psychologically urgent, an ingeniously ambiguous gesture of expiation for a dominant idea that has been warping the book's direction." *House*, like Holgrave at end, "turns conservative" as a way of evading its deepest implications. Novel is " 'about' the risks of artistic imagination." "If Hepzibah illustrates the futility of Hawthornian art in the nineteenth century, Clifford and Holgrave may be said to illustrate the flaws and dangers of the artistic temperament."

Cronkhite, G. Ferris. "The Transcendental Railroad." *New England Quarterly* 24 (September 1951): 306–28. Discussion of railroad in "Flight of Owls" chapter.

Crowley, John H. "Hawthorne's New England Epochs." *ESQ* 25, no. 2 (1979): 59–70. *House* built on historical foundation of *The Whole History of Grandfather's Chair*.

Cunliffe, Marcus. "*The House of the Seven Gables*." In *Hawthorne Centenary Essays*, edited by Roy Harvey Pearce, 79–101. Columbus: Ohio State Univ. Press, 1964. Divides *House* into three themes: "Evil, Lineage, and Impermanence."

An "evil deed may have far-reaching consequences. . . . Family pride and acquisitiveness are deplorable, whether or not they involve wrongdoing. . . . Family pride, even when not actively harmful, is absurdly out of place in the American context of rapid social change."

Curran, Ronald T. " 'Yankee Gothic': Hawthorne's 'Castle of Pyncheon.' " *Studies in the Novel* 8 (Spring 1976): 69–79. Analysis of Hawthorne's use of gothic themes. Compares *House* to *Udolpho*, *The Monk*, *Wuthering Heights*, and *The Castle of Otranto*.

Dahl, Curtis. "The Architecture of Society and the Architecture of the Soul: Hawthorne's *The House of the Seven Gables* and Melville's *Pierre*." *University of Mississippi Studies in English* n. s., 5, (1984–1987): 1–22. Compares Hawthorne and Melville and their uses of architectural imagery and symbolism. Compares Judge's country estate to Saddle Meadows in *Pierre*.

Dameron, J. Lasley. "Hawthorne's *The House of the Seven Gables*: A Serpent Image." *Notes and Queries* 6 (July–August 1959): 289–90. Gives possible source for image of Judge as snake. Scene where Judge associated with serpent may have come from *Blackwood's* where Alexander Gardner wrote a "memoir on the subject of the fascinating power of serpents."

Dauber, Kenneth. "*The House of the Seven Gables*." In *Rediscovering Hawthorne*, 118–48. Princeton, NJ: Princeton Univ. Press, 1977. Words in *House* "express; they do not denote." Because of replications and duplications an "incident multiplies in its own image, leading back into itself . . . *The House of the Seven Gables* goes nowhere, which is at once its virtue and the reason why, ultimately, it fails." Ending "forced."

Davis, Sarah I. "The Bank and the Old Pyncheon Family." *Studies in the Novel* 16, no. 2 (Summer 1984): 150–66. *House* "deals with the inheritance from the Bank controversy in New England and projects a resolution of its injustices." The controversy was the defeat of the Second United States Bank and the indictment of its president, Nicholas Biddle. "Both Clifford and Jaffrey . . . subsume characteristics of Biddle.

DeSalvo, Louise. "*The House of the Seven Gables*." In *Nathaniel Hawthorne*, 77–96. Atlantic Highlands, NJ: Humanities, 1987. Fictional Pyncheon family "directly analogous" to Hawthorne's family. By "inventing" Matthew Maule "Hawthorne shifts the legend from being woman-centered to being man-centered." This "effectively obliterates . . . all of those *women* who were persecuted for witchcraft in Puritan New England." Narrator "misrepresents" Hepzibah's fate as a class rather than a gender issue. Narrator's tone hostile toward Hepzibah.

Dillingham, William B. "Structure and Theme in *The House of the Seven Gables*." *Nineteenth-Century Fiction* 14 (June 1959): 59–70. When episodes and digressions are considered thematically *House* "takes on a unity not recognizable when it is viewed solely as a narrative." The "real theme" which is projected by antithesis "concerns the necessity of man's participation in what Holgrave terms 'the united struggle of mankind.' " Antitheses include: poverty versus riches; "the present with the past, aristocracy with democracy, youth with age, greed with unselfishness, the complex with the simple, appearance with reality, pride with humbleness, the isolated with the unisolated."

Donohue, Agnes McNeil. "*The House of the Seven Gables*: 'An Uncontrollable Mischief.' " In *Hawthorne: Calvin's Ironic Stepchild*, 68–94. Kent, OH: Kent State Univ. Press, 1985. Discussion of Hawthorne's third person narrative, symbols, structure, and characters in *House*.

Dooley, Patrick K. "Genteel Poverty: Hepzibah in *The House of the Seven Gables*." *Markham Review* 9 (Winter 1980): 33–35. Hepzibah "a remarkable picture of how the upper class saw itself and looked down upon the lower classes in nineteenth-century New England society." Key differences between new and old orders is attitude toward work—Hepzibah embarrassed, Phoebe not. Dooley uses Veblen's *The Theory of the Leisure Class*, while arguing that Hawthorne "actually sides with the old gentility."

Dryden, Edgar A. "Hawthorne's Castle in the Air: Form and Theme in *The House of the Seven Gables*." *ELH* 38, no. 2 (June 1971): 294–317. The "sense of homelessness" is the "original impulse or basic theme of Hawthornian Romance, and gives the familiar metaphor of the house of fiction a special ontological dimension."

Eigner, Edwin M. "Character." In *The Metaphysical Novel in England and America: Dickens, Bulwer, Melville, and Hawthorne*, 67–109. Berkeley: Univ. of California Press, 1978. Compares *House* to *Faerie Queen*—especially the "House of Pride" episode.

Emry, Hazel Thornburg. "Two Houses of Pride: Spenser's and Hawthorne's." *Philological Quarterly* 33 (January 1954): 91–94. In first chapter Hawthorne refers to house as "gray feudal castle"—this is clue that Spenser's "House of Pride" in *The Faerie Queene* is "source of exact physical details for the Pyncheon house."

Erlich, Gloria C. "Fathers, Uncles, and Avuncular Figures." In *Family Themes and Hawthorne's Fiction: The Tenacious Web*, 104–45. New Brunswick, NJ: Rutgers Univ. Press, 1984. *House* most "home—and family-centered" of Hawthorne's novels. Jaffrey Pyncheon a "toweringly oppressive paternal figure." Relates Hawthorne's own family situation to his fiction. Holgrave and Clifford artists, Judge "anti-artist." Discussion of narrator—"positively gloats" over Judge's death.

Fairbanks, Henry G. "Hawthorne and the Machine Age." *American Literature* 28 (May 1956): 155–63. Analysis of railroad image in *House*.

Farmer, Norman, Jr. "Maule's Curse and the Rev. Nicholas Noyes: A Note on Hawthorne's Source." *Notes and Queries* 11 (June 1964): 224–25. Account of curse delivered during Salem trials "which matches perfectly that employed by Hawthorne . . . but which was most certainly not directed at John Hathorne." The famous "blood to drink" curse uttered by Sarah Good and aimed at Nicholas Noyes.

Fleck, Richard F. "Industrial Imagery in *The House of the Seven Gables*." *Nathaniel Hawthorne Journal* 4 (1974): 273. Close reading of romance "uncovers a significant number of industrial images which, along with the railroad, collectively function . . . as metaphors of mental states." Examples include "steel-spring" of shop bell, "inflammable gas," and electricity.

Fogle, Richard H. "*The House of the Seven Gables*." In *Hawthorne's Imagery: The 'Proper Light and Shadow' in the Major Romances*, 48–91. Norman: Univ. of Oklahoma Press, 1969. Characters "incomplete in themselves." "Together they make up a design." *House* "has a dominant sunshine-storm, or light-darkness, pattern, originating in the physical properties of the house itself." Hepzibah and Judge "mirror images." Judge "false sun god." Clifford "is not ready to face the broad sunshine of reality, whether human or divine."

———. "Nathaniel Hawthorne: *The House of the Seven Gables*." In *Landmarks of American Writing*, edited by Hennig Cohen, 111–20. New York: Basic, 1969. Characters as "pictures," and discussion of role of portraits.

———. "*The House of the Seven Gables*." In *Hawthorne's Fiction: The Light and the Dark*, 122–39. Norman: Univ. of Oklahoma Press, 1975. Continuity of guilt primary theme closely linked with the secondary theme: "conservatism and the new spirit of radical democracy." Pyncheons aristocrats and Maule's plebeians. Phoebe "is closest to the center of human nature. A conservative in the best sense, she represents the truth of the heart." The Holgrave-Phoebe union is "union of head and heart." Judge portrait "not wholly successful"—Hawthorne excessive in his description. His hatred "manifests itself in a too persistent and obtrusive irony."

Fossum, Robert H. "The Impalpable Now: *The House of the Seven Gables* and *The Blithedale Romance*." In *Hawthorne's Inviolable Circle: The Problem of Time*, 127–49. Deland, FL: Everett / Edwards, 1972. Critical of *House*. Hawthorne's "artistry sadly disproportionate to his moral." Characterization suffers from "aesthetic anemia."

Frank, Albert J. von, and John R. Byers, Jr. "*The House of the Seven Gables*: An Unlikely Source." *PMLA* 89 (October 1974): 1114–15. "Forum" exchange on Byers's essay. Frank not convinced that Leslie's story is source for *House*. Byers responds.

Gallagher, Susan Van Zanten. "A Domestic Reading of *The House of the Seven Gables*." *Studies in the Novel* 21, no. 1 (Spring 1989):1–13. Reads *House* within norms of nineteenth-century "cult of domesticity" as seen within popular fiction.

Gatta, John, Jr. "Progress and Providence in *The House of the Seven Gables*." *American Literature* 50 (March 1978): 37–48. Essential shape of the book "progressive and optimistic."

Gerber, John C. "A Critical Exercise in the Teaching of *The House of the Seven Gables*." *Emerson Society Quarterly* 25 (1961): 8–11. Suggestions for a "varied critical attack" on *House* in an undergraduate course.

Gilmore, Michael T. "Hawthorne." In *The Middle Way: Puritanism and Ideology in American Romantic Fiction*, 114–30. New Brunswick, NJ: Rutgers Univ. Press, 1977. As opposed to *Scarlet*, in *House* art "becomes a substitute for the sermon, and it falls to the figure of the artist to teach the truths that it was once the province of the ministry to preach."

———. "The Artist and the Marketplace in *The House of the Seven Gables*." In *American Romanticism and the Marketplace*, 96–112. Chicago: Univ. of Chicago Press, 1985. (First appeared in *ELH* 48, no. 1 [Spring 1981]:172–89.) Relationship of artist to buyers in *House* similar to Hawthorne's own desire to sell—"Hawthorne is using Hepzibah to explore his own ambivalence about courting the public in order to make money."

Gollin, Rita K. "The Romances." In *Nathaniel Hawthorne and the Truth of Dreams*, 140–213. Baton Rouge: Louisiana State Univ. Press, 1979. Romance "presents the dream of the house." Pyncheons described as "a race of dreamers, and Clifford is the most melancholy and ineffectual of Hawthorne's long line of wasted and delicate dreamers." Dreaming essential to Clifford's sanity.

Gray, Richard. " 'Hawthorne: A Problem': *The House of the Seven Gables.*" In *Nathaniel Hawthorne: New Critical Essays,* edited by A. Robert Lee, 88–109. Totowa, NJ: Barnes and Noble, 1982. Finds three problems with *House:* "tone and attitude"; "structure, its center of consciousness or organizing principle"; and "theme or subject"—"what is the book about"?

Griffith, Clark. "Substance and Shadow: Language and Meaning in *The House of the Seven Gables.*" *Modern Philology* 51 (February 1954):187–95. Hawthorne creates characters using either "substance words" or "shadow words." For example, "iron," "massive," and "granite" versus "sluggishness," "mouldy," and "shadowy."

Gross, Seymour L. "Introduction." Nathaniel Hawthorne's *The House of the Seven Gables,* vii–x. New York: Norton, 1967. Part of fascination of *House* lies in the way it "serves as a theatre for the rival claims made upon Hawthorne of democratic expectancy and the conservative impulse, pragmatism and estheticism, a deterministic view of history and a belief in man's capacity to resist the pressures of inheritance."

Gross, Theodore L. "Nathaniel Hawthorne: The Absurdity of Heroism." In *The Heroic Ideal in American Literature,* 18–33. New York: Free Press, 1971. (First appeared in *Yale Review* 57 [Winter 1968]: 182–95.) Finds that "entire novel is a movement away from the pompous, the pretentious, the heroic." Discusses absurdity of characterizations.

Gupta, R. K. "Hawthorne's Treatment of the Artist." *New England Quarterly* 45 (March 1972): 65–80. Compares Holgrave and Coverdale. Both "tease and manipulate human sensibilities out of a cold and passionless curiosity and are therefore guilty of the unpardonable sin of violating the sanctity of the human heart."

Gustafson, Judith A. "Parody in *The House of the Seven Gables.*" *Nathaniel Hawthorne Journal* 6 (1976): 294–302. *House* parodies romance conventions. Phoebe parody of type found in popular literature—the literature which "expressed through its sunny ingenues the sentimental ideals of domestic bliss."

Gysin, Fritz. "Paintings in the House of Fiction: The Example of Hawthorne." *Word and Image* 5, no. 2 (April–June 1989): 159–72. Colonel's paintings provide the "connecting link of all the stories and sketches of earlier events with the present [1840's]." First detailed description of portrait "cannot quite escape the picturesque style of the Dutch genre paintings." Examines three aspects of the portraits: "the special relationship between painting and death, the concern with surface and substance, and the status of the picture as an object."

Harris, Kenneth Marc. " 'Judge Pyncheon's Brotherhood': Puritan Theories of Hypocrisy and *The House of the Seven Gables.*" *Nineteenth-Century Fiction* 39, no. 2 (September 1984): 144–62. Analyzes Puritan theories of hypocrisy of John Cotton, Jeremy Taylor, Thomas Hooker, Thomas Shepard, William Cobbett, and others, and compares Hawthorne's use of this hypocrisy theme in *House.* Analyzes "linguistic scheme."

Havens, Elmer A. " 'The Golden Branch' as Symbol in *The House of the Seven Gables.*" *Modern Language Notes* 74 (January 1959): 20–22. Recounts legend of Aeneas's and Sibyl's visit to Hades in sixth book of *Aeneid* and its relationship to *House.*

Hawthorne, Manning. "*The House of the Seven Gables* and Hawthorne's Family History." *Literary Half-Yearly* 7, no. 1 (January 1966): 61–66. Discussion of history of original Hathornes in Salem, the Ingersoll house, persons who contributed to characterization in *House*.

Herzog, Kristin. "The Home-Based Power of Women and Maules." In *Women, Ethnics, and Exotics: Images of Power in Mid-Nineteenth-Century American Fiction*, 16–28. Knoxville: Univ. of Tennessee Press, 1983. Unless proud Pyncheon spirit admits primitive Maule spirit into house and bends to its level, it can only decay. Hepzibah "important milestone" because *House* is "first notable American novel in which a single woman is a major character." Hepzibah not a parody—she has dignity. Alice is exotic while Phoebe "represents simple reality" or nature.

Hoffman, Daniel G. "Paradise Regained at Maule's Well." In *Form and Fable in American Fiction*, 187–201. New York: Oxford Univ. Press, 1961. No single controlling symbol in *House*. *House* "lacks the unification of tone" found in *Scarlet*. Holgrave Hawthorne's "most optimistic character." Basic flaw of *House* is that happy ending "contradicts [Hawthorne's] own fundamental conception of 'the truth of the human heart.' "

Holland, J. Gill. "Hawthorne and Photography: *The House of the Seven Gables*." *Nathaniel Hawthorne Journal* 8 (1978): 1–10. Gives possible sources of daguerreotype of Judge Pyncheon. General discussion of nineteenth-century views on photography, electricity, and mesmerism.

Horne, Lewis B. "Of Place and Time: A Note on *The House of the Seven Gables*." *Studies in the Novel* 2 (Winter 1970): 459–67. *House* as variation of the "theme of spiritual trial and growth."

Houston, Neal B., and Roy E. Cain. "Holgrave: Hawthorne's Antithesis to Carlyle's Teufelsdröckh." *Research Studies* (Washington State University) 38, no. 1 (March 1970): 36–45. Hawthorne uses Holgrave "to refute the philosophy of progress of Thomas Carlyle's *Sartor Resartus*." Chapter 12 of *House* "reveals Holgrave and his philosophy of progress most clearly."

Humma, John B. " 'Time Passes' in *To the Lighthouse*: 'Governor Pyncheon' in *The House of the Seven Gables*." *Ball State University Forum* 20 (Summer 1979): 54–59. Influence of Hawthorne's narrative technique in "Governor Pyncheon" chapter on Virginia Woolf.

Hutner, Gordon. "*The House of the Seven Gables* and the Secret of Romance." In *Secrets and Sympathy: Forms of Disclosure in Hawthorne's Novels*, 64–101. Athens: Univ. of Georgia Press, 1988. Naming secrets "lies at the root of the problem of organizing the several styles, plots, and themes of *Seven Gables*." Within novel there are two kinds of secrets—"determinate and not—to be associated with the other oppositions that undergird the novel's structure. These two kinds of secrets warrant two forms of disclosure—'ostensible' and 'more subtle'—that reflect the romance's two temporal frames, past and present."

Idol, John L., Jr. "Clifford Pyncheon's Soap Bubbles." *American Notes and Queries* (New Haven) 23 (November / December 1984): 39–41. Soap bubbles relate to artist Edward Malbone whom Hawthorne made the creator of miniature of Clifford. There is reference to Malbone blowing soap bubbles in a letter from his sister recorded in Dunlap's *History of the Arts of Design in the United States*.

Jacobs, Edward Craney. "Shakespearean Borrowings in *The House of the Seven Gables*." *Nathaniel Hawthorne Journal* 7 (1977): 343–46. Hepzibah prayer scene borrowed from Claudius's prayer scene in *Hamlet*. Hepzibah's soliloquy similar to Hamlet's contemplation of suicide. In chapter 8 there is reference to *King Lear*.

Jaffe, David. "The Miniature that Inspired Clifford Pyncheon's Portrait." *Essex Institute Historical Collections* 98, no. 4 (October 1962): 278–82. Evidence that miniature is by Edward Malbone and of William Seton. Gives biographical details on Seton.

Johnson, Claudia D. " 'The Sun, As You See, Tells Quite Another Story': *The House of the Seven Gables*." In *The Productive Tension of Hawthorne's Art*, 67–82. University: Univ. of Alabama Press, 1981. Hawthorne circumvents "inescapable tragedy" by "bathing" conclusion in "artificial light." The return to Eden in conclusion is Hawthorne's attempt to "return to the belief that imagination can change even the darkest truths." The return in the "conclusion of a story that freely uses the materials of descent, result[s] in a negation of the theme."

Johnson, W. Stacy. "Hawthorne and *The Pilgrim's Progress*." *JEGP* 50, no. 2 (April 1951): 156–66. Clifford compares Judge to Giant Despair; House a Doubting Castle.

Junkins, Donald. "Hawthorne's *The House of the Seven Gables*: A Prototype of the Human Mind." *Literature and Psychology* 17 (1967): 193–210. Romance universally relevant because it "dramatically symbolizes the multiple functions of the human mind as they interrelate in the mind's struggle against fragmentation and toward wholeness." House represents mind, four inhabitants represent four basic psychological functions, and emergence of characters from house at conclusion is "a symbol of the process of individuation as it occurs in the regenerative human psyche."

Kaplan, E. Ann. "Hawthorne's 'Fancy Pictures' on Film." In *The Classic American Novel and the Movies*, edited by Gerald Peary and Roger Shatzkin, 30–41. New York: Frederick Ungar, 1977. Discussion of 1940 movie by Joe May—movie emphasizes social rather than supernatural. Many changes in plot: Hepzibah becomes Clifford's lover, trial scene added where Clifford is found guilty, and ending a double wedding between Phoebe and Holgrave and Hepzibah and Clifford.

Karlow, Martin. "Hawthorne's 'Modern Psychology': Madness and its Method in *The House of the Seven Gables*." *Bucknell Review of Science and Literature* 27, no. 2 (1983): 108–31. Uses R. D. Laing's *The Divided Self* to show that plot is "an elaborate, though somewhat mechanical, *psychomachia*." Clifford is true self while Jaffrey is false self of one personality.

Kaul, A. N. "Nathaniel Hawthorne: Heir and Critic of the Puritan Tradition." In *The American Vision: Actual and Ideal Society in Nineteenth-Century Fiction*, 139–213. New Haven, CT: Yale Univ. Press, 1963. *House* "explores the cultural past . . . in economic terms," illustrated by the "underlying relation between the religious motivation and the economic drives of Puritan polity." Witchcraft a "convenient instrument of covetous policy."

Kehler, Joel R. "*The House of the Seven Gables*: House, Home, and Hawthorne's Psychology of Habitation." *ESQ* 21 (1975): 142–53. Action of novel mainly an effort to find a "home" or "dream house."

Kleiman, E. "The Wizardry of Nathaniel Hawthorne: *Seven Gables* as Fairy Tale and Parable." *English Studies in Canada* 4, no. 3 (Fall 1978): 289–304. Artist "must become . . . a magician or wizard himself"—an "alchemist of the imagination." Hawthorne's imagination the "metaphysical battleground" where witches and wizards confront Puritans.

Klinkowitz, Jerome F. "In Defense of Holgrave." *Emerson Society Quarterly* 62 (Winter 1971): 4–8. Holgrave's change defensible—he "prepares for the 'setting sunshine' of the conclusion." Close reading of Alice Pyncheon's story shows "his actions are consistent with the novel's theme and development."

————. "Ending the *Seven Gables*: Old Light on a New Problem." *Studies in the Novel* 4 (Fall 1972): 396–401. Critique of Battaglia's "*The* (Unmeretricious) *House of the Seven Gables*."

————. "Hawthorne's Sense of an Ending." In *The Practice of Fiction in America: Writers from Hawthorne to the Present*, 11–18. Ames: Iowa State Univ. Press, 1980. (First appeared in *ESQ* 19, no. 1 [1973]: 43–49.) Concludes that *House* ending "demonstrates the same thesis as his other romances, only in an obverse manner." Ending "not a total anomaly."

Levy, Alfred J. "*The House of the Seven Gables*: The Religion of Love." *Nineteenth-Century Fiction* 16 (December 1961): 189–203. *House* a "book with faith in young people . . . fundamentally, optimistic."

Levy, Leo B. "Picturesque Style in *The House of the Seven Gables*." *New England Quarterly* 39 (June 1966): 147–60. Uses James's definition of "picturesque." In *House*, "picturesque more complex than James allows"—"it is an important technique in dramatizing the crisis of a decaying, aristocratic society."

Liebman, Sheldon W. "Point of View in *The House of the Seven Gables*." *ESQ* 19, no. 4 (1973): 203–12. Discussion of "ambiguity of narration." Comparison of legendary and historical—reader must choose between two points of view. Reader must "decide to trust either legend or history and abide by that choice on all the important issues of the book."

Lubbers, Klaus. "Metaphorical Patterns in Hawthorne's *The House of the Seven Gables*." In *Literature und Sprache der Vereinigten Staaten*, edited by Hans Helmcke, Klaus Lubbers, and Renate Schmidt-von Bardeleben, 107–16. Heidelberg, Germany: Carl Winter, 1969. Analysis of "prominent verbal patterns" like "rusty," "venerable," "patched," and "sphere." Discussion of metaphors of jail, stream of life, and world as theater.

Luedtke, Luther S. "Hawthorne's Oriental Women: The First Dark Ladies." In *Nathaniel Hawthorne and the Romance of the Orient*, 165–93. Bloomington: Indiana Univ. Press, 1989. "Eastern atmosphere" in Holgrave's legend, and Hepzibah's turban is a "droll parody of Oriental splendor."

MacAndrew, Elizabeth. "The Victorian Hall of Mirrors." In *The Gothic Tradition in Fiction*, 151–239. New York: Columbia Univ. Press, 1979. Compares *House* to Dostoyevsky's *The Double*.

McPherson, Hugo. "The New England Myth: A Mirror for Puritans." In *Hawthorne as Myth-Maker: A Study in Imagination*, 132–45. Toronto: Univ. of Toronto Press, 1969. (First appeared as "Hawthorne's Mythology: A Mirror for Puritans." *University of Toronto Quarterly* 28 [April 1959]: 267–78.) Relation of *House* to Greek myths—"The pattern of *Seven Gables* . . . is fundamentally related to the quest pattern of the mythological tales."

McWilliams, John P., Jr. "Broken Lines." In *Hawthorne, Melville, and the American Character: A Looking-Glass Business*, 107–29. Cambridge: Cambridge Univ.

Press, 1984. Pyncheon family character types: Matthew Maule is "underside" of Judge's character and Holgrave has "inherited Puritan virtues."

Male, Roy R., Jr. " 'From the Innermost Germ' the Organic Principle in Hawthorne's Fiction." *ELH* 20 (1953): 218–36. Analysis of mechanical and organic images. Colonel Pyncheon's house with sundial is illustrative of mechanical Puritan society.

———. "Evolution and Regeneration: *The House of the Seven Gables*." In *Hawthorne's Tragic Vision*, 119–38. New York: Norton, 1957. "Central metaphor" in *House* "drawn from the process of evolution."

Mariano, Josefina T. "Nathaniel Hawthorne's Symbolism of Black and White as a Synthesis of Permanence and Change in *The House of the Seven Gables* and *The Marble Faun*." *Diliman Review* (Philippine Islands) 18 (July 1970): 268–83. Through symbolism of black and white, Hawthorne illustrates how "life is an interplay of light and shadow" which sometimes contrasts, and sometimes synthesizes "past and present, permanence and change." Mirror image "contributes to the interplay and synthesis of contrary colors of white and black.

Marks, Alfred H. "Who Killed Judge Pyncheon? The Role of the Imagination in *The House of the Seven Gables*." *PMLA* 71 (June 1956): 355–69. Judge died "because he had mistaken a substance for a shadow." He mistook Clifford for a ghost and died of fright.

———. "Hawthorne's Daguerreotypist: Scientist, Artist, Reformer." *Ball State Teachers College Forum* 3 (Spring 1962): 61–74. Includes historical background on daguerreotyping.

Matthews, James. W. "The House of Atreus and *The House of the Seven Gables*." *Emerson Society Quarterly* 63 (Spring 1971): 31–36. Compares *House* to a number of Greek tragedies, including the *Oresteia* and *The Eumenides*.

Meikle, Jeffrey L. "Hawthorne's Alembic: Alchemical Images in *The House of the Seven Gables*." *ESQ* 26, no. 4 (1980): 173–83. Hawthorne "consciously structured" *House* as alchemical drama. Pyncheon elm "tree of 'universal matter.' " Hawthorne often uses word "rust." Colonel described in terms of iron. Holgrave plays role of mercury "whose 'chemical marriage' with the seed of gold produces the philosopher's stone."

Michelson, Bruce. "Hawthorne's House of Three Stories." *New England Quarterly* 57 (June 1984): 163–83. [Reprinted in this volume.] *House* shows "itself to be about fiction" (metafiction). Also a discussion of the ghost story genre.

Milton, John R. "The American Novel: The Search for Home, Tradition, and Identity." *Western Humanities Review* 16 (1962): 169–80. Complexities and possibilities of the "home" theme first suggested in *House*. Railroad "an effective symbol of the fresh beginning." In train scene "Hawthorne almost caught the migratory nature of the American people and the important ambivalence in the American novel: we are homeless because we have fled from our traditional home, but we immediately begin the search for a new home."

Mizruchi, Susan L. "From History to Gingerbread: Manufacturing a Republic in *The House of the Seven Gables*." In *The Power of Historical Knowledge: Narrating the Past in Hawthorne, James, and Dreiser*, 83–134. Princeton, NJ: Princeton Univ. Press, 1988. Characters and narrator "evade a present they are too ineffectual to meet by retreating into a mythic past." There is "exile of history at the novel's close." Narrator is mythmaker.

Moore, Robert. "Hawthorne's Folk-Motifs and *The House of the Seven Gables*." *New York Folklore Quarterly* 28 (September 1972): 221–33. Enumerates witch motifs.

O'Connor, William Van. "Hawthorne and Faulkner: Some Common Ground." In *The Grotesque: An American Genre, and Other Essays*, 59–77. Carbondale: Southern Illinois Univ. Press, 1962. *Absalom, Absalom!* and *The Sound and the Fury* "bear some comparison" to *House*.

Orel, Harold. "The Double Symbol." *American Literature* 23 (1951): 1–6. Double symbol is light and time in Judge Pyncheon's death scene.

Pearce, Roy Harvey. "A Sense of the Present: Hawthorne and *The House of the Seven Gables*." In *Gesta Humanorum: Studies in the Historicist Mode*, 55–74. Columbia: Univ. of Missouri Press, 1987. Puts romance "firmly in the context of Hawthorne's career." Hawthorne's central theme is "discovery of self in a culture whose worshipful devotion to the idea of self had increasingly become nominal."

Pearson, Norman Holmes. "The Pynchons and Judge Pyncheon." *Essex Institute Historical Collections* 100, no. 4 (October 1964): 235–55. Discussion of letters between Hawthorne and Olivers and Pynchon, who were offended by romance.

Person, Leland S., Jr. "*The Scarlet Letter* and *The House of the Seven Gables*: Resisting the Seductive Power of Art." In *Aesthetic Headaches: Women and a Masculine Poetics in Poe, Melville, and Hawthorne*, 122–45. Athens: Univ. of Georgia Press, 1988. In both novels "the power of male art to reach the heart or 'wellspring' of a female audience looms large." In Holgrave's story to Phoebe, "male discourse possesses an essentially phallic power to penetrate and 'master' the mind of a female listener."

Platizky, Roger S. "Hepzibah's Gingerbread Cakes in *The House of the Seven Gables*." *American Notes and Queries* (New Haven) 17 (1979): 106–08. Ned Higgins "unifying principle" in romance.

Porte, Joel. "Hawthorne." In *The Romance in America: Studies in Cooper, Poe, Hawthorne, Melville, and James*, 95–151. Middletown, CT: Wesleyan Univ. Press, 1969. *House* "can be read . . . as a fable explaining the nature and function of romance."

Ragan, James F. "Hawthorne's Bulky Puritans." *PMLA* 75 (1960): 420–23. "Body Imagery" in Hawthorne; especially body of Judge Pyncheon.

———. "Social Criticism in *The House of the Seven Gables*." In *Literature and Society: Nineteen Essays by Germaine Bree and Others*, edited by Bernice Slote, 112–20. Lincoln: Univ. of Nebraska Press, 1964. In *House* Hawthorne works out "beauty-versus-practicality theme in detail" begun in Bellingham's garden in *Scarlet*. Old world gentility "ignored Nature's requirement of utilitarianism." For Hawthorne, "the greatest evil in American social history occurred when Puritan values outlived the age of faith."

Reed, Amy Louis. "Self-Portraiture in the Work of Nathaniel Hawthorne." *Studies in Philology* 23, no. 1 (January 1926): 40–54. Coverdale, Holgrave, and Kenyon "fairly close to Hawthorne's own character." His "young heroes and his mature villains" both varieties of self-portraiture.

Rees, John O., Jr. "Elizabeth Peabody and 'The Very A B C': A Note on *The House of the Seven Gables*." *American Literature* 38 (January 1967): 537–40. Reference to "the very A B C" through Hepzibah is reference to new teaching methods, particularly Charles Kraitsir's method found in *The Significance of the Alphabet* and taken up by Elizabeth Peabody. Hawthorne may be satirizing these new teaching methods.

Reid, Alfred S. "Hawthorne's Ghost-Soul and the Harmonized Life." *Furman Studies* 12, no. 1 (November 1964): 1–10. In *House*, Hawthorne "stresses the lack of harmony between Clifford's outer or 'animal' substance and the inner or spiritual essence, which gives the 'animal' its life." Phoebe, however, "has an ideal constitution." Compares Matthew Maule to Hamlet.

Reynolds, David. "Hawthorne's Cultural Demons." In *Beneath the American Renaissance: The Subversive Imagination in the Age of Emerson and Melville*, 249–74. New York: Knopf, 1988. Train scene "dialectic engagement with and detachment from antebellum popular culture." Several images—"pamphlet novels, penny papers, spiritualism, electricity, mesmerism, the justified criminal—are among those that constituted the most problematic issues of the modern scene."

Rice, Julian C. "The Unimpaled Butterfly: Redemption in *The House of the Seven Gables*." *Journal of Evolutionary Psychology* 2, nos. 1–2 (August 1981): 48–62. Hawthorne conscious of archetypal pattern of world's great religions and wisdom traditions. In *House*, "the emphasis is on the second stage of transition . . . from experience to enlightenment." The house "expresses a desire for rigidified permanence." "The wisdom tradition . . . tells us that our desire for fixity is an unnatural *hubris*."

Ringe, Donald A. "Hawthorne's Psychology of the Head and the Heart." *PMLA* 65 (March 1950): 120–32. Cold, speculative, intellectuals commit sin of isolation which destroys. Holgrave achieves balance between heart and head and is saved.

Rodnon, Stewart. "*The House of the Seven Gables* and *Absalom! Absalom!*: Time, Tradition, and Guilt." *Studies in the Humanities* 1, no. 2 (Winter 1969–70): 42–46. Six parallels between two novels: both family-centered, panoramic, chronicled stories; both loaded with symbolism; both have "mordant, ironic humor"; both show effect of strong central character from past on a young person in story's present; both explore decline of tradition; and both reflect a "special view of the nature of good and evil."

Rozsnyai, R. "The Romance of Either / Or: Hawthorne's *The House of the Seven Gables*." *AUS-PEAS* 1 (1980): 103–38. Romances "shaped by the Kierkegaardian ambiguity of choice." In *House*, romance structured around a central metaphor (house) "which is not fixed," but unstable and continually shifting. There is no unified movement "which could provide the romance with a structural pattern"; rather the shifting nature of the house metaphor is "a means to establish levels of meaning," and provide clues to "decode" them.

Rubey, Dan. "Reading the Surface of the World: Photography and Perception in Hawthorne's *House of the Seven Gables*, Teshigahara's *Woman in the Dunes*, and Antonioni's *Blow- Up*." *Selecta: Journal of the Pacific Northwest Council on Foreign Languages* (Missoula) 7 (1986): 123–30. In the three works photographers are main characters who "investigate the relationship between visual perception, art, the self, and the social."

St. Armand, Barton Levi. "The Golden Stain of Time: Ruskinian Aesthetics and the Ending of Hawthorne's *The House of the Seven Gables*." *Nathaniel Hawthorne Journal* 3 (1973): 143–53. In "Lamp of Memory" chapter in *The Seven Lamps of Architecture*, "Ruskin enunciates an aesthetic which counters the early Holgrave's philosophy of transience and which parallels the cautious conservatism to which the later Holgrave is converted."

Sachs, Viola. "The Myth of America in Hawthorne's *House of the Seven Gables* and *Blithedale Romance*." *Kwartalnik Neofilologiczny* 15, no. 3 (1968): 267–83. Analysis of *House* "reveals Hawthorne's attempt to deal with the American experiment, and to confront the Ideal, that is the vision of the New Land, with the Reality."

Schoen, Carol. "The House of the Seven Deadly Sins." *ESQ* 19, no. 1 (1973): 26–33. Similarity in Hawthorne's method of treating each of the Seven Deadly Sins illuminates his overall plan. First chapter in each sequence introduces situation which "permits the action of a particular vice to be displayed prominently[;] the central chapter presents either a way of life that is completely free of that sin, or alternatively, a life thoroughly corrupted by it; and the final chapter sums up the extremely limited capacity of the characters to confirm their sinful attitudes within the boundaries necessary for successful living."

Schriber, Mary Suzanne. "Nathaniel Hawthorne: A Pilgrimage to a Dovecote." In *Gender and the Writer's Imagination: From Cooper to Wharton*, 45–85. Lexington: Univ. Press of Kentucky, 1987. Female characters used as "symbols of the culture's values." Alice and Hepzibah "ladies"; Phoebe "middle-class woman." Hepzibah spinster and thus "displaced from woman's sphere." "Phoebe replicates 'the American girl' of Cooper." Hepzibah comic while Phoebe represents hope.

Schroeder, John W. " 'That Inward Sphere': Notes on Hawthorne's Heart Imagery and Symbolism." *PMLA* 65 (March 1950): 106–19. In *House* heart appears three times as mansion and twice as prison.

Scoville, Samuel. "Hawthorne's Houses and Hidden Treasures." *ESQ* 19, no. 2 (1973): 61–73. Threshold scenes often portentous. Discussion of the many entrances and exits.

Sherbo, Arthur. "Albert Brisbane and Hawthorne's Holgrave and Hollingsworth." *New England Quarterly* 27 (December 1954): 531–34. Brisbane, who is associated with animal magnetism and Fourierism, could be model for both Holgrave and Hollingsworth. Concludes that Hawthorne's increased knowledge of Fourierism may have led to the more "sympathetically portrayed" Holgrave followed by the "more sombrely conceived Hollingsworth."

Smith, Allan Gardner Lloyd. "Immured in the Past: *The House of the Seven Gables*." In *Eve Tempted: Writing and Sexuality in Hawthorne's Fiction*, 45–59. London: Croom Helm, 1984. Finds saturation of text by idea of inheritance "generates a particular kind of bio-architectural metaphor, in which the self is seen as a building, containing the inner life (or death) of the person."

Smith, Henry Nash. "The Morals of Power: Business Enterprise as a Theme in Mid-Nineteenth-Century American Fiction." In *Essays on American Literature in Honor of Jay B. Hubbell*, edited by Clarence Gohdes, 90–107. Durham, NC: Duke Univ. Press, 1967. Judge's lust for money and power identifies him with rising commercialism of which Emerson declared Napoleon to be the type. Portrayal of Judge "to strongly clouded by emotion to be accepted as merely an abstract denunciation of greed."

Smith, Julian. "A Hawthorne Source for *The House of the Seven Gables*." *American*

*Transcendental Quarterly* 1 (1969): 18–19. Hawthorne's *Legends of the Province House* source for *House*.

Stanton, Robert. "Hawthorne, Bunyan, and the American Romances." *PMLA* 71 (1956): 155–65. Comments on the allusions to Bunyan in the "Flight of Two Owls" chapter.

Stein, William Bysshe. "The New American Faust." In *Hawthorne's Faust: A Study of the Devil Archetype*, 123–41. Gainesville: Florida Univ. Press, 1953. Maule's curse, "as objectified in the seven-gabled mansion, is the Faustian symbol." The house also symbol of Pyncheons' Faustian desire.

Steinbrink, Jeffrey. "Hawthorne's Holgravian Temper: The Case Against the Past." *American Transcendental Quarterly* 31 (Summer 1976): 21–23. Holgrave "represents one aspect of Hawthorne's complex attitude toward history."

Sterne, Richard Clark. "Hawthorne's Politics in *The House of the Seven Gables*." *Canadian Review of American Studies* 6 (Spring 1975): 74–83. Discussion of Ned Higgins, Matthew Maule, and Jim Crow and Scipio.

Stineback, David C. " 'The fluctuating waves of our social life': Nathaniel Hawthorne's *The House of the Seven Gables*." In *Shifting World*, 43–60. Lewisburg, PA: Bucknell Univ. Press, 1976. *House* fails as romance but succeeds as realistic novel because of "persistent incompatibility, despite the author's overt intentions, of history and morality."

Stoehr, Taylor. "Hawthorne and Mesmerism." *Huntington Library Quarterly* 33 (1969): 33–60. Discusses relationship between colonial witchcraft and mesmerism in Hawthorne's time.

Stone, Edward. "Hawthorne's Other Drowning." *Nathaniel Hawthorne Journal* 2 (1972): 231–37. Hepzibah's "entrance on stage" parallels description of drowning of young Concord woman from Hawthorne's notebooks. Serves as basis for drowning scene in *Blithedale*.

———. "Hawthorne's House of Pyncheon: A Theory of American Drama." In *Artful Thunder: Versions of the Romantic Tradition in American Literature in Honor of Howard P. Vincent*, edited by Robert J. DeMott and Sanford E. Marovitz, 69–84. Kent, OH: Kent State Univ. Press, 1975. *House* "first American Democratic tragedy."

Stubbs, John C. "*The House of the Seven Gables*: Hawthorne's Comedy." In *The Pursuit of Form: A Study of Hawthorne and the Romance*, 101–19. Urbana: Univ. of Illinois Press, 1970. Clifford and Hepzibah pair of "mock lovers." Hawthorne mocks Holgrave's "stiff-necked radicalism." Clifford and Hepzibah "almost farcical representation of the love of Holgrave and Phoebe." Structure of *House* "depends on a rhythm of straightforward presentation counterpointed with comic inversion."

Sundquist, Eric J. " 'The home of the dead': Representation and Speculation in Hawthorne and *The House of the Seven Gables*." In *Home as Found: Authority and Genealogy in Nineteenth-Century American Literature*, 86–142. Baltimore: Johns Hopkins Univ. Press, 1979. *House* revenges death of Matthew Maule by "gleefully presiding over the demise of Judge Pyncheon, only to turn around and implicate its narrator, through his association with Holgrave, in the necromatic act with which the cycle of guilt originated."

Swanson, Donald R. "On Building *The House of the Seven Gables*." *Ball State University*

*Forum* 10 (Winter 1969): 43–50. Discusses sources for *House* found in Hawthorne's notebooks and life.

Tatar, Maria M. "Masters and Slaves: The Creative Process in Hawthorne's Fiction." In *Spellbound: Studies on Mesmerism and Literature*, 189–229. Princeton, NJ: Princeton Univ. Press, 1978. Holgrave characterized as man "of remarkable physical attractiveness," while mesmerism subjects consistently depicted as "defenseless, ethereal virgins." Holgrave's interest in art, mesmerism, and social reform suggests that a connection exists between these three vocations. Mesmerism well suited to romance.

————. "The Houses of Fiction: Toward a Definition of the Uncanny." *Comparative Literature* 33, no. 2 (Spring 1981): 167–82. Uses Freud's idea of "Das Unheimliche." Defines uncanny as "something familiar or old-established in the mind that has been estranged by the process of repression." *House* "peculiar American variant of the Gothic Romance." Hidden deed secret which is "matrix for the uncanny events." "The curse thus derives its power from the absence of the document and the presence of the portrait."

Tharpe, Coleman W. "The Oral Storyteller in Hawthorne's Novels." *Studies in Short Fiction* 16 (1979): 205–14. Discussion of Holgrave's "legend of Alice Pyncheon." Story functions as vehicle by which Phoebe becomes aware of "tradition of her family and by which Holgrave releases his own repressed emotions resulting from his growing love for Phoebe and his sense of guilt at being a Maule."

Tharpe, Jac. "House of Secret Knowledge." In *Nathaniel Hawthorne: Identity and Knowledge*, 110–24. Carbondale: Southern Illinois Univ. Press, 1967. For Hawthorne the only source of truth is "intuition applied to the eyes and face," a method used often in *House*.

Thomas, Brook. "*The House of the Seven Gables*: Hawthorne's Legal Story." In *Cross-Examinations of Law and Literature: Cooper, Hawthorne, Stowe, and Melville*, 45–70. Cambridge: Cambridge Univ. Press, 1987. (First appeared in *University of Mississippi Studies in English* n. s., 5, [1984–1987]: 249–71.) Comparison of Judge to contemporary legal system. Compares the death of Judge Pyncheon to the murder of Captain Joseph White in 1830.

————. "*The House of the Seven Gables*: Hawthorne's Romance of Art." In *Cross-Examinations of Law and Literature: Cooper, Hawthorne, Stowe, and Melville*, 71–90. Cambridge: Cambridge Univ. Press, 1987. (First appeared as "*The House of the Seven Gables*: Reading the Romance of America." *PMLA* 97 [March 1982]: 195–211.) Holgrave's conversion at end shows "how the artist's desire to find eternal truths can lead to political conservatism." Description of Colonel's motives for building house "can be read allegorically as Hawthorne's self-conscious comment on his own motives in constructing" *House*. Like colonel's house, romance "becomes a monument to its founder, an attempt to resist the flow of time."

Travis, Mildred K. "Past vs. Present in *The House of the Seven Gables*." *Emerson Society Quarterly* 58 (1970): 109–11. Finds pervasive use of "antithesis between the past and present."

Vance, William L. "Tragedy and 'The Tragic Power of Laughter': *The Scarlet Letter* and *The House of the Seven Gables*." *Nathaniel Hawthorne Journal* 1 (1971):

232–54. *House* "tragicomedy in the modern sense . . . by accident." Hepzibah's entrance "elaborately comic."

Waggoner, Hyatt H. *"The House of the Seven Gables."* In *Hawthorne: A Critical Study*, 160–87. Cambridge, MA: Belknap, 1963. *House* more deliberately written than *Scarlet*. "The house is both setting and symbol: it is the antagonist in a drama of good and evil." Discussion of Hawthorne's use of circle and Eden imagery. Discussion of Hawthorne's "ambiguity device"—"allowing multiple interpretations of a single incident." Reads ending nonironically.

Waterman, Arthur E. "Dramatic Structure in *The House of the Seven Gables.*" *Studies in the Literary Imagination* 2 (1969): 13–19. "[C]onscious theatrical framework" in *House*. Entrances, exits, and chapter endings "tantamount to scenic divisions." Uncle Venner and Ned like chorus figures. *House* has five-act structure.

Westbrook, Perry D. "Nathaniel Hawthorne." In *Free Will and Determinism in American Literature*, 29–37. Rutherford, NJ: Farleigh Dickinson Univ. Press, 1979. Compares *House* to Oliver Wendell Holmes's *Elsie Venner*. Each concerned with themes of will and transmitted guilt.

Wheelock, Alan S. "The House of Pride." *Essex Institute Historical Collections* 112, no. 4 (October 1976): 306–32. Relationship between first Pyncheon and architect similar to relationship between Samuel McIntire (American architect and woodworker) and his patrons. Discussion of Knox estate and Hawthorne's views on moral dimensions of architecture.

Whelan, Robert Emmet, Jr. *"The House of the Seven Gables*: Allegory of the Heart." *Renascence* 31 (Winter 1979): 67–82. *House* as allegory similar to Bunyan's *Holy War*. In allegory Hepzibah represents "Unregenerate Will," Phoebe represents "Love," Clifford represents "Spirit or the Unselfish Principle," Judge Pyncheon represents "Flesh or the Selfish Principle," and Holgrave represents "Introspective Intellect and Conscience."

Yates, Norris. "Ritual and Reality, Mask and Dance Motifs in Hawthorne's Fiction." *Philological Quarterly* 34 (January 1955): 56–70. Analysis of Jim Crow and the organ player.

Yoder, R. A. "Transcendental Conservatism, and *The House of the Seven Gables.*" *Georgia Review* 28 (Spring 1974): 33–51. Compares the politics of Emerson and Hawthorne.

# Index

♦